Die Before You Die

A Rumi-Inspired Journey Through Grief and Love

MOSTAFA DARVISHI

ISBN: 979-8-89570-093-8

Printed in Canada

For permissions, inquiries, and speaking engagements:

msdarvishi@gmail.com

Dedication

To the loving memory of my parents
And
To my beloved wife

Epigraph

"Die, die in this love, die.
In this love, if you die, your soul will be received."
Jalal al-Din Rumi

بـمـیـریـد، بـمـیـریـد، در ایـن عشق بـمـیـریـد
در ایـن عشق چون مـردیـد، هـمـه روح پـذیـریـد
جلال الـدیـن رومی (مـولـوی)

Contents

Foreword

The wound is where the Light enters you.

—Rumi

Grief is not a detour. It is not a dysfunction to be corrected or a weakness to be hidden. It is a sacred path, a firewalk that transforms the soul if we allow it. But few are willing to accompany us through that fire without offering prescriptions, timelines, or tidy conclusions. Fewer still can stand beside our sorrow and simply say, "You are not alone."

This book does exactly that.

In Die Before You Die, Mostafa Darvishi offers us a gift that is as rare as it is necessary: a map drawn not from theory, but from the terrain of lived heartbreak. He does not speak about grief from a distance—he speaks through it, as someone who has walked its lonely corridors, who has knelt in the silence of unanswered prayers, and who has wept into the lap of poetry when language failed.

He is not a therapist, not a psychologist, not a spiritual master. And that is precisely why his voice carries such quiet power. He does not write from a podium. He writes from the floor, from the ashes, from the trembling edge where love meets loss. He writes like someone who has died a little and chosen to live anyway.

What makes this work extraordinary is its weaving of two great rivers: the contemplative beauty of Rumi and the grounded clarity of modern psychology. Each chapter becomes a gentle bridge between the heart's devastation and its capacity to heal. There is space here—for sorrow, for memory, for rage, for silence. There is no rush to move on, only an invitation to push through.

I have walked with many grievers in my life. I have listened to the ache of countless hearts who thought their pain would never soften. And I have longed for a book like this, one that holds the hand without gripping it, one that offers light without denying the darkness.

If you are holding this book, chances are you have loved someone so deeply that their absence changed the shape of your world. Let this book walk with you. Let it sing to your soul. Let it remind you that even in your pain, you are accompanied by Rumi's eternal voice, by the pulse of poetry, and by a fellow traveler whose sorrow has become a source of beauty.

May this book be your companion, as it has already become mine.

With deep reverence,

Mostafa Darvishi

The Author

Acknowledgement

There are no words vast enough to encompass the love that shaped this book. And yet, in the trembling silence where words break down, this book was born.

To my **mother**, my first guide into the soul of Rumi, this is your voice, echoing across the pages. I was a child, barely tall enough to reach the bookshelves, when you began pouring verses into me like warm milk at night. You didn't explain the metaphors. You simply let me feel them, your voice quivering as you sang of longing, of union, of the Beloved. You were not just my mother. You were the gatekeeper of my soul's first awakening. The one who gave me both the alphabet and the ache. You planted Rumi in my bones long before I understood the harvest he would one day become.

When you and Father left this world, something in me collapsed. It wasn't only that I missed you, it was that I no longer recognized the sky without your gaze beneath it. I wandered the ruins of language, searching for home, for warmth, for meaning. In that shattering silence, I opened Rumi again, and I wept not for answers, but for how gently he held my grief, just as you once held me. You returned through his verses. Your lullabies, your prayers, your fierce love, all of it was there, waiting.

This book was written for every soul who has ever wept and wondered if the pain would ever make sense. It was written for those who walk through the valley of grief with empty hands and torn hearts. It was written in the shadow of loss, but also in its light. Because grief, I have learned, is not the opposite of love. It is what remains when love has no more place to go. And you, my dear reader, are not alone in this ache.

I bow in deep gratitude to the translators of Rumi, especially Coleman Barks[1], Kabir Helminski[2], and Jawid Mojaddedi[3], who became midwives for this book by bringing Rumi's fire into the hearts of modern seekers. And to the psychologists, therapists, mystics, and spiritual companions whose works stitched my brokenness into something resembling wholeness, you know who you are, and I hold your guidance sacred.

And to **Rumi**, beloved master of the invisible, thank you for reminding us that even in our sorrow, we are never alone. The wound, after all, is where the Light enters.

And lastly, to **my beloved wife**, the quiet flame in my life whose love teaches me daily what it means to remain tender in a world that bruises. Your passion, your listening, your faith in this journey became the bridge between my past and my becoming. This book would not exist without the sanctuary of your love. In your eyes, I found the courage to write again, to love again, and to live again.

From the ache of goodbye to the miracle of reunion in this life or the next, may these words serve as a lamp on the path of whoever needs them.

---

1. **Coleman Barks** is an American poet and former literature faculty member at the University of Georgia. Although he neither speaks nor reads Persian, he is a popular interpreter of Rumi, rewriting the poems based on other English translations.
2. **Kabir Edmund Helminski** is the author of several books on contemporary Sufism, a translator of Sufi poetry, and is the co-founder and co-director of Threshold Society.
3. **Jawid Mojaddedi** is professor of Religion at Rutgers University. His area of research is early and medieval Sufism. Born in Kabul, Afghanistan, and raised from the age of five in Great Britain, he completed his studies at the University of Manchester, receiving his Ph.D. in 1998.

About the Author

Mostafa Darvishi is not a psychologist, nor a therapist, nor a spiritual master. He is a man whose heart was broken, whose words faltered, and who, for a time, lost language itself. Yet through grief, he found a new tongue, one carved from tears, poems, and the gentle echo of love that survives beyond loss.

Mostafa's journey began at age six, when his mother, her voice soft and steady, first poured Rumi's ghazals into the vessel of his young soul. Those early lullabies were not entertainment, they were invitations to the infinite. By age ten, he had memorized hundreds of Rumi's poems. When he recited a ghazal aloud and was punished for it, he discovered that words can wound, but the soul still remembers.

He followed the echo of those words into academia, earning a Ph.D. in Electrical & Electronics Engineering from Polytechnique Montréal, specializing in the effects of cosmic radiation on spacecraft electronics. Now, a recognized expert in microelectronics, an adjunct professor at academia, and a leader in advanced technology development, Mostafa continues to honor his love of languages—Persian, English, French, and Portuguese, each learned with the hunger his mother first nourished.

Yet academic success could not shield him from the ache of his mother's loss and then his father's soon after. The heartbeat of his life, once steady, stuttered. No words could map the emptiness he felt. It was in that silence that he opened Rumi's *Masnavi* again—not as a scholar, but as a mourner. And there, amid verses steeped in longing and union, he found something he thought lost: companionship. Permission to weep. Permission to be broken.

This book, *Die Before You Die: A Rumi-Inspired Journey Through Grief and Love*, offers no prescriptions—only presence. It is not built on theory, but on truth: the simple, sacred truth that grief can be a path to transformation if we allow it to be. It bridges the rigor of modern psychology—mindfulness, acceptance, post-traumatic growth—with the soul's longing that Rumi so tenderly speaks to.

If you who hold this book feel abandoned in your sorrow, know this: you are not broken. If you mourn someone that sorrow cannot contain, know this too: your grief is not only sorrow—it is love remade. And if you feel a longing you can't describe, believe this: that longing is your soul remembering home.

Mostafa walks alongside you in these pages—not as a guide, but as a companion who has walked through his own darkness and discovered that, in grief, we may not only lose—we may *become*. For grief is not the opposite of love—it is what becomes of love when the ones we love have gone.

A Note on the Rumi Translations in This Book

Throughout the pages of this book, you will encounter many luminous quotes attributed to Jalal al-Din Muhammad Rumi—words that have crossed centuries, cultures, and languages to stir hearts around the world. Yet it is important to gently clarify, with both reverence and responsibility, that many of these familiar English versions are not literal, word-for-word translations of Rumi's original Persian writings.

Rumi composed his mystical poetry in 13th-century Persian, primarily in texts such as the *Masnavi-ye Manavi*[1], the *Divan-e Shams-e Tabrizi*[2], and *Fihi Ma Fih*[3]. However, the versions widely known and loved today—particularly those translated or interpreted by Coleman Barks and others—are often poetic paraphrases. These renditions aim not at linguistic fidelity, but at evoking the emotional and spiritual essence of Rumi's teachings. In the process, much of the historical, cultural, and Sufi-specific context has been simplified or reimagined for contemporary audiences.

These adaptations, while beautiful and soul-stirring, are not literal translations—and should not be taken as such. In this book, whenever possible, we have included the closest authentic Persian verses and cited

---

1. The Masnavi-ye Ma'navi (meaning "The Spiritual Couplets") is a monumental 13th-century Persian poem by the Sufi mystic Jalal al-Din Rumi, revered as a profound work of Islamic mysticism and the longest single-authored mystical poem. Composed of six books containing some 25,000 verses, it functions as a spiritual guide for Sufis, teaching the path to union with God through stories, fables, and profound philosophical insights into love, selflessness, and divine reality.
2. Divan-i Kabir, also known as Divan-i Shams and Divan-i Shams-i Tabrizi, is a collection of poems written by the Persian poet and Sufi mystic Rumi. A compilation of lyric poems written in the Persian language, it contains more than 40,000 verses and over 3,000 ghazals.
3. The Fihi Ma Fihi or Fīhi Mā Fīhi, lit. "It Is What It Is" or "In It What Is in It" is a Persian prose work of 13th century Sufi mystic and Iranian poet Jalāl al-Dīn Muḥammad Rūmī. The book has 72 short discourses.

their sources, to preserve the sacred origin of Rumis' voice and to honor the deep mystical tradition from which they emerged.

Rumi himself was no stranger to paradox. His words often move in spirals—toward the heart, not the mind. He invites us to taste the meaning, not merely parse the syntax. It is in that spirit that we offer both the modern English renderings and the original Persian texts: not as competing versions, but as two wings of the same bird—one carrying sound, the other carrying silence.

Let them both guide you home.

Introduction: When the Heart Breaks Open

A Rumi-Inspired Journey Through Grief and Love

"Don't grieve. Anything you lose comes round in another form."

— Rumi

A Cup of Sorrow, A Flame of Love

We never plan to become students of sorrow. It comes uninvited, like a sudden nightfall that steals the warmth from a sunny afternoon. My grief journey was not a choice, but a collapse. I was 24 when my mother passed away. She had suffered for months, immobilized by a broken hip, her world confined to a bed. I watched her strength fade day by day, unable to do anything but sit by her, talk to her, and offer my helpless love. Her body eventually surrendered not to the fracture, but to the flu. It was a quiet, devastating end. I did not know then that my heart, too, had fractured.

My father, broken by the loss of his lifelong companion, spiraled into grief. He was a quiet man but deeply bound to my mother. I watched him drown in cigarettes and silence, smoking away the emptiness. Within months, he was gone, too. In that short window of time, I became an orphan. My life split in two: before grief and after.

Grief has many faces—sadness, rage, numbness, confusion. But perhaps its cruelest mask is invisibility. The world kept turning, yet I felt like a ghost in it. Friends disappeared. The phone stopped ringing. Days bled into nights. And I, someone who had studied science and engineering, who understood how systems and logic worked, could not figure out how to get out of bed.

My Mother, My First Guide to Rumi

But long before loss, there had been poetry.

I was six when I first tasted the nectar of Rumi, poured gently into my soul by my mother's voice. She would sing his ghazals like lullabies, her voice a trembling echo of generations of Persian mysticism. I was too young to grasp the meanings, but I felt the longing. I felt the beauty. By ten, I had already memorized hundreds of Rumi's poems, with my mother as my first teacher. She saw my hunger for language and nurtured it.

One memory is still vivid: I recited a ghazal of Rumi at school, proud and innocent, only to be punished by the principal who found it inappropriate. But I didn't care. Rumi's words had already claimed me. They spoke to a deep, ancient part of me that neither school nor society could touch. It wasn't just poetry. It was home.

That early bond with Rumi became the undercurrent of my life. I was enthusiastic about Persian literature, even as I pursued engineering. I was captivated by language, by soul, by beauty. My academic journey eventually took me to Polytechnique Montréal, where I earned a PhD in Electronics Engineering. But no matter how far I went, I carried the rhythm of Rumi's poetry like a heartbeat.

Grief That Left Me Wordless

When my parents died, that heartbeat stuttered.

Language—my greatest companion—failed me. In the face of grief, it neither could articulate the emptiness, nor could translate the ache.

I was broken, not just by loss, but by the loss of meaning. What does life mean without those who loved you first, who shaped your soul? What is the purpose of ambition, of learning, of becoming, when the ones you want to share it with are gone?

It was then that Rumi returned, not through academic study, but through tears. I opened the *Masnavi* again, not as a student, but as a mourner. And I found there, in those verses, not answers—but companionship. Permission to weep. Permission to be lost. Permission to trust that love doesn't end, it transforms.

"This moment is all there is. Don't wait for tomorrow. Dive in now."
— **Rumi**

Why This Book? Why Now?

This book is born not of expertise but of experience. I am not a psychologist. I am not a spiritual master. I am simply someone who lost everything and slowly found his way back to life through grief, through poetry, through music, and through love.

This book is for anyone who has lost someone they loved so deeply that the world itself seemed to dissolve. It is for those who are still grieving—whether days or decades later. It is for those who want to do more than "move on"; they want to move **through**, to grow, to transform.

If you feel abandoned in your pain, you are not alone.

If you feel empty and confused, you are not broken.

If you feel a longing you can't describe, you are awakening.

This book offers no prescription. But it offers a path. A gentle path, illuminated by both the science of psychology and the soul of Rumi.

The Meaning Behind the Title: "Die Before You Die"

The title of this book, *Die Before You Die*, is not a dramatic metaphor. It is a sacred command; a spiritual call echoed through centuries of mystic tradition. The words originate from a quote by the Prophet of Islam, Muhammad, who is reported to have said:

موتوا قبل أن تموتوا

"Die before you die."

These simple, paradoxical words have echoed across time, through Sufi hearts and tongues, finding perhaps their most poetic echo in the work of Mawlana Jalal al-Din Rumi.

In one of his most transcendent ghazals, Rumi implores:

بمیرید بمیرید در این عشق بمیرید

Die, die in this love, die.

در این عشق چو مردید همه روح پذیرید

In this love, if you die, your soul will be received.

This call to "die" is not a call to end our physical lives. It is a call to surrender, to release the false self, the ego, the clinging, the illusion of permanence. It is about letting go of who we thought we were so that we may encounter who we truly are.

In the context of grief, this death happens uninvited. Loss strips away the illusions we held about safety, permanence, and control. But in this forced surrender, there is also an invitation: to awaken. To be transformed.

Choosing this title was not merely an artistic decision. It was the most accurate way I could describe what happened to me after the death of my parents. A part of me did die. But another part began to stir, slowly, like a seed cracking open underground.

Die Before You Die is not just the name of this book. It is the path this book invites you to walk.

The Meeting of Psychology and Poetry

In recent decades, psychology has deepened its understanding of grief. We no longer view mourning as a linear process or a checklist of stages. Instead, grief is now seen as a nonlinear, deeply personal journey. Modern frameworks such as the **Dual Process Model** emphasize the dynamic movement between "loss-oriented" and "restoration-oriented" coping. You cry one moment and go grocery shopping the next. You feel hopeful in the morning and desolate by evening.

Concepts like **continuing bonds** validate the enduring connection we feel to those we've lost. You may still talk to them in your mind. You may dream of them, hear their advice, feel their presence. This is not dysfunction. It is love.

And then there is **post-traumatic growth**: the idea that, in the aftermath of loss, some people do not simply recover—they evolve. They become deeper, wiser, and more compassionate. Their priorities shift. Their souls expand.

These psychological truths resonate deeply with Rumi's teachings. Rumi does not shy away from pain. He invites it in. He honors it. His grief over the loss of Shams[1] became the very soil from which the *Masnavi* grew.

"You have to keep breaking your heart until it opens."

— **Rumi**

What You Will Find in This Book

This book is divided into four parts, each one walking with you through the layered journey of grief:

- **Part I: Understanding the Grief Within** explores the emotional, psychological, and spiritual dimensions of mourning.

- **Part II: Walking Through the Fire** delves into the raw, overwhelming emotions of loss—from despair to guilt to the terrifying silence.

- **Part III: Finding Meaning in the Pain, Not Just Moving On** draws on Rumi's vision and modern psychology to help you understand how love can endure, how the soul can grow.

- **Part IV: Returning to Life, Gently** shows how you can begin again, transformed by sorrow but not trapped in it.

Each chapter weaves modern psychological theory with Rumi's mystic wisdom, along with personal reflections and invitations for contemplation.

---

1. **Shams** refers to **Shams of Tabriz**, aka, **Shams Tabrizi** or **Shams-e-Tabrizi**. The name *Shams* is derived from Arabic, meaning "sun." Rumi regarded Shams as a sun who illuminated his once-dark world upon entering his life.

The Door Is Already Open

If you are reading this book, you have already begun.

You have survived something unspeakable. You have asked the question: *How do I live now?* This book cannot answer that for you. But it can walk beside you as you find the answer in yourself.

Rumi reminds us that grief is not a punishment. It is a doorway. Loss does not mean the end of love. It means we are being asked to expand our understanding of it.

So, come. Sit with me. Sit with your pain. Sit with your longing. You are not alone.

Let us listen together, not for solutions, but for the deeper music beneath the silence.

"The wound is the place where the Light enters you."

— **Rumi**

Part I: Understanding the Grief Within

Chapter 1:
What Is Grief, Really?

Grief is the deep, acute pain we feel when something—or someone—we love is gone. It's not just sadness: it's a profound emotional response that may echo through our thoughts, bodies, and days. As Psychology Today explains, grief may encompass guilt, confusion, yearning, and physical symptoms like fatigue or heartache—because "*it is a reflection of what we love*". It's not confined to the death of a person; grief can follow any significant loss—an identity, a relationship, a dream. There is no fixed timeline, no one-size-fits-all process; some endure acute grief, while others may face prolonged grief where pain lingers and disrupts life long-term. In reality, grief isn't a path we walk through in stages—it's the wrenching reshaping of our inner world, uniquely and unpredictably tailored to each life it touches.

Definitions of Grief, Mourning, and Bereavement

Grief is one of the most universal yet deeply personal experiences a human being can undergo. It is both ordinary and extraordinary. Across cultures, continents, and centuries, people have faced the death of loved ones with rituals, tears, silences, and songs. But even with its shared human nature, grief feels—at its core—uniquely isolating. Why? Because every relationship is distinct. Every love is different. And so, every grief must be, too.

Modern psychology offers us a vocabulary to begin exploring this terrain:

- **Grief** is the emotional response to loss. It encompasses a broad spectrum of feelings: sadness, anger, guilt, anxiety, relief, confusion, and even numbness. It is not a single emotion but a storm of them. George A. Bonanno[1], a leading psychologist in bereavement research, emphasizes that grief is a flexible, adaptive response—one that doesn't follow a single script.

- **Mourning** refers to the external expression of grief. It includes rituals, customs, and shared cultural or religious practices that give form to internal sorrow—like funerals, wearing black, or periods of withdrawal. According to anthropologist Margaret Mead[2], mourning allows society to witness and validate loss, providing structure and meaning in the face of chaos.

- **Bereavement** is the state of having lost someone significant. It is the condition of being deprived through death. The Oxford Handbook of Bereavement (Stroebe, Hansson, Schut, & Stroebe, 2008) defines bereavement as a psychological, social, and physical experience that includes grief and mourning.

These three terms work together. Bereavement is the condition, grief is the internal experience, and mourning is how that experience is shared or expressed.

---

1. **George A. Bonanno** is a professor of clinical psychology at Teachers College, Columbia University, U.S. He is responsible for introducing the controversial idea of resilience to the study of loss and trauma. He is known as a pioneering researcher in the field of bereavement and trauma.
2. **Margaret Mead** was an American cultural anthropologist, author and speaker, who appeared frequently in the mass media during the 1960s and the 1970s. Mead was a communicator of anthropology in modern American and Western culture and was often controversial as an academic.

But none of these definitions can fully capture the reality of loss. Psychology attempts to organize what Rumi lived and expressed through poetry:

There is a sorrow in my heart, unknown to anyone...

— **Rumi**

Rumi knew what modern therapists and neuroscientists confirm: grief is not merely a response to loss—it is a spiritual unraveling, a breaking open of the self.

Neuroscientific studies using fMRI scans show that the brain processes social pain, such as the death of a loved one, in ways similar to physical pain (Eisenberger & Lieberman, 2004). The anterior cingulate cortex, in particular, activates during grief, explaining why loss can feel like a bodily wound.

Psychologically, grief can be both acute and chronic. The **acute phase** may bring intense longing and emotional dysregulation. In some cases, prolonged grief disorder (PGD)—recognized in the DSM-5-TR[1]—can emerge when these symptoms persist, deeply impairing function.

But this unraveling can also be transformative. As existential psychologist Viktor Frankl[2] wrote, "In some ways suffering ceases to be suffering at the moment it finds a meaning."

---

1. DSM-5-TR is the standard classification of mental disorders used by mental health professionals in the United States.
2. **Viktor Emil Frankl** was an Austrian neurologist, psychologist, philosopher, and Holocaust survivor, who founded logotherapy, a school of psychotherapy that describes a search for a life's meaning as the central human motivational force. Logotherapy is part of existential and humanistic psychology theories.

Shams Tabrizi echoes this to Rumi:

"Try not to resist the changes that come your way. Instead, let life live through you."
— **Shams Tabrizi**

Common Myths and Misconceptions

Despite the universality of grief, many of us carry damaging myths about how we "should" grieve. These misconceptions not only distort our expectations of ourselves but also make the grieving process more isolating.

Here are some of the most common myths:

1. Grief follows a predictable, linear path. This myth stems from a misunderstanding of Elisabeth Kübler-Ross's[1] five stages: denial, anger, bargaining, depression, and acceptance. These were originally intended to describe terminally ill patients, not the bereaved.

Contemporary research supports a non-linear model. The **Dual Process Model** (Stroebe & Schut, 1999) suggests people oscillate between loss-oriented and restoration-oriented processes. Some days are focused on the pain of the loss; others involve adapting to new roles and routines.

Rumi offers poetic insight:

"Don't get lost in your pain, know that one day your pain will become your cure."

— **Rumi**

---

1. **Elisabeth Kübler-Ross** was a Swiss-American psychiatrist, a pioneer in near-death studies, author, and developer of the five stages of grief, also known as the "Kübler-Ross model". In 1970, Kübler-Ross delivered the Ingersoll Lecture at Harvard University, focusing on her book, On Death and Dying.

2. You should be "over it" by now. There is often social pressure to "move on." However, grief has no universal timeline. Some mourn intensely for months, others for years. Neimeyer's[1] **Meaning Reconstruction Theory** emphasizes that grief involves rebuilding a personal narrative after loss, which takes time.

Studies show that even years later, reminders of the deceased can trigger fresh waves of emotion. This is not regression—it's part of the ongoing process of integration.

3. Expressing emotions is a sign of weakness. In many cultures, emotional restraint is valorized. But research shows that suppressing grief can lead to **complicated grief**, a condition associated with depression, anxiety, and somatic symptoms (Shear et al., 2007).

Rumi insists:

"The wound is the place where the Light enters you."

— Rumi

Allowing emotion is essential. Tears can be holy. Laughter can be sacred.

4. Staying "strong" means not crying. This misconception can be especially harmful to men, who are often expected to grieve stoically. But

---

1. **Robert A. Neimeyer**, PhD, directs the Portland Institute for Loss and Transition; actively practices as a trainer, consultant, and coach; and has published extensively on grieving as a meaning-making process.

grief requires vulnerability. Brené Brown's[1] work on shame and resilience highlights that emotional openness builds strength, not weakness.

5. Continuing bonds are unhealthy. Contrary to earlier models that encouraged "letting go," contemporary grief theory—like the Continuing Bonds Model (Klass, Silverman, & Nickman, 1996)—validates maintaining emotional ties with the deceased. Talking to the departed, honoring their memory, or even sensing their presence can be healthy expressions of love.

Rumi himself never let go of Shams. Shams became his inner companion, his muse, his spiritual mirror:

"The minute I heard my first love story, I started looking for you…"

— Rumi

The Uniqueness of Every Loss

Every grief is different because every relationship is different. The death of a parent, a child, a spouse, or a friend is experienced not just through roles, but through the emotional tapestry each relationship weaves.

Two siblings mourning the same mother may grieve entirely differently. Why? Because different memories, needs, and meanings shaped their bond. The **Relational-Cultural Theory** developed by Jean Baker Miller[2] and others supports this: human connection is central to psychological development, and each connection forms a unique matrix of emotion.

---

1. **Brené Brown** is a researcher and storyteller who's spent two decades studying courage, vulnerability, shame, and empathy.
2. **Jean Baker Miller** was a psychiatrist, psychoanalyst, social activist, feminist, and author. She wrote Toward a New Psychology of Women, which brings psychological thought together with relational-cultural theory.

Robert Neimeyer's Meaning Reconstruction theory argues that grief involves reshaping the narrative of self in light of the absence. If your identity was partially anchored in the person lost, their absence demands not just mourning—but redefinition.

My mother gave me the gift of Rumi. That bond was not merely maternal; it was poetic, sacred, and cultural. Losing her meant losing a voice that once formed my soul. My father's grief became a mirror for my own, and when he passed, I lost not only a parent but the only witness to the fullness of my loss. Rumi captured this uniqueness in each heartbreak:

"When the soul lies down in that grass, the world is too full to talk about."

— **Rumi**

Even silence has a different shape depending on who is gone.

Psychologists also point out the role of **attachment styles** (Bowlby, 1969; Mikulincer & Shaver, 2007) in shaping grief. Those with secure attachment may grieve openly and gradually find resolution. Those with avoidant or anxious attachment may suppress grief or feel overwhelmed.

But no theory can fully explain the ache of absence. It is a singular silence.

"Be like a tree and let the dead leaves drop."

— **Rumi**

هر چه می‌خواهی بگذار و بگذر

مولوی

Letting go is not forgetting. It is growing roots deeper into life.

Grief Through the Lens of Trauma

When grief is sudden, violent, or prolonged, it can overlap with trauma. The American Psychological Association defines trauma as an emotional response to a terrible event like death, an accident, or a natural disaster. Trauma in grief often manifests when the death was unexpected, untimely, or accompanied by helplessness or horror—such as with accidents, suicide, or medical negligence.

In my case, the long suffering of my mother and the painful helplessness of watching her decline created a trauma imprint. This was not only a loss, but a drawn-out rupture. After her death, my father's spiral into grief mirrored my own trauma. His chain-smoking and heartbreak left me with a double wound, a collapse of my emotional infrastructure.

Clinical psychologist Dr. Janina Fisher[1] notes that trauma is not just what happens to us, but what happens inside us in response. Your nervous system likely went into chronic stress: hypervigilance, sadness, numbness. Loss stacked on top of loss. It is grief entangled with trauma.

Rumi's verses often allude to death as a form of awakening. When viewed through trauma theory, we see how grief can rewire us—fracture our old world—and also become the ground of spiritual reconstruction.

"Be patient where you sit in the dark. The dawn is coming."

— **Rumi**

---

1. **Janina Fisher**, PhD, is assistant education director of the Sensorimotor Psychotherapy Institute, an EMDR International Association (EMDRIA) consultant, and a former instructor at the Trauma Center, a clinic and research center founded by Bessel van der Kolk.

Grief Rituals and the Body-Soul Connection

Throughout human history, cultures have used ritual to metabolize grief. Ritual gives form to the formless pain, a rhythm to the chaos. From wailing women in African villages to the "Ashura" mourning ceremonies of Shia Islam, from Buddhist cremation chants to Jewish sitting shiva, grief becomes embodied in collective ritual.

Modern psychology supports the power of rituals. Grief rituals—even invented ones—provide:

- A sense of agency

- Emotional containment

- Social validation

- Symbolic closure

Research by Norton & Gino (2014) shows that people who perform grief rituals report more emotional stability, even if the ritual has no religious meaning. Writing a letter, lighting a candle, walking to a meaningful place— each becomes a language the body speaks when the tongue cannot.

In my grief, perhaps my ritual became turning to Rumi. Reading Masnavi was a sacred act. Each ghazal was a ceremony. When others left, Rumi remained.

"There is a candle in your heart, ready to be kindled. There is a void in your soul, ready to be filled."

— **Rumi**

Rumi understood that mourning needs music, poetry, dance, and silence. His **Sama**[1], the whirling dance of the dervishes, is not merely a performance—it is a ritual of rebirth. Death is not just an end. It is the falling away of form, the turning of the soul.

Case Studies in Grief

Clinical Case Study 1: Sarah's Frozen Grief

Sarah was a 38-year-old graphic designer who went to therapy six months after her younger brother died in a car accident. Her outward composure was startling—she spoke with calmness and even joked during sessions. However, beneath this was a profound emotional numbness. She hadn't cried once since his death. Friends praised her strength, but Sarah admitted to feeling like a "ghost moving through life."

Her therapist recognized the signs of **disenfranchised grief**—grief that isn't acknowledged or validated. Because Sarah's family emphasized "getting on with life," she felt ashamed of any displays of sorrow. In therapy, she was guided through somatic experiencing and expressive writing exercises, helping her reestablish an emotional connection with her loss.

Rumi's verse became a turning point:

"Don't grieve. Anything you lose comes round in another form."

— Rumi

When read aloud in session, Sarah broke down. Her first tears were not only of sadness, but relief. In that moment, the frozen grief began to thaw.

---

1. Sama is a Sufi ceremony performed as part of the meditation and prayer practice dhikr. Sama means "listening", while dhikr means "remembrance".

Clinical Case Study 2: Ahmad and the Phantom Presence

Ahmad, a 50-year-old engineer, lost his wife to a sudden heart attack. Months after her death, he began to sense her presence. He reported that she would sit beside him, especially during his morning coffee. Friends worried he was "losing it," and he feared admitting this would make him seem unstable.

However, his therapist, informed by the **Continuing Bonds Theory**, reassured Ahmad that this was not uncommon. Many bereaved individuals report hearing the voice or sensing the presence of their loved ones. Rather than pathologizing the experience, therapy focused on creating a symbolic space for his ongoing bond with his wife.

Ahmad later said that allowing himself to talk to her—write her letters, and even smile at her favorite chair—was the most healing part of his journey.

Rumi's poetry validated this:

"Goodbyes are only for those who love with their eyes. Because for those who love with heart and soul, there is no such thing as separation."

— Rumi

Personal Reflection: A Room Full of Echoes

In the wake of my parents' deaths, the emptiness of my shared home became a mirror of my inner world. Their absence echoed through rooms once filled with quiet conversation, my mother's poetry recitations, my father's coughing, the soft sounds of companionship.

Friends who once checked in began to fade away, consumed by the current of their own lives. I was left not only with sorrow, but with a gnawing sense of invisibility. It was as though my grief rendered me invisible to the world. But one thing remained: Rumi!

In the silence, you turned to the Masnavi—not only as a book but as a companion, a lantern. Each verse brought breath to rooms that felt suffocated by loss. You weren't just reading Rumi; you were hearing your mother again. Her voice, her rhythm, her love encoded in syllables and song.

"Don't you know yet? It is your light that lights the world."

— **Rumi**

These words were not metaphors. They were balm. They were truth.

Reflective Practices and Meditations

These exercises are meant to gently guide the reader through the emotional and spiritual terrain of Chapter 1.

Reflective Practice 1: Naming the Loss

Objective: To define and clarify what was lost and how it is being carried

Instructions:

- Take a notebook or journal and write down:
  - Who did you lose?
  - What roles did they play in your life? (Parent, companion, teacher, mirror?)

- o What parts of yourself feel altered or absent since their departure?

- o What do you miss that feels intangible—touch, presence, voice?

Reflection Prompt:

"What part of my inner world now echoes with their silence?"

Reflective Practice 2: The Grief Timeline

Objective: To map the emotional shifts over time

Instructions:

- Draw a horizontal timeline.

- Mark key moments: the day of loss, the first month, the first year, anniversaries, holidays.

- Along this line, mark emotional peaks and valleys. Use colors or symbols.

- Where were you most numb? Most tearful? Most at peace?

Reflection Prompt:

"What did I learn about myself in these valleys and peaks?"

Reflective Practice 3: A Letter to the Departed

Objective: To continue bonds and process unfinished words

Instructions:

- Write a letter to your loved one.

- Say what was left unsaid. Ask questions. Express anger, love, fear, and longing.

- If it feels right, read it aloud.

Closing Prompt (from Rumi):

"Try to be a rainbow in someone's cloud. Let that someone be your own soul."

— Rumi

Meditation: The River of Grief (10 minutes)

Objective: To ground and soothe the nervous system

Guided Visualization:

- Sit comfortably. Close your eyes.

- Imagine a river flowing before you. It is wide, slow-moving, calm.

- Into this river, place your grief. Visualize its color, weight, shape.

- Watch it float downstream—not to disappear, but to become part of the greater current.

- Say softly: "My grief belongs to the river. I am allowed to rest."

"Be like a tree and let the dead leaves drop."

— Rumi

Cross-Cultural Grief Rituals and Mourning Traditions

Grief is a universal human experience, yet the ways in which societies mourn and honor the dead are shaped profoundly by culture, history, and spiritual belief. Across the world, grief rituals serve not only to honor the departed but also to offer structure, containment, and collective meaning to the bereaved. These rituals embody the very essence of what Rumi speaks of when he says:

"Don't get lost in your pain, know that one day your pain will become your cure."

— Rumi

1. Iranian Shi'a Traditions and the Forty-Day Mourning Period

In many Iranian families, the mourning period traditionally spans forty days, mirroring ancient pre-Islamic and Islamic customs. Ceremonies are held on the 3rd, 7th, and 40th days after the funeral, each marked with poetry recitation (often including Rumi), Qur'anic chanting, and communal prayer. This structure gives mourners a framework—a rhythm—to their sorrow.

The 40-day mourning period is echoed in Rumi's own worldview. His grief over the loss of Shams of Tabriz transformed into the vast river of his poetry, and he once wrote:

"With life as short as a half-taken breath, don't plant anything but love."

— Rumi

2. Mexico's Día de los Muertos (Day of the Dead)

Rather than suppressing grief, Día de los Muertos transforms it into a celebration. Families build altars (ofrendas) adorned with marigolds, candles, favorite foods of the departed, and personal mementos. Children are encouraged to engage with death as a continuation of life, not as its termination.

This joyful reverence reminds us of Rumi's counsel:

"Why should I be unhappy? Every parcel of my being is in full bloom."

— **Rumi**

3. Japanese Buddhist Mourning (Otsuya and Obon)

In Japan, mourning is both formal and continuous. The initial wake, or *otsuya*, allows family and friends to gather, express condolences, and reflect on the life of the departed. Annual *Obon* festivals welcome the spirits of ancestors with lanterns, dances, and food offerings.

There is a profound emphasis on *ancestral continuity* and *ritual remembrance*—not unlike Rumi's continuous bond with Shams and his transformation of loss into sacred union.

4. West African Grief Traditions (Ghanaian Funerals)

In Ghana, funerals are elaborate and often festive events, especially for elders who have lived long lives. They are seen as life transitions rather than terminations. Coffins may be shaped as animals, cars, or symbolic objects. Community support is immense—grief is not a private event but a shared, public honoring.

As in Rumi's verse:

"Try not to resist the changes that come your way. Instead, let life live through you."

— **Rumi**

5. Jewish Mourning Practices (Shiva and Kaddish)

In Judaism, the first week of mourning—*Shiva*—offers a structured setting for grief. Mourners stay home, avoid daily obligations, and are visited by the community. For eleven months, mourners recite the *Kaddish*, a prayer that praises life and God—not death—underscoring the transformative journey of grief.

This ongoing ritual rhythm parallels the Masnavi's emphasis on transformation:

"You were born with wings, why prefer to crawl through life?"

— **Rumi**

6. Tibetan Sky Burial and the Transmigration of the Soul

In some Tibetan Buddhist traditions, death is not an end, but a passage. Sky burials—where the body is offered to vultures—are based on the belief that the soul continues and the body is merely a temporary vessel.

These practices align with Rumi's recurring message of soul over body:

"I died as mineral and became a plant, I died as plant and rose to animal... I died as man and became an angel. What have I lost by dying?"

— **Rumi**

7. Contemporary Grief Rituals in the West

In Western psychology, a renewed interest in grief rituals has emerged, especially among those coping with ambiguous loss or disenfranchised grief. Practices like planting a memorial tree, creating digital tributes, writing legacy letters, or participating in grief circles are gaining popularity.

These modern rituals are rooted in **Narrative Therapy** and **Ritual Theory**, where symbolic action is used to help individuals reauthor their lives and integrate loss into a new identity.

Universal Lessons from Ritual

The universal lessons taken from ritual can be categorized as follows:

- **Containment**: Rituals provide a safe psychological and cultural space for the chaos of grief.

- **Continuity**: They create a bridge between past and present, life and death, presence and absence.

- **Community**: Whether in silence or in celebration, mourning rituals often draw support from collective experience.

Rumi knew this deeply:

"Don't you know yet? It is your Light that lights the world."

— Rumi

These grief rituals, from ancient Persia to modern digital spaces, affirm that the pain of separation is both uniquely individual and profoundly universal.

Designing Your Own Grief Ritual: Exercises in Meaning-Making

Creating a personal grief ritual can serve as a profound act of meaning-making, transformation, and healing. Rituals help give form to the formless, language to the unspeakable, and a sense of rhythm to the overwhelming chaos of loss.

The following exercises draw from psychological frameworks such as **Ritual Theory**[1], **Narrative Therapy**[2], and **Somatic Psychology**[3], while being inspired by the contemplative and soul-reaching vision of Rumi.

"With life as short as a half-taken breath, don't plant anything but love."

— **Rumi**

Exercise 1: The Grief Altar

Purpose: To create a sacred, physical space to honor your loved one and process your emotions.

Instructions:

1. Choose a quiet corner of your home.

2. Select meaningful objects: a photograph, a piece of clothing, a candle, a poem, dried flowers, or something your loved one cherished.

3. Arrange them with intention. You may place a verse from Rumi or a quote that consoles you.

4. Spend 5–10 minutes a day in front of this altar. Breathe deeply. Say aloud something you wish you had said. Or simply sit in silence.

---

1. Ritual theory posits that focused social interactions, known as rituals, are fundamental to all social dynamics, shaping beliefs, morality, and culture by generating group emotions and linking them to symbols.
2. Narrative therapy is a form of counseling where a therapist collaborates with a client to externalize problems, viewing them as separate from the person's identity, and then helps the client re-author their life story to focus on their strengths, values, and alternative futures.
3. Somatic psychology is a body-centered psychotherapy that views the mind and body as deeply connected and uses physical awareness and movement to address emotional and physical trauma and stress.

Reflection Prompt:

"What unspoken words rise in me when I sit before this altar?"

Exercise 2: Creating a Personal Mourning Ritual

Purpose: To develop a meaningful action or sequence that marks your ongoing love and mourning.

Instructions:

- Choose a time of day (e.g., sunrise, bedtime) or a meaningful date (e.g., birthdays, anniversaries).

- Choose an activity that feels sacred: lighting incense, writing in a journal, singing a melody, reciting Rumi's poetry.

- Repeat this ritual regularly. It doesn't need to be elaborate—consistency is key.

Rumi Prompt:

"When the soul lies down in that grass, the world is too full to talk about."

Exercise 3: The Grief Walk

Purpose: To externalize grief through physical movement, inspired by walking meditation and somatic release.

Instructions:

1. Choose a quiet walking path (park, cemetery, shoreline, or even around your block).

2. As you walk, bring your attention to the sensations in your body—your feet, your breath, your heart.

3. Each step is a prayer. Each breath is a remembrance. Speak your loved one's name if you feel moved.

Optional: Carry a small token that reminds you of them—a stone, a photo, a flower.

Rumi Reflection:

"The wound is the place where the light enters you."

Exercise 4: A Ritual of Release

Purpose: To symbolize letting go of guilt, anger, or sorrow while honoring what remains.

Instructions:

1. Write a letter expressing what you are ready to release— unspoken anger, lingering questions, regrets.

2. Read it aloud in a safe and private space.

3. Then, choose a release action:

   o Burn the letter safely.

   o Bury it beneath a tree or flowerbed.

   o Tear it and scatter it into moving water.

Rumi Prompt:

"Be like a tree and let the dead leaves drop."

Exercise 5: Planting Memory

Purpose: To create something living that continues in honor of your loved one.

Instructions:

1. Choose a plant, tree, or flower to plant in their memory.

2. Involve others if it feels right.

3. Say a few words or read a poem as you plant it.

As you water and care for this plant, it becomes a symbol of both loss and continuity—a living ritual.

Rumi Reflection:

"Don't grieve. Anything you lose comes round in another form."

— Rumi

Closing Ritual Thought

Grief rituals do not end grief. They hold it. They cradle the parts of us that cannot yet speak or make sense of the pain. These practices are bridges—not to forget, but to integrate.

"You were born with wings. Why prefer to crawl through life?"

— Rumi

Summary and Reflection: Embracing the Landscape of Grief

Grief is not a single path, but a vast terrain—unpredictable, raw, and uniquely shaped by each soul's journey. In this chapter, we have explored the psychological, cultural, and spiritual foundations of grief, mourning, and bereavement. We have learned to dismantle common myths, appreciate the singularity of every loss, and recognize grief as a deeply human, deeply sacred experience.

From trauma theory to Rumi's spiritual metaphors, we've seen that grief is not a sign of weakness or a problem to be fixed—it is an invitation to transformation. It is the echo of love reverberating in the empty spaces.

Across cultures, grief rituals serve as both balm and bridge. They help us contain chaos, channel sorrow, and create meaning. Whether through an altar of remembrance or a solitary walk through the woods, the act of ritual gives form to the formless, allowing us to begin weaving grief into the fabric of our identity.

"Grief can be the garden of compassion. If you keep your heart open through everything, your pain can become your greatest ally in your life's search for love and wisdom."

— **Rumi**

As you reflect on your own losses—whether fresh or buried deep in the past—consider what grief means to you now. Not just as pain, but as presence. Not just as absence, but as love remembered. Let your grief speak, and you may find that within it lies the seed of something sacred, something eternal.

Reflection Questions

1. What is one myth about grief you believed before reading this chapter?

2. How has your understanding of mourning and bereavement shifted?

3. What ritual or cultural practice resonated most with your heart?

4. If you were to create your own grief ritual, what might it include?

5. What would Rumi say to your grief today?

Write, ponder, sit in silence—let the conversation begin.

"This moment is all there is. Don't wait for the next moment to begin living."

— **Rumi**

Chapter 1 Summary: What Is Grief, Really

Grief is not a detour from life—it is life asking us to feel more deeply. In this opening chapter, we began to meet grief not as a problem to fix but as a companion to walk beside. We explored how Rumi's mystical lens and contemporary grief psychology both invite us to turn toward our pain, not away from it. We named the many faces of loss—visible and invisible—and rooted ourselves in a compassionate framework for the journey ahead. The threshold has been crossed. The path unfolds now not with certainty, but with sincerity.

Chapter 2:
The Psychology of Loss

Grief, though universal, expresses itself in ways as diverse as the people who bear it. Behind our sorrow lies an intricate psychological architecture—an interplay of memory, emotion, identity, and attachment. While no one model fully captures the depth of loss, several frameworks have helped clinicians, mourners, and scholars alike understand the shape that grief often takes.

In this chapter, we will examine three of the most respected psychological models of grieving: the Dual Process Model of Stroebe and Schut, Worden's Four Tasks of Mourning, and Acceptance and Commitment Therapy (ACT).

As with all aspects of this book, we will continually reflect on Rumi's teachings, which—though centuries old—mirror the wisdom modern psychology is just beginning to articulate.

The Dual Process Model (Stroebe & Schut)

Developed in the 1990s by Margaret Stroebe[1] and Henk Schut[2], the **Dual Process Model** revolutionized our understanding of grief by emphasizing that mourning is not linear. Rather, people oscillate between two primary types of coping:

1. **Loss-Oriented Coping** – dealing directly with the grief itself, yearning, sadness, and memories.

---

1. **Margaret Stroebe** is a professor at the Department of Clinical and Health Psychology, Utrecht University, and the Department of Clinical Psychology and Experimental Psychopathology, University of Groningen, The Netherlands.
2. **Henk Schut** is the coordinator of the international Master Clinical Psychology (CP) of the department of clinical psychology at Utrecht University.

2. **Restoration-Oriented Coping** – focusing on rebuilding life, adapting to new roles, and reengaging with the world.

This dynamic movement, called **oscillation**, is normal and healthy. The griever is not expected to "move on" in a straight line, but rather to dance—sometimes painfully—between moments of sorrow and moments of renewal.

"Don't grieve. Anything you lose comes round in another form."

— **Rumi**

This quote echoes the model's core: life after loss is not about replacing what is gone but allowing the movement between remembering and living.

Applications in Real Life

- A person might spend one morning crying over old letters and the afternoon paying bills or going to work.

- Some days are drenched in mourning; others feel almost normal.

- The model reminds us not to pathologize these shifts—they are signs of healing, not regression.

Rumi's Mirror of Oscillation

Rumi's poetry often explores the paradoxical nature of the human experience—joy and sorrow, union and separation, light and shadow. This duality parallels Stroebe & Schut's model.

"Try not to resist the changes that come your way. Instead, let life live through you."

— **Rumi**

Grief, then, is not something to conquer, but to move through. Like the whirling dervish[1], we circle between presence and absence, between past and future.

The Tasks of Mourning (Worden's Model)

Grief counselor J. William Worden[2] proposed a structured, active process to help mourners work through their grief. His model outlines **four tasks** that support emotional processing and reintegration:

1. **Accept the Reality of the Loss**

   The first task is confronting the stark truth: they are gone. This involves both cognitive recognition and emotional assimilation. Denial is natural in early grief, but must gradually soften for healing to begin.

2. **Process the Pain of Grief**

   Rather than avoiding pain, Worden urges mourners to feel it—fully, deeply. Suppression or distraction may delay recovery.

3. **Adjust to a World Without the Deceased**

   This includes internal, external, and spiritual adjustments:

   o   Internally: Who am I now without them?

---

1. A dervish, darvesh, or darwīsh is a member of a Sufi fraternity, or more broadly a religious mendicant, who chose or accepted material poverty. The latter usage is found particularly in Persian and Turkish as well as in Tamazight, corresponding to the Arabic term faqīr.
2. **William Worden** is a Fellow of the American Psychological Association and holds academic appointments at the Harvard Medical School and at the Rosemead Graduate School of Psychology in California. He is the author of Personal Death Awareness; Children & Grief: When a Parent Dies, and is coauthor of Helping Cancer Patients Cope.

- Externally: How do I manage life tasks that they once handled?

- Spiritually: What meaning do I make from this loss?

4. **Find an Enduring Connection While Moving Forward**

   The goal is not detachment, but integration. The love and memory of the deceased can become part of one's evolving story, carried with rather than left behind.

Psychological Integrity and Grief

This model helps us see grief not as a passive wound but as a journey of responsibility. Each task represents active participation in the soul's healing.

"Be like melting snow—wash yourself of yourself."

— Rumi

Rumi's words align with this model's essence: the tasks are acts of spiritual melting, where ego dissolves and a new self-understanding is born.

Acceptance and Commitment Therapy (ACT): Allowing Pain, Choosing Life

ACT, a modern behavioral therapy developed by Steven C. Hayes[1] and colleagues, centers around one vital principle: **suffering stems not from pain itself, but from our attempts to avoid it.**

---

1. **Steven C. Hayes** is an American clinical psychologist and Nevada Foundation Professor at the University of Nevada, Reno Department of Psychology, where he is a faculty member in their Ph.D. program in behavior analysis.

ACT teaches us six core processes that support psychological flexibility. In the context of grief, three are especially transformative:

1. **Acceptance** – Letting feelings be there, even when painful. This echoes Rumi's invitation:

"This being human is a guest house. Every morning a new arrival... Welcome and entertain them all."

— **Rumi**

Acceptance in ACT is not resignation, but spaciousness—the willingness to hold grief gently without needing to fix it.

2. **Cognitive Defusion** – Separating ourselves from the content of our thoughts. Instead of believing "I can't go on," we learn to see it as, "I'm having the thought that I can't go on." This subtle shift can create immense relief.

3. **Values-Based Living** – Even in grief, we can choose to act in alignment with our deepest values: love, connection, creativity, service. ACT encourages us to **move toward** what matters, even if sorrow travels with us.

Integrating ACT with Rumi's Path

Rumi's spiritual vision parallels ACT's premise: transformation comes not by escaping pain, but by befriending it.

"Don't get lost in your pain, know that one day your pain will become your cure."

— **Rumi**

Through acceptance, defusion, and values-driven action, the mourner becomes not a prisoner of grief, but a participant in healing.

Toward Integration

Together, these models—Stroebe & Schut's oscillation, Worden's tasks, and ACT's mindfulness—paint a picture of grief not as a static tragedy but as a living process of becoming.

In their depths, these frameworks affirm what Rumi has always whispered: that sorrow is not an ending, but a threshold.

"With life as short as a half-taken breath, don't plant anything but love."

— Rumi

Grief is not an interruption of life. It *is* life—more raw, more tender, more alive. And in working with it, we shape not only our sorrow but our soul.

RUMI'S CIRCLE: Spiritual Reflections & Guided Practices Inspired by Rumi

Rumi's circle is indeed a guided meditation practice, aka, *In the Circle of Those Who Mourned Before You*

"You were never alone in your sorrow."

— Rumi

Practice:

Create a quiet space. Sit or lie comfortably. Close your eyes. Imagine yourself surrounded by ancestors who have known grief. Feel their presence.

Ask them silently, "What do you want me to know about mourning?" Allow any message, image, or sensation to arise.

Reflection Prompt:

- Who showed up in your circle?

- What were you given, shown, or told?

- How did it feel to be witnessed in your sorrow?

Journal your insights afterward.

VOICES OF GRIEF

This collection presents a few global perspectives on mourning, drawn from diverse cultures, languages, ethnicities, and races, to highlight the shared experience and universal nature of grief.

Japan – "In the Silence, We Bow"

Mizuki, 62

"Grief is quiet, but not absent."

Ritual: Daily altar visits for 49 days.

Insight: "Even when I could not cry, I still showed up."

Rumi's Echo:

"The wound is the place where the light enters you."

— Rumi

Mexico – "We Dance with the Dead"

Diego, 39

"Grief isn't hidden. It's carried and celebrated."

Ritual: Día de los Muertos altars, food, laughter.

Insight: "Our dead just stepped into the next room."

Rumi's Echo:

"Every parcel of my being is in full bloom."

— Rumi

Somalia – "I Could Not Cry Aloud"

Hani, 47

"I lost my sister—and my home."

Ritual: Qur'anic recitation alone, baking ancestral bread.

Insight: "My grief lives quietly here—but it is still fed."

Rumi's Echo:

"One day, your pain will become your cure."

— Rumi

FROM THE FIELD: Personal Exploration & Practice Tools

Integration Exercise: Mapping Your Cultural Grief Story

Explore your grief's cultural roots and personal form. Write freely or use the prompts below:

1. What grief traditions did your family or culture pass down?

2. Were emotions expressed or silenced? How did this shape your way of grieving?

3. What rituals brought comfort—or didn't? Would you reclaim or redesign any?

4. Are there songs, poems, prayers, or proverbs from your heritage that you can turn to now?

Tip: Use Rumi's poetry as a bridge between your sorrow and soul.

Imagine him whispering across time:

"You were never alone in your sorrow."

— Rumi

Reflection & Integration

To begin this journey of reflection, we start by exploring how psychological understanding and soulful insight can come together in the face of loss. Bridging these two realms offers a more compassionate and holistic way to engage with grief—one that honors both the mind's need for clarity and the soul's longing for meaning.

Bridging Psychology and the Soul After Loss

Understanding grief through psychological models offers a vital framework—but true integration happens when these insights are brought into personal experience. Reflection and integration are not about solving grief like a puzzle; rather, they are about *making space* for grief to unfold meaningfully.

This section invites you to slow down, turn inward, and gently examine your relationship with loss. Through guided reflections, journaling prompts, and embodied practices, you'll explore how your grief speaks to your unique emotional world—while drawing from the wisdom of both contemporary psychology and Rumi's centuries-old teachings.

Reflective Questions

Use these questions for quiet contemplation, therapy sessions, or support group discussions. They are grouped by the psychological models introduced in this chapter and are intended to help you connect your inner experience with each framework.

1. The Dual Process Model (Stroebe & Schut)

- Can you recall recent moments of **oscillation** between sorrow and re-engagement? How did those shifts feel in your body?

- Do you ever judge yourself for "functioning too well" or "not grieving enough"? What would it mean to accept this ebb and flow?

- Are there restorative activities (work, art, laughter) that you've avoided, believing they dishonor your grief? Might Rumi's view of the soul's expansion offer a gentler permission?

2. Worden's Four Tasks of Mourning

- Which of the four tasks—acceptance, pain processing, life adjustment, or connection—feels most present for you now?

- What adjustments have you already made (internally or externally) to life without your loved one?

- In what ways are you still bonded to the person you lost? How can that connection evolve without trapping you in the past?

3. ACT (Acceptance and Commitment Therapy)

- What painful thoughts or emotions do you find yourself resisting or avoiding? How might you practice acceptance rather than control?

- Can you name one **core value**—love, presence, creativity, kindness—that still lights your path, even in grief?

- What does it mean to "move forward with the pain," rather than waiting for the pain to disappear first?

4. Rumi's Spiritual Insight

- How do Rumi's metaphors (guest house, melting snow, whirling dervish) resonate with your emotional state?

- "Die before you die"—what in your old self has been shed through this loss?

- In what ways has this grief called you toward a more authentic or loving version of yourself?

Guided Journaling Prompts

These prompts are designed for longer-form self-exploration. Find a quiet space, let your thoughts unfold freely, and return to these entries over time as your grief evolves.

1. **Describe your own oscillation** between sorrow and survival. What do these movements reveal about how you're healing?

2. **Write a dialogue** between you and your grief. What would it say to you? What would you say in return?

3. **List five ways your life has changed** since your loss—emotionally, spiritually, relationally. Which of these changes feels like a burden? Which, if any, feel like growth?

4. **Reimagine your future self** three years from now. What qualities of strength, compassion, or meaning might emerge from the heartbreak you now carry?

5. **Recount a memory or dream** involving your loved one. What unspoken message or wisdom might it contain for your current moment?

Embodied and Creative Practices

These rituals and exercises are designed to bring your reflection into movement, creativity, and sensory experience—key aspects of healing that words alone may not reach.

A. The Grief Oscillation Calendar

Create a visual grief diary:

- Choose two colors—one for days you feel deeply connected to your loss (loss-oriented), and another for days when you feel engaged with life (restoration-oriented).

- At the end of each week or month, reflect on the pattern. Does it surprise you? Validate you? What kind of balance feels most nourishing?

B. Rumi-Inspired Breath Meditation

Sit in stillness for 10–15 minutes daily. As you inhale, say silently:

"This grief is a guest."

As you exhale:

"I welcome it in."

This gentle mantra mirrors Rumi's *Guest House*, reminding you that emotions, even painful ones, are visitors—not invaders.

C. Worden's Tasks Collage

On paper or digitally, create a collage that represents the four mourning tasks:

- Use colors, photos, symbols, or words.

- Let this be both a visual journal and a ritual offering—something you can return to in difficult times to track your progress.

D. Values Clarification Circle (ACT Practice)

Draw three intersecting circles labeled:

- *What truly matters to me*

- *What soothes or grounds me*

- *What I want to offer to the world*

In the center, write the values or themes that overlap. Then, choose **one small action** you can take this week that embodies these values, even in the presence of grief.

Final Reflection: Pain as Portal

"Don't get lost in your pain, know that one day your pain will become your cure."

— Rumi

Grief, when resisted, can feel like drowning. But when honored as a sacred process, it becomes a crucible—one that softens us into tenderness, humility, and depth.

Let this chapter be a map, not a prescription. Let it point you toward the movement, meaning, and mystery in your own path. And most of all, let it remind you that you are not broken—you are becoming.

Grief Across Borders: Cross-Cultural Case Studies

While modern psychology often frames grief in individual terms, mourning is also deeply social and shaped by cultural traditions, spiritual cosmologies, and historical memory. What we grieve—and how we grieve it—varies widely around the world. Yet beneath these surface differences lies a shared human ache, and a shared yearning for meaning.

Let us journey across cultures to witness how the psychology of loss, Worden's tasks, ACT principles, and Rumi's wisdom find echo in diverse mourning traditions.

Japan: Silent Strength and the Ritual of Memory

Cultural Context: In Japan, grief is often expressed with *gaman*—a value of endurance, dignity, and emotional restraint. Outward expressions of pain are minimized to maintain harmony.

Ritual Example: The **Obon Festival** is an annual Buddhist tradition where ancestral spirits are believed to return home. Families clean graves, light lanterns, and perform *Bon Odori* dances to honor the dead.

Psychological Lens:

- Obon creates a **restoration-oriented space** for communal memory.

- The silence of *gaman* may inhibit Worden's second task (processing pain), but communal rituals act as gentle containers for sorrow.

- ACT's emphasis on values aligns with *giri* (duty) and *ninjo* (emotion): actions taken in grief honor relational integrity.

Rumi Parallel:

"Silence is the language of God. All else is poor translation."

— Rumi

Here, silence is not absence—it is reverence.

Mexico: Día de los Muertos and Joyful Grief

Cultural Context: In Mexican tradition, **Día de los Muertos** (Day of the Dead) merges pre-Columbian and Catholic practices. Far from morbid, it is colorful, playful, and intimate.

Ritual Example: Families build **ofrendas** (altars) with photos, candles, marigolds, and favorite foods of the deceased. Parades, skull art, and shared meals create a connection between generations.

Psychological Lens:

- This is an active embodiment of Worden's **Task 4**: maintaining bonds while living forward.

- Restoration and loss are *not separated*—they dance together.

- ACT's principle of acceptance is woven into the culture: death is not an interruption of life, but part of its rhythm.

Rumi Parallel:

"Why should I be unhappy? Every parcel of my being is in full bloom."

— Rumi

Joy in mourning isn't a contradiction—it is a celebration of the eternal.

India: Reincarnation, Detachment, and Sacred Fire

Cultural Context: In many Hindu traditions, death is seen as **moksha**—liberation of the soul. Grief is sacred, but *impermanence* is a guiding truth.

Ritual Example: Cremation ceremonies are conducted at the Ganges or sacred ghats. After 13 days, the family completes **shraddha**, a rite to aid the soul's passage and help the living resume worldly life.

Psychological Lens:

- Acceptance is embedded in philosophy: sorrow is acknowledged, but non-attachment is taught.

- Worden's first and third tasks (acceptance and adjustment) are spiritually integrated.

- ACT's cognitive defusion aligns with *viveka*—discerning the soul from thought and form.

Rumi Parallel:

"You were born with wings, why prefer to crawl through life?"

— Rumi

Grief is real, but not final. Fire is not an end—it is a release.

Ghana: Dancing With the Departed

Cultural Context: Among many Ghanaian groups, especially the Akan, funerals are lavish, multiday celebrations. Death is both solemn and *festive*— a passage into ancestorhood.

Ritual Example: Coffins are often shaped like fish, cars, or symbols of the person's life. Music, dance, and attire transform grief into spectacle.

Psychological Lens:

- Mourning is **collective and expressive**, aiding emotional catharsis (Worden Task 2).

- Social rituals support oscillation (Dual Process Model): mourning interweaves with music, laughter, and movement.

- ACT's emphasis on action aligns with communal, values-driven expression of legacy and continuity.

Rumi Parallel:

"Dance, when you're broken open. Dance, if you've torn the bandage off."

— Rumi

Here, movement is both metaphor and medicine.

Reader-Inspired Vignettes

(Note: These stories are representative composites drawn from real-life accounts to preserve privacy.)

✉ Yasmin, 35 – Iran/Germany

"When my father died, I moved between two languages of grief—Farsi and German. In Farsi, grief is poetic. We say 'delam tang shode' (my heart has become tight). In German, everything is so quiet, orderly. My therapist helped me blend both: I wrote letters to my father in Persian, but I also created a structure—walks, meditation—to feel his absence with care. I think Rumi saved me. His poems felt like messages written by my father from the beyond."

Framework Match: Oscillation (Stroebe & Schut), ACT Acceptance, Rumi's Guest House

Darius, 62 – United States

"After my wife died, I didn't cry for six months. I thought I was coping. Then I walked into a grocery store and saw her favorite cereal. I broke down in the aisle. My grief counselor explained that this was my body catching up. I started using ACT practices—labeling my thoughts, not judging them. I even began reading Rumi. He doesn't try to fix your grief. He just stands beside you and whispers, 'Yes, this too belongs.' That saved me."

Framework Match: ACT Cognitive Defusion, Worden Task 2 (Processing), Dual Process Model

Leila, 29 – Tunisia/Canada

"When my mother passed, my aunts held mourning chants for 40 nights. We cooked her favorite dishes and told stories. In Montreal, none of my friends knew what to say. I felt lost—like my culture of grief didn't fit in. Then I began creating my own ritual: Friday night candles, Rumi readings, and cooking her recipes. It became sacred. I'm still grieving, but I'm not lost anymore."

Framework Match: Ritual Integration, Worden Task 4 (Continuing Bonds), ACT Values Work

Integration Exercise: Mapping Your Cultural Grief Story
Reclaiming Memory, Meaning, and Mourning from Your Lineage

Every grief story is personal—but it is also ancestral. Behind your tears are echoes of the way your people, family, and culture have held loss across generations. This exercise invites you to reflect on the cultural and familial blueprint you inherited around grief—and how you might carry it forward, rework it, or heal what was never spoken.

Find a quiet space. Light a candle, play music from your heritage, or sit with a photo of an ancestor or loved one. Let your body feel rooted in time and place. Then reflect deeply on the following questions—not just with your mind, but with your whole being.

What are your cultural or familial traditions around mourning?

- What were the customs, rituals, or beliefs around death and mourning in your family? Were there ceremonies, specific clothing, foods, or periods of silence?

- How did your family mark time in grief—three days, 40 days, a year? Were these timelines comforting or constraining?

- Were there gendered roles in grief (e.g., women weeping, men remaining stoic)?

- How did your family talk—or not talk—about death?

Write about:

A memory of a funeral, a story you were told about how your grandparents mourned, or how your cultural group views the afterlife. What is passed down to you, and what might you want to carry forward—or let go?

Were you encouraged to express or suppress emotion?

- Growing up, what was your family's or culture's message about crying, anger, or talking about loss?

- Were you praised for "being strong" or "holding it together"?

- Were emotions like guilt, rage, or despair allowed space—or labeled as shameful or "too much"?

Explore:

How this emotional pattern may have shaped your grieving style today. Do you tend to internalize grief? Do you seek community or solitude? Consider writing a letter to your younger self, naming what they were taught and gently offering a new way forward.

What rituals or phrases brought you comfort? Are there any you want to reclaim or redesign?

- Were there mantras, blessings, songs, foods, prayers, or gestures associated with mourning in your tradition?

- Did someone in your family model a ritual of remembrance that felt meaningful—lighting a candle, wearing black, cooking a favorite dish of the deceased, keeping a photo on the altar?

- Are there traditions you felt disconnected from, or wanted but didn't receive?

Reclaim + Redesign

Create or adapt a ritual that feels healing to you now. This might be weekly journaling with your ancestors, setting up a seasonal shrine, dancing to ancestral music, or hosting a gathering where grief is named and honored. Let this be an act of both grief and creativity.

What stories from your ancestry—like poetry, songs, or rites—could guide your grief journey today?

- Were there elders, poets, storytellers, or spiritual figures in your lineage who spoke of death with beauty, sorrow, or wisdom?

- Are there lullabies or mourning songs you remember hearing? Proverbs about grief? Sacred texts or myths that made space for sadness?

- How did your people find meaning in suffering or connect with those who passed on?

Create a Soul Archive:

Gather 2–3 pieces of ancestral wisdom that resonate with your grief journey. This could include a poem, sacred verse, folktale, or family saying. Copy them into your journal. Reflect: *What is the deeper teaching here? What does my lineage want me to know about loss?*

Reflection Prompt: A Letter to Your Lineage

Write a letter beginning with:

"Dear ancestors, I am grieving now, and I want to remember how you grieved before me…"

Let the letter be a space where you honor what was wise, name what was painful, and envision how your grief might become a bridge between worlds—past, present, and future.

Rumi as a Soul-Companion

Use Rumi's poetry as a bridge between your own heart and your cultural memory. Across borders and centuries, his words remind us that grief is a threshold, not a dead end. Try reading this line aloud in your native language, if possible:

"You were never alone in your sorrow."

Imagine Rumi as a soul-friend, a mystic elder from the broader human family, placing his hand gently on your back and guiding you home—not just to healing, but to wholeness.

Printable Grief-Mapping Worksheet

Use this worksheet to explore your personal and cultural grief inheritance. Write freely—this is for your heart's unfolding.

Title: "Tracing My Cultural Grief Landscape"

1. Mourning Traditions from My Family or Culture

What were the rituals or customs after someone passed away?

☐ Funeral rites

☐ Memorial gatherings

☐ Special foods or fasting

☐ Mourning clothes (e.g., black, white)

☐ Time-bound rituals (e.g., 3, 7, or 40 days)

Reflections:

My people mourned by...

One tradition I want to carry forward is...

One I may want to question or release is...

2. Emotional Expression in My Upbringing

When grief or sadness arose, I was taught to:

☐ Stay strong

☐ Cry quietly or alone

☐ Express openly

☐ Avoid the topic

Reflections:

Growing up, my grief was seen as...

Now, I tend to deal with grief by...

I wish I had been told...

3. Words, Symbols, or Gestures of Comfort

Were there comforting phrases, prayers, songs, or objects?

☐ Specific blessings or verses

☐ Music, chants, or poetry

☐ Keepsakes (e.g., photos, jewelry)

☐ Shared meals or storytelling

Reflections:

What comforted me most was...

One ritual or gesture I want to reclaim or create is...

4. Ancestral Teachings or Guidance About Loss

- My ancestors taught me (through stories, poems, songs, etc.) that death means...

One story I remember about death or mourning is...

Today, I believe grief means...

5. Integration Prompt

Write a short letter beginning with:

"Dear ancestors, I carry this sorrow and I seek your wisdom..."

Printable Grief Ritual Design Template

Now it's time to design a sacred space to honor your grief—rooted in your soul, your story, and your lineage.

1. Name of Ritual (optional):

Example: "Evening of Memory," "Circle of Tears," "Feast of the Remembered," "The Silent Bowl"

2. Purpose or Intention of the Ritual:

What is this ritual for? (e.g., honoring a specific loved one, releasing pain, connecting with memory, asking for ancestral guidance, etc.)

3. Location & Setting:

Where will you perform this ritual?

☐ Home altar

☐ Outdoor space

☐ Sacred room or religious place

☐ Virtual / group ritual

☐ Other: _____

Describe the space. Will there be candles, incense, music, and photos?

4. What Will Be Included:

Choose the components that resonate:

☐ Lighting a candle

☐ Reading Rumi's poetry or sacred texts

☐ Playing specific music or chanting

☐ Writing a letter to the deceased or your past self

☐ Preparing or sharing food

☐ Silence or meditation

☐ Offering flowers, stones, or symbolic items

☐ Reciting personal or ancestral blessings

☐ Sharing stories aloud

List any specific poems, objects, or steps you want to include:

5. Timeframe and Repetition:

- Will this be a one-time ritual?

- Or a recurring one (e.g., monthly, on anniversaries, seasonally)?

This ritual will happen on: _____

I will return to it: ☐ Once ☐ Monthly ☐ On anniversaries ☐ Seasonally
☐ When I need it

6. Closing the Ritual:

How will you end the ritual with care and gentleness?

☐ A blessing or whisper of thanks

☐ Ringing a bell or sound

☐ Hugging oneself or others

☐ Journaling

☐ A walk in nature

Final Reflection:

After doing this ritual, I want to feel more…

I want to remember that…

My grief is…

Guided Meditation: Meeting Your Grief Ancestors
"In the Circle of Those Who Mourned Before You"

Best done seated comfortably or lying down, in a quiet space. You may light a candle or place a photo of an ancestor or loved one nearby.

Begin. Close your eyes. Take a deep breath…

Feel the ground beneath you—your spine supported, your heart still tender, your breath steady. Sense the long line of people behind you. Parents, grandparents, great-grandparents. Some you may have known. Some you have only heard stories of. Some remain unnamed—but all have known grief.

Breathe in… Breathe out…

Imagine yourself standing in the center of a circle. One by one, your grief ancestors begin to arrive. You don't need to know their names. You only need to feel their presence.

- One places a shawl over your shoulders—perhaps the shawl they wore when mourning their own loss.

- One hands you a small object: a flower, a stone, a thread of prayer beads.

- Another speaks softly: "We've been here too. We know the sorrow."

Notice what your body feels. Are you held? Are you weeping? Are you still?

"The wound is the place where the light enters you."

— Rumi

Now ask silently: "What do you want me to know about grieving?"

Wait. Listen. Perhaps you receive a message, a feeling, or just a sense of being deeply understood.

When you're ready, thank them. Whisper your own grief into the circle and let it be witnessed.

Slowly return… to your body… to this moment… to this breath.

Open your eyes. Journal your reflections.

- Who came?

- What were you shown or told?

- What do you carry forward?

Interview Dialogues: Grief Across Cultures

These fictionalized but *authentically grounded* conversations are composites based on real cultural traditions and lived experiences, offering a window into how grief is shaped and honored globally. They could be placed in shaded boxes or as sidebars in the book.

Mizuki, 62, Japan – "In the Silence, We Bow"

On Buddhist death rituals and restrained emotional expression in Japan

Q: How did you mourn your mother's death?

A: In Japan, we are quiet in our grief. There is not a lot of open crying in public. But we show our love in ritual. I visited her altar every morning for 49 days. I lit incense, rang the bell, and talked to her spirit. Even when I could not cry, I still showed up.

Q: Was it healing?

A: Yes. The silence became a kind of companionship. And every year on Obon, I feel her come home with the other ancestors. That is enough.

Reflection: Rumi writes, *"Your task is not to seek for love, but to find all the barriers within yourself that you have built against it."*
Mizuki's ritual became a doorway through silence—breaking the barrier between the visible and the unseen.

Diego, 39, Mexico – "We Dance with the Dead"

On Día de los Muertos and collective remembrance

Q: What does grief look like for you?

A: Grief isn't something to hide. It's something we carry and decorate. Every year, my family builds an ofrenda with photos, flowers, favorite foods of our loved ones. We laugh, cry, tell stories. My grandfather's cigar is always on the altar—still unlit, still full of spirit.

Q: What helps most?

A: Community. Color. The sense that our dead are not "gone." They just stepped into the next room. Día de los Muertos lets us feel close without needing to "move on."

Reflection: Rumi once asked, "*Why should I be unhappy? Every parcel of my being is in full bloom.*"

Diego's grief is not hidden in black. It is dressed in marigold. It blooms annually—and so, he says, does his grandfather's memory.

Hani, 47, Somalia (living in Canada) – "I Could Not Cry Aloud"

On refugee loss, exile, and cultural displacement in grief

Q: How do you experience grief as a Somali woman far from home?

A: It is layered. I lost my sister in the war, but I also lost my home. When she died, we did the *Qur'anic recitations* over Zoom. It was… empty. No wailing, no coffee ceremonies, no neighbors arriving barefoot from next door.

Q: What helps now?

A: I write her name in Somali in my journal every morning. I recite surahs for her. I started baking our old bread again, even if I eat it alone. My grief lives quietly here—but it is still fed.

Reflection: Rumi said, *"Don't get lost in your pain. Know that one day, your pain will become your cure."*

For Hani, ritual becomes a reclamation. Even in exile, grief finds a home.

Suggested Practice: Create Your Own Cultural Dialogue

After reading these stories, reflect:

- What would your story sound like in this format?

- How would you describe your grief through the lens of your culture or personal history?

- Try interviewing yourself or a family member using the same questions.

Prompt:

- "What does grief look like for you?"

- "What rituals or customs helped you mourn?"

- "What do you carry forward from your ancestors?"

You may be surprised by what emerges—what wisdom lives in your story, and how it echoes those around the globe.

Chapter 2 Summary: The Psychology of Loss

Grief is shaped not only by what we lose, but *where* and *who* we come from. In Chapter 2, we explored the powerful cultural tapestries that influence how we mourn, remember, and express pain. We honored ancestral rituals, silenced traditions, and personal grief maps. Through reflection exercises and cross-cultural storytelling, we began reclaiming the layered wisdom of our heritage. Rumi's universal voice reminds us: even across centuries and continents, sorrow speaks a common language—and the soul always listens.

Chapter 3:
Rumi and the Souls Perspective on Loss

Loss is not just an emotional event—it is a spiritual reckoning. It turns the heart inward and demands a deeper inquiry into the nature of life, love, and being. In the depths of grief, many have turned to spiritual traditions for answers, seeking solace not just in psychological frameworks but in soul language. Among the many guides who have walked this path, Rumi stands as a beacon for those yearning to find the divine in their suffering.

In this chapter, we turn to the timeless wisdom of Jalal al-Din Rumi, whose poetry does not deny pain but transfigures it. His vision does not offer escape but instead offers an invitation—to journey inward, to befriend impermanence, and to awaken to the Beloved that exists beyond the veil of loss. Alongside Rumi's insights, we will also explore how modern depth psychology and transpersonal theories echo his call: that beneath every sorrow lies a path to union, that the pain of separation carries within it the seed of spiritual awakening.

"Don't Grieve. Anything You Lose Comes Round in Another Form."

"Don't grieve. Anything you lose comes round in another form."

— **Rumi**, *Ghazal 1662, Divan-e Shams*

At the heart of Rumi's spiritual psychology lies one of his most quoted and deceptively simple teachings: **"Don't grieve. Anything you lose comes round in another form."** This line, with its gentle imperative and expansive promise, invites us to reimagine the very nature of grief, attachment, and transformation. But what does it truly mean—not just poetically, but psychologically and spiritually—to be told not to grieve in the face of profound loss?

This subsection unpacks Rumi's teaching through the lenses of modern grief theory, trauma studies, attachment psychology, and mystical insight, ultimately illuminating a path that does not bypass sorrow but transcends it through depth, perspective, and soulful surrender.

The Psychological Meaning Beneath the Poetry

At first glance, Rumi's instruction—"don't grieve"—might sound like spiritual bypassing or suppression. But when examined more deeply, it becomes clear that he is not invalidating grief; he is **transfiguring** it. Rumi does not deny pain—in fact, his poetry often bathes in it. What he offers instead is a transpersonal lens: one that sees the soul's evolution as continuous, and all losses as transformations rather than terminations.

Modern psychological frameworks can help us interpret this more clearly.

1. Post-Traumatic Growth (PTG)

Research into **Post-Traumatic Growth** (Tedeschi & Calhoun, 1996)[1] shows that many individuals report significant personal development following major loss. These include:

- Increased appreciation for life

- More meaningful relationships

---

1. **R.G. Tedeschi**, and **L.G. Calhoun**, (1996), The posttraumatic growth inventory: Measuring the positive legacy of trauma. J. Traum. Stress, 9: 455-471. https://doi.org/10.1002/jts.2490090305.

- Greater sense of inner strength

- Spiritual or existential growth

Rumi's teaching anticipates this modern finding. Loss may shatter one's life narrative—but from those shards, a deeper truth can emerge. This is not consolation; it is transformation.

"Grief can be the garden of compassion. If you keep your heart open through everything, your pain can become your greatest ally in your life's search for love and wisdom."
— **Rumi**

2. Attachment Theory and Transformation

From an **attachment psychology** perspective, we grieve most intensely when the loss threatens a core attachment—whether to a person, role, belief, or identity. Yet, secure attachment doesn't mean clinging. It means being able to internalize the presence of the other, even in their absence.

What Rumi offers is the ultimate secure attachment—not to the temporal form, but to the **essence** behind all forms. His teaching helps re-anchor the grieving psyche to something enduring: not the impermanent body or role, but the unbreakable bond of **presence, meaning, and soul memory**.

The Metaphysics of Form and Transformation

To Rumi, the world of forms is ever-shifting, but **nothing is truly lost**. Everything returns—albeit in a new robe. This is a deeply **Sufi**

metaphysical view rooted in the belief in divine unity (*tawhīd*) and the perpetual unfolding of God through manifestation.

"Why do you weep? That which you lose returns again in another way. It is not gone. It is transformed."

— **Paraphrased from Rumi's Masnavi**

Modern Parallel: Energy and Continuity

Even modern physics offers a poetic echo: **energy is never destroyed; it merely changes form.** When someone we love dies, their physical presence ceases—but their **energy** continues:

- In the way we speak, love, and create.

- In the memories that shape our values.

- In the legacies they leave behind.

In trauma therapy, especially in **meaning-making practices** (e.g., Neimeyer, 2001)[1], the most healing question becomes:

"How is my relationship to them changing, not ending?"

Rumi would answer:

"They are now everywhere, not just somewhere".

— **Rumi**

A Sufi Reframing of Grief

---

1. **Robert A. Neimeyer,** "The language of loss: Grief therapy as a process of meaning reconstruction." (2001).

Grief, to Rumi, is not a deviation from the spiritual path—it is **the path itself**. Every form we lose pulls us closer to **what is formless, eternal, and beyond separation**.

"You were born with wings, why prefer to crawl through life?"

— **Rumi**

In his cosmology, every loss is a kind of death—and every death a rebirth. Grieving is, therefore, an initiation into higher awareness, deeper love, and the relinquishment of illusions. As in the **whirling of the dervish**[1], each spin toward the inner center requires a letting go of the outer edge.

Grieving Without Grasping

"Don't grieve" does not mean "don't feel." Rather, it means:

Don't become so identified with the loss that you lose your ability to be present to life's renewal.

This aligns with **Acceptance and Commitment Therapy (ACT)**, where the goal is not to eliminate suffering, but to hold it lightly, while turning toward life-affirming values.

ACT therapist Russ Harris[2] writes:

"The goal is to live a rich, meaningful life while accepting the pain that inevitably comes with it."

---

1. The whirling of the dervish is a Sufi meditation practice from the Mevlevi order, where members spin in a trance-like state as a form of spiritual communion and prayer to achieve divine unity.
2. **Dr. Russ Harris** is one of Australia's foremost practitioners and trainers of Acceptance and Commitment Therapy (ACT), a mindfulness-based psychological therapy that aims to help you to reduce stress, overcome fear and find fulfilment.

Rumi whispers the same:

"Open your hands. Let the form go. Something truer is on the way."

— Rumi

Experiential Sidebar: Rumi's Circle – An Inner Dialogue on Loss

Visualize yourself sitting across from Rumi. You are holding your loss in your lap—heavy, fragile. He looks at you, not with pity, but with knowing.

Rumi: "Tell me what you miss."

You: "Their voice. Their laughter. The way they made me feel whole."

Rumi: "Have you noticed how your tears carry their voice now? How your laughter remembers them? How your brokenness is opening you to something even vaster?"

You: "But I don't want vaster. I want *them.*"

Rumi (softly):

"Anything you lose… comes round in another form.
Not the same. But not less. Let yourself be changed."

Reflection Questions

- What is something or someone you've lost that returned in a new form—through memory, insight, art, relationships, or dreams?

- In what ways are you being invited to grow through this transformation?

- What parts of your identity are ready to be shed, like old skins, so something deeper can emerge?

RUMI'S CIRCLE: Featured Reflection

"Don't Grieve. Anything You Lose Comes Round in Another Form."

— **Rumi**, *Ghazal 1662, Divan-e Shams*

Loss often arrives like an unexpected storm—stripping away what felt permanent, safe, or essential. Whether it is the death of a loved one, the end of a relationship, or the collapse of a role or identity we've long inhabited, loss leaves behind a haunting silence. In that silence, grief echoes.

And yet, in the midst of that ache, Rumi offers us this astonishing line:

"Don't grieve. Anything you lose comes round in another form."

These words are not an erasure of sorrow, nor are they an invitation to detach from the pain. Instead, they are a deep spiritual orientation—a compass pointing us toward the transformative potential within the experience of loss.

For Rumi, grieving is not only natural, it is sacred. But it is also not the final station on the soul's journey. Loss, in his view, is not annihilation; it is metamorphosis. What leaves us through one door, re-enters our life—or consciousness—through another.

This teaching sits at the crossroads of Sufi mysticism and modern psychology. It reminds us that everything in life is in motion—and that even the most painful departures may contain a quiet promise of return, though not in the same form we once knew.

To understand this paradox—and to allow it to hold meaning in the face of real suffering—we must widen the lens through which we view grief.

We must learn to see as the soul sees: beyond form, beyond time, and beyond endings.

In the following pages, we'll explore how this single line from Rumi encapsulates a powerful psychological truth: that transformation often disguises itself as loss, and that grieving is not only an act of mourning, but an invitation to perceive the hidden continuity in all things.

The Soul's Perspective on Loss

Rumi does not command us to deny our sorrow. He invites us to see it through the lens of spiritual transformation. Loss, he says, is not the end of something—it is the transmutation of form. Whether in love, identity, or the physical absence of someone dear, Rumi insists: nothing truly vanishes. It evolves!

Psychological Resonance

Modern frameworks such as **Post-Traumatic Growth (PTG)**, **Attachment Theory**, and **Acceptance and Commitment Therapy (ACT)** echo this wisdom:

- **PTG** shows that suffering can birth more profound empathy, insight, and purpose.

- **Attachment Theory** teaches us to internalize the love we've lost as an enduring presence.

- **ACT** encourages us to accept pain without becoming it, and to turn toward what matters.

Loss changes us. But not always in ways that diminish. In Rumi's world and in therapeutic reality, grief can become the gateway to awakening.

"Grief is the garden of compassion. If you keep your heart open through everything, your pain can become your greatest ally."

— **Rumi**

FROM THE FIELD: Trauma and Return

VOICES OF GRIEF: Omar (Jordan)

"When my mother died, I thought the sun went out. I couldn't pray, eat, or speak. But over time, her voice came back in my breath. I sing the songs she used to hum while cooking. It's like she changed form and moved into my heartbeat."

Omar's reflection exemplifies how the essence of our loved ones' lives on not metaphorically, but biologically, spiritually, and psychologically. They return in gestures, sounds, insights, even dreams.

Practice & Integration Tools
Exercise: "What Form Has Returned?"

1. **Recall a loss** that still feels raw or unresolved. Hold it in awareness gently, without judgment.

2. **Ask**: *Has anything from that loss come back in another form?*

   o A habit or phrase they used?

   o A new relationship that opened after their departure?

   o A shift in your own identity, values, or vocation?

3. **Reflect** in writing or drawing: *What has been lost and what has been reborn?*

Guided Meditation: "Transformation Through the Garden Gate"

(5–10 minutes, can be read aloud or recorded)

- Sit comfortably. Close your eyes.

- Visualize a garden—an ancient one. Its gate is open. You carry your grief with you as a small bundle in your arms.

- As you enter the garden, notice how the air changes. Time bends. The earth pulses with stories.

- Find a quiet stone bench and sit. Place your bundle beside you. Whisper to it:

  "I have not abandoned you. I am watching you transform."

- Slowly, the bundle dissolves. In its place grows a plant—maybe a flower, tree, or vine. Touch it. Smell it. What does it teach you?

- When ready, leave the garden with this new form growing within you. Let it shape your next step.

Rumi's Whisper

"Why do you stay in prison when the door is so wide open?"

— **Rumi**

Let this chapter—and this meditation—be a soft nudge toward the open door. Not to forget. But to remember differently.

Summary

This single line from Rumi "Don't grieve. Anything you lose comes round in another form" carries a world of psychological and spiritual insight. It does not ask you to silence your tears. It asks you to trust them. It suggests that the soul's journey is not interrupted by loss but *advanced* through it. And it gently guides you to open your heart, not only to the memory of what was, but to the *mystery of what is becoming*.

Rumi offers no shortcut through the valley of grief. But he walks beside us with a lantern, illuminating the path not away from loss, but deeper into life.

Mortality and Impermanence in Rumi's Poetry

"Try not to resist the changes that come your way. Instead, let life live through you."

— Rumi

Rumi's work is steeped in the language of transience. Rather than resisting mortality, he embraced it as the essence of life's beauty and the threshold to spiritual awakening. In his universe, impermanence was not a threat to joy—it was its very condition. Everything in the world, he teaches, is in a state of **becoming and unbecoming**. And the more deeply we understand this dance of arrival and departure, the more compassionately we can meet our own grief.

Modern psychology, too, increasingly recognizes that confronting mortality can deepen presence, sharpen our values, and clarify meaning. The rise of existential therapy, death awareness practices, and the integration of Buddhist impermanence teachings into contemporary clinical models echoes what Rumi declared centuries ago: **the awareness of death is a medicine, not a poison**.

Rumi on the Ephemeral Nature of Life

Across his works—especially in the *Masnavi* and the *Divan-e Shams*—Rumi weaves impermanence not as a melancholy thread but as a shimmering, golden law of the soul's journey.

"Try to learn to let what is simply be. The soul unfolds not in permanence, but in passing through."

— *Masnavi, Book 3*

Or again:

"With life as short as a half-taken breath, don't plant anything but love."

In this poetic economy, there is no wasted grief. Every sorrow is a reminder that life is not owned but **borrowed**, and this impermanence calls us to **live more fully, not less**.

Death as a Return, Not a Departure

Perhaps Rumi's most radical gift is his **reversal of death's narrative**. To Rumi, death is not the end, it is the return. His famous metaphor compares the body to a cage and the soul to a bird. Death is not destruction; it is **release**.

"Don't cry at my grave, I'm not there. I did not die."

— **Attributed to Rumi**

This sentiment reframes death not as annihilation, but as **reunion with the Beloved**, a release from illusion, from the temporary, and into the eternal.

Echoes in Modern Psychological Frameworks

We begin our exploration of modern psychological frameworks with those that face mortality head-on. Existential and meaning-based therapies invite us to see grief not just as a wound, but as a portal to deeper understanding, purpose, and transformation—an echo of ancient wisdom now reflected in contemporary thought.

1. Existential Psychology & Meaning-Based Therapies

Existential theorists like **Irvin Yalom**[1] argue that our confrontation with mortality can be one of the most powerful forces for transformation. Knowing that life ends can paradoxically awaken a deeper sense of **aliveness, purpose, and choice**.

This echoes Rumi's insight:

"Die before you die, so when death comes, you have already known its secret."

In therapeutic settings, clients who work through their fears of death often report greater **freedom, clarity of priorities**, and deeper compassion for themselves and others.

---

1. **Irvin David Yalom** is an American existential psychiatrist who is an emeritus professor of psychiatry at Stanford University, as well as author of both fiction and nonfiction.

2. Mindfulness & Buddhist Psychology

Contemporary mindfulness approaches (e.g., MBSR, MBCT) emphasize **impermanence (anicca)** as one of the central truths of existence. From this view, clinging causes suffering, and release brings peace.

Rumi intuitively expressed this centuries earlier:

"Don't grieve for what is passing. Everything that disappears is making room for something new."

The shared insight across cultures and modalities is this: **Impermanence is not a flaw in the system—it is the system.**

Sufi Cosmology and the Cycles of Becoming

In Sufi metaphysics, human life is part of an **unfolding spiral of creation and return**. Everything visible is temporary and in movement, while the **unseen**—the Beloved, the Source, the Real—is the only constant. This cosmology sees death as a stage in the soul's evolution, not its termination.

"You were born with wings, why prefer to crawl through life?"

Rumi invites us to see the soul not as trapped by death but **liberated through it**. His poetry offers a language for those who feel the weight of grief but long for glimpses of meaning within it.

Death as the Mirror of Life

In Rumi's poetic universe, **death is not the end** but a threshold—a veil through which the soul passes into deeper dimensions of reality. He does not speak of death with dread but with intimacy, awe, and even longing.

For Rumi, **mortality is the key that unlocks the deeper meaning of existence**. He urges us not only to accept impermanence but to live fully in its light—because it is only through loss and transience that we awaken to the eternal.

Modern psychology increasingly echoes this view. The field of **existential psychology**, as advanced by thinkers like Irvin Yalom, Viktor Frankl[1], and Rollo May[2], posits that **awareness of mortality can awaken a more meaningful life**. Rather than paralyzing us, the knowledge that we and everything we love will pass away can catalyze profound insight, purpose, and spiritual maturity.

Rumi and psychology converge here: both recognize that impermanence is not a problem to solve, but a truth to embrace.

Rumi's Death as a Wedding Night

"When the soul lies down in that grass, the world is too full to talk about."

— Rumi

The night Rumi died, December 17, 1273, is still celebrated by the Mevlevi Order as **Shab-e Arus**, or *"The Wedding Night."* It is not the anniversary of a death, but of **union with the Divine Beloved**. Rumi taught that death was not a rupture, but a reunion—a return to the Source.

---

1. **Viktor Emil Frankl** was an Austrian neurologist, psychologist, philosopher, and Holocaust survivor, who founded logotherapy, a school of psychotherapy that describes a search for a life's meaning as the central human motivational force.
2. **Rollo Reece May** was an American existential psychologist and author of the influential book Love and Will. He is often associated with humanistic psychology and existentialist philosophy, and alongside Viktor Frankl, was a major proponent of existential psychotherapy.

This is not a metaphor to him. It is a radical spiritual truth:

Just as a drop rejoins the ocean, the soul rejoins what it has never truly been separated from.

This reframing allows grievers to **view loss not as annihilation, but as a transformation of connection**. The form of the beloved changes— but the essence remains accessible, if not visible.

In modern grief therapy, such ideas are echoed in concepts like **continuing bonds** (Klass, Silverman, & Nickman, 1996)[1], which suggest that maintaining an internal, symbolic relationship with the deceased is not pathological; it's human. Rumi was centuries ahead of this: for him, death does not sever the relationship; it reveals its deeper, formless dimension.

Impermanence as the Path to Presence

"Try to learn to let what is simply be."

— Rumi

Rumi's view of impermanence is not limited to death. He writes passionately about the transitory nature of all things: youth, beauty, fortune, suffering, seasons of the heart. His poetry reminds us that **clinging to what must change is the root of suffering**—and that **surrender is the path to liberation**.

"Don't grieve. Everything you love will probably be lost, but in the end, love will return in another way."

---

1. **D. Klass, P. R. Silverman, & S. L. Nickman,** (Eds.). (1996). Continuing bonds: New understandings of grief. Taylor & Francis.

In ACT (Acceptance and Commitment Therapy), this principle is also central: **pain is part of life**, and resistance to it deepens suffering.

The goal is not to eliminate discomfort, but to open up to the full spectrum of human experience—joy and sorrow, gain and loss—with compassion and presence.

Rumi knew this. His poems whisper of a mysterious rhythm:

- What is taken will return.

- What is born must die.

- What dies gives birth again.

This rhythm is not to be feared. It is to be *danced with*.

Modern Western cultures often shy away from death. But traditional societies, like Maya's[1], frequently integrate **death rituals and ancestral communication** as part of the healing process. This aligns beautifully with Rumi's invitation to engage death not as taboo, but as a teacher.

Reflection & Practice: Sitting with Impermanence

A guided Contemplation: "The River's Edge" is suggested as follows.

- Sit in stillness. Imagine your life as a river—flowing, always changing. Along its banks are the faces you've loved, the dreams you've chased, the losses you've mourned.

- Now ask yourself: *What have I tried to hold on to that was meant to pass?*

---

1. The Maya civilization was a Mesoamerican civilization that existed from antiquity to the early modern period.

- Breathe.
- As the current moves, allow yourself to soften.
- Feel the river carry both your sorrow and your strength. Let go, gently.
- Say quietly to yourself: *"I allow the river of life to shape me. I trust the tide."*

Before moving on to the next section, let's intersperse this section with more tools such as journaling prompts, cross-cultural insights, or visual meditations. Indeed, interspersing this section with experiential tools will allow readers to emotionally and spiritually engage with the material, not just intellectually.

Below are thoughtfully designed inserts—journaling prompts, cross-cultural insights, and visual meditation exercises, each crafted to deepen the reader's integration of the themes of mortality, impermanence, and transformation through the lens of Rumi and modern psychology.

Reflection Journal: Mapping Impermanence in My Life

☐ **Prompt 1:**

Think of a time you resisted a change in your life—a breakup, a move, the loss of a job or role, the death of a loved one.

- What were you most afraid to let go of?
- How did holding on shape your suffering?
- What eventually changed—inside or outside of you?

☐ **Prompt 2:**

Recall a moment when something or someone returned to you "in another form."

- Did it come as a dream, a synchronicity, a different relationship, or a new layer of wisdom?

- How might Rumi's words, *"Don't grieve. Anything you lose comes round in another form,"* apply here?

☐ **Prompt 3:**

What are the "forms" you now carry within you from those you have lost?

- Are there gestures, recipes, sayings, or songs that live on in you?

☐ **Closing Reflection:**

Let your journaling end with the question: *"If impermanence is the law of life, what is the one thing that remains?"*

Cross-Cultural Insight: Impermanence as Teacher

☐ **Buddhist Practice (Tibetan Vajrayana Tradition)**

In many Tibetan Buddhist practices, students meditate in charnel grounds—sites of decomposition—to directly confront the impermanence of the body. The practice is not morbid. Instead, it is designed to awaken the **preciousness of this fleeting life**. Rumi echoes this bold intimacy with death when he writes:

"Don't run away from grief, o soul. Look for the remedy inside the pain."

☐ Japanese Aesthetics – Wabi-Sabi

Wabi-Sabi is the art of finding beauty in the imperfect, impermanent, and incomplete. Cracked teacups, faded wood, fallen leaves—these are not seen as broken, but as bearers of **soul and story**.

In grief work, this worldview allows us to honor our scars as signs of lived love. Try this: Next time you see something decaying—a dried flower, an old photo—pause. Ask: *What beauty does its transience reveal?*

☐ Mexican Día de los Muertos (Day of the Dead)

Rather than suppress grief, Día de los Muertos celebrates it. Through food, music, and altar-building, families **invite their ancestors home** once a year.

The veil between worlds thins, and the living commune with the departed—not as ghosts, but as kin. What if your grief was an altar, not a tomb?

Visual Meditation: The Sand Mandala

In Tibetan Buddhism, monks painstakingly create sand mandalas over days or weeks, only to sweep them away in a ritual of **impermanence**.

☐ Try this Visualization:

- Close your eyes.
- Imagine building a mandala—each grain a memory, a longing, a hope.
- Let your breath become your brush.
- Slowly, lovingly, sweep it away.
- As it dissolves, hear Rumi whisper:

    "Why do you stay in prison when the door is so wide open?"

93

☐ Integration Note:

This meditation helps loosen the mind's grip on permanence. It allows grief to move—not to erase, but to evolve.

FROM THE FIELD: Therapist's Note

Dr. Salma Rashid (Islamic Psychotherapist, London)

"Many of my grieving clients feel guilty about moving on—as if their love depended on staying sad. I often bring them Rumi. His words offer permission to feel joy again—not as betrayal, but as proof that the soul, like love, is unkillable. We explore how the one they lost is not 'gone' but woven into their breath, their choices, their next kindness."

Reflection Prompt:

- What parts of yourself have been shaped by someone who is no longer physically present?

- How might your future carry their presence forward—*in another form?*

RUMI'S CIRCLE: Living Impermanence Through Art

Create something—a collage, a sand pattern, a painted rock. Then, after a moment of gratitude… destroy it. Let it go.

Watch what arises.

Fear? Resistance? Grief? Relief?

This is impermanence as a teacher.

This is presence as practice.

RUMI'S CIRCLE: Embodied Practice—"Turning with Loss"

The ritual dance of the Mevlevi Order (*Inspired by the Whirling Dervishes* (*Sema*)) is more than aesthetic, it's a sacred turning toward truth. The whirling mimics the cosmos and the soul's rotation around love. When we grieve, we are similarly spun between absence and presence, death and rebirth.

Practice:

- Stand barefoot on the earth or floor.

- Begin slowly turning clockwise with arms open wide.

- Let one palm face the sky (receiving) and one toward the earth (grounding).

- As you turn, repeat internally:

  "What I lost… becomes what I become."

Let yourself stop naturally. Sit in stillness. Notice the internal echoes.

Design Tip: Style this as a circular motif with flowing lines around the text, evoking movement.

Visual Metaphor: The Phoenix Mandala

Image Prompt: In the center, a phoenix rising from ashes. Around it, Rumi's quote:

"Try to learn to let what is always moving move through you."

Reflection Exercise:

- Draw or paint your own version of the phoenix.

- Inside its wings, write names or moments you've lost.

- In the flames below, write what has changed in you because of those losses.

- In the sky above, write what you are ready to receive or become.

This creates a **living mandala** of impermanence, grief, and becoming.

VOICES OF GRIEF: "Stories of Becoming"

A series of short quotes or micro-narratives from diverse grievers about how something or someone returned to them "in another form."

Sample Quotes:

- ☐ *"My grandmother died before I had kids, but I see her in the way I braid my daughter's hair. It's like her hands are mine now."*—Nadia, Morocco

- ● *"When my best friend died, I couldn't sleep. Then I started writing letters to her. Now those letters are a blog helping others. She became my purpose."*—David, Canada

- ☐ *"In my culture, we say, 'You live in the names of those who speak you.' My father's name is still in my mouth. So he lives."*—Laila, Syria

Prompt for Reader:

- When has grief shaped you into something new?

- What form might your loved one or lost self be taking now—in your work, your words, your heart?

Design Tip: Place these voices in a highlighted text block with a soft, translucent background—perhaps parchment-style or dusky blue tones—evoking a sense of memory.

Mini Meditation: "The Formless Whisper"

◆ **Close your eyes**. Breathe gently. Imagine someone or something you've lost.

◆ Visualize them not as a solid body, but as light, fragrance, wind.

◆ Ask silently: *"In what form do you visit me now?"*

◆ Sit and listen—not for language, but for a whisper in sensation.

This meditation opens the soul's ear to the unseen forms loss takes—intuition, synchronicity, creative spark, ancestral presence.

Design Tip: Feature this on a textured background resembling clouds or light mist.

Creative Writing Prompt: "Letters to the Formless"

Write a letter to what you lost—but address it in its new form.

• If it's a person, address it to "The Song You Became" or "The Quiet Strength I Now Feel."

• If it's a role or identity, write to "The Space You Left Behind" or "The Fire That Reforged Me."

End the letter with: *"Thank you for coming back to me."*

🖉 This technique supports grief integration through metaphor and re-mapping.

Somatic Inquiry: "Grief as River, Not Stone"

Touch your heart gently with both hands.

- Ask: *"What part of me still wants to hold on?"*

- Ask: *"What part of me is ready to let flow?"*

Imagine grief not as a rock lodged in the chest, but as a **river**. It can be fierce, but it moves.

"You were born with wings. Why prefer to crawl through life?"

— Rumi

Let grief move *through* you, not *become* you.

RUMI'S CIRCLE: "The Form Beneath the Form"

"With life as short as a half-taken breath, don't plant anything but love."

— Rumi

Contemplative Art Practice

✎ **Materials**: A blank sheet of paper and colored pencils or markers.

- Draw a symbol of what you lost. Let it emerge intuitively— perhaps a name, a date, a broken object, or a heart.

- Now, draw what came into your life afterward—a friend, a feeling, a talent, a silence.

- Connect the two with a spiral, wave, or thread.

- Title your piece: "The Form Beneath the Form."

This practice taps into Jungian archetypal work—making the invisible visible through creative expression. In Rumi's world, what is *lost* returns in *disguise*.

Cross-Cultural Wisdom: "Loss Across the Traditions"

Grief takes many forms across world cultures. Here, we offer wisdom from spiritual traditions that echo Rumi's vision of impermanence and return.

§ **Tibetan Buddhism**: The *Bardo Thödol* (Tibetan Book of the Dead) teaches that consciousness passes through states between death and rebirth. Loss is part of a sacred cycle—not an end.

❉ **Mexican Día de los Muertos**: Ancestors return to feast and dance with the living. The form may change, but the bond remains.

☽ **Islamic Sufism** (Rumi's path): *Fanaa* (annihilation of the ego) leads to *Baqaa* (eternal subsistence in God). Death becomes a doorway to Oneness.

🕯 **Hinduism**: The *Bhagavad Gita* reminds us, *"The soul is neither born, and it never dies... it simply passes into new forms."*

↺ These traditions affirm that grief is not failure—it's a gateway to connection with something larger, timeless, and often beyond the intellect.

Journal Reflection: "When I Became New"

Prompt the reader with soul-deep questions that guide insight and integration:

- What part of me died when I lost _____?

- What part of me was born afterward?

- How might my grief be shaping the next version of myself?

- If Rumi sat with me now, what would he see in the ashes of my sorrow?

💡 Encourage them to *write with candlelight or in silence*, inviting inner stillness. Frame this practice as a "Letter to the Self That Is Becoming."

Guided Visualization: "The Garden of Returning"

❀ A gentle, somatic visualization that can be read aloud or recorded for personal listening.

"Close your eyes. Imagine walking through a fog… something is missing. The air is thick with longing.

Then, a shape emerges—not what you lost, but what it became. It might be music. A tree. A child's laughter. A warm wind.

It speaks to you—not in words, but in presence.

You sit together in a garden that was planted by your grief.

And you understand… it never left. It simply returned in another form."

📌 **Design Tip**: Frame this visually with a border of petals or leaves gently turning into stars—evoking transmutation and cyclical rebirth.

"Sound of Loss" Practice—Somatic Vocalization

🎙 This experiential exercise is inspired by both polyvagal theory and Sufi devotional practices like *zikr* (chanting the names of God).

✦ **Instructions:**

- Sit with eyes closed.

- Inhale deeply. As you exhale, let out a tone, any sound, that feels like your grief.

- Repeat 5–7 times.

- Then, shift to humming or chanting a simple phrase such as "I am becoming."

⚖️ This blends **somatic release** (used in trauma recovery) with **devotional practices** (used in Sufism and many mystical paths). Let the body *speak what words cannot*.

Callout: "The Alchemy of Disappearance"

Rumi said:

"Don't get lost in your pain. Know that one day your pain will become your cure."

🍄 Prompt for Discussion or Reflection:

- What in your life seemed like a curse at the time but shaped you into someone stronger or more tender?

- Could your grief itself become medicine—for yourself or others?

◇ Encourage readers to find one action—small or symbolic—through which their pain might serve someone else: planting a tree, writing a song, holding space for another.

Visual Map: "The Shape of Losses Past"

☐ Create a visual *timeline or constellation* of previous losses, charting:

- What was lost?

- What came in its place?

- What quality was developed? (e.g., courage, empathy, solitude, awareness)

Connect them with curved lines—representing the flowing, nonlinear path of soul growth.

📌 This can be a **fold-out insert** or a guided template offered at the back of the book.

RUMI'S CIRCLE: "Loss as an Invitation to Divine Intimacy"

"You were born with wings, why prefer to crawl through life?"—Rumi

✦ Intimacy Exercise: The "Letter to the Beloved"

🖊 This writing prompt blends Attachment Theory with Sufi spiritual love:

- Write a letter to your lost loved one as if they are still listening.
- Say what remains unsaid. Whisper the secrets, sorrows, or thanks.
- Then write a second letter—from the Beloved to you. Imagine they respond not with judgment, but with pure grace.

🕊 This exercise transforms grief into a dialogue, deepening the continuing bond while acknowledging impermanence. Psychologically, it supports **emotional processing and relational closure**.

Visual Styling Tip: Include a parchment-style callout box titled "Your Soul Correspondence," framed with soft brushstroke borders.

VOICES OF GRIEF: "Grievers Across Time & Place"

📖 First-person stories or mini-interviews that offer **cross-cultural resonance**.

From India: A Granddaughter's Ritual

"In our house, when my grandfather died, we didn't say goodbye. We gathered in silence for 13 days. Every morning, we sang songs he loved. By the end, his absence had become music in the walls."

From the American Southwest: The Empty Chair

"We set a place at the table for my sister every Christmas. Not out of superstition, but to remember she's still part of us. That chair doesn't make us sad—it anchors us."

From West Africa: The Mourning Dance

"My aunt wailed in the yard and tore her clothes. Then, two days later, we danced. The drums said, 'She lives in the music now.' I understood grief not as sorrow, but movement."

These stories act as **soul mirrors**, expanding empathy while normalizing diverse grief practices. They ground the abstract in *embodied wisdom*.

JOURNAL PROMPT: "What Returned?"

"Don't grieve. Anything you lose comes round in another form."

✦ **Writing Inquiry:**

- Think of something or someone you lost deeply.

- What (if anything) came in its place?

- Was there a new friend, a purpose, an inner strength, a silence that taught you to listen?

- If you imagined the loss as a *teacher*, what was its lesson?

▐ Encourage a "stream-of-consciousness" style, no editing, just flow. This allows unconscious connections to emerge.

SOMATIC PRACTICE: "Embodied Transmutation"

⃞♀ This gentle body-based ritual draws from trauma-informed yoga and Rumi's whirling metaphor of transformation.

The Movement:

1. Stand with feet grounded, arms at sides.

2. Inhale deeply. As you exhale, slowly turn in a small clockwise circle.

3. Place one hand on your heart, the other over your belly.

4. Whisper aloud:

> *"What was lost… is changing form."*
> *"I allow space for what is becoming."*

✺ Repeat three times, each time with slightly more movement.

This exercise brings **somatic integration** to the existential truth of impermanence.

VISUAL MEDITATION: "The Shifting Sands"

✦ **Design Element: Full-Page Illustration or Fold-Out**

Create a minimalist illustration showing:

- A sand mandala in its complete form.

- Then, a hand gently blowing it away.

- The grains of colored sand drift into the sky and re-form into stars.

📌 Caption: *"The shape has changed, but the essence remains."*

This image anchors the idea that what we grieve is never truly gone but only transformed. It draws on Buddhist sand mandala rituals and Rumi's elemental symbolism.

EXPERIENTIAL RITUAL: "Light the Lost Into Becoming"

🕯 A simple but profound fire ritual for letting go, inspired by Rumi's reverence for burning as sacred transformation.

✦ **Instructions:**

1. On small slips of paper, write:

   o The name of what was lost.

   o The feeling it left behind.

   o What it may be turning into (e.g., strength, compassion).

2. Fold each slip gently, breathe into it, and place it in a fireproof bowl or outdoor flame.

3. As it burns, whisper:

"May this loss become light."

"May what was taken return in another form."

This practice honors **symbolic release** and **neuro-emotional rewiring** through gesture and visualization.

DESIGN FEATURE: "The Morphing Thread"

📌 A subtle, symbolic thread motif can be visually interwoven throughout the pages of this chapter.

- On each page, a faint thread runs along the margin.
- It frays, knots, loops, and eventually glows, symbolizing the journey of loss into light.

💡 This creates continuity not just of content, but of experience— readers feel guided even between words.

Following this section, we will expand the experiential dimension further, honoring the soul of this section— "Don't grieve. Anything you lose comes round in another form"—by giving readers **multiple, embodied, and soul-nourishing ways** to feel into this transformation. These tools speak to **emotional integration, spiritual insight, and psychological restoration**, offering a bridge between Rumi's mystical worldview and today's trauma-informed healing models.

FROM THE FIELD: "Therapists on Loss and Transformation"

💬 **A Sidebar Featuring Reflections from Psychotherapists & Healers**

"When a client says, 'I feel like part of me died,' I invite them to explore what might be trying to be born in that space. This echoes Rumi's belief in the soul's regenerative rhythm."
— *Dr. Leila N., grief therapist, Toronto*

"In somatic therapy, we often ask, 'Where is your loss living in the body?' Once that's known, transformation can begin. Rumi reminds us that what breaks open can also let in light."

— *Aminah F., trauma-informed yoga guide, Cairo*

"Many of my patients begin their healing by reclaiming the smallest ember: a ritual, a scent, a phrase. Rumi's line—'Anything you lose comes round in another form'—is less poetic metaphor, more neurological truth."
— *Dr. Paul V., integrative psychiatrist, San Francisco*

◇ These voices support readers in knowing their grief is not only valid—but also a shared human threshold into wholeness.

TOOLBOX: "Grief & Form-Shift Tracker"

▣ A worksheet-style practice for ongoing reflection and journaling.

Instructions: Over time, track how a significant grief may be *changing shape* in your life.

WHAT WAS LOST	INITIAL EMOTION	WHAT'S EMERGING NOW	POSSIBLE FORM IT'S TAKING
A relationship	Grief, numbness	More solitude and intuition	Stronger inner boundaries
A home or homeland	Displacement	Longing for rootedness	Starting a garden, community
A belief or identity	Confusion	Spaciousness	Deeper faith, spiritual openness

♥ Use this tool monthly. Healing may be slow, nonlinear, or invisible—but these quiet transformations matter.

𝓢 You may label this visual sidebar as:

"Tracking the Return: How Loss Morphs Over Time"

RUMI'S CIRCLE: "Whispers of Becoming"

🎧 **Audio Companion Suggestion** (For future audiobook or website companion)

Create a soundscape titled *"Whispers of Becoming"* that pairs Rumi's poetry with music and guided imagery. Include lines like:

"Try not to resist the changes that come your way. Instead, let life live through you."

"Don't grieve… it will return. Maybe not as you expect—but as you need."

🔊 Backed by ney[1], flute or soft daf[2] drum rhythms, this meditation lets listeners absorb the **truth of impermanence in the language of the body and breath**.

📌 If this is for print, include a QR code or short URL to access the companion audio.

VISUAL CALLIGRAPHY PANEL: "Return in Another Form"

A hand-lettered page or spread using **Sufi-inspired calligraphy or Eastern geometric design**.

Text:

"Don't grieve. Anything you lose comes round in another form."
— **Rumi**

📐 Surround this phrase with visual symbols of transmutation:

- A seed becoming a flower

- A broken vase forming a mosaic

- The moon in different phases

- A phoenix in subtle silhouette

🏛 **Design Tip**: This can function as a *mini-poster* or journal insert. Use gold accents and indigo tones to invoke mysticism and warmth.

---

1. Ney is an end-blown flute that figures prominently in traditional Persian, Turkish, Jewish, Arab, and Egyptian music. In some of these musical traditions, it is the only wind instrument used.
2. Daf, also known as dâyere and riq, is an Iranian frame drum musical instrument, also used in popular and classical music in Persian-influenced South and Central Asia, such as in Afghanistan, Azerbaijan, and Turkey.

SHADOW PRACTICE: "Meeting the Doubter"

🕯 Loss can awaken parts of us that resist Rumi's message. Honor that complexity.

✦ Inner Dialogue Exercise:

1. Close your eyes and imagine the part of you that doesn't believe anything will "return."

2. Ask: "What do you most fear?"

3. Now imagine your inner Beloved (or guide) responds—not to correct you, but to *sit beside* your grief.

4. Record the dialogue in your journal:

   o What did the doubting part say?

   o How did the Beloved respond?

⬤ Inspired by **Internal Family Systems** and **Sufi companionship with the self**, this exercise helps integrate rather than bypass emotional reality.

CROSS-CULTURAL VISUAL GALLERY: "Loss Transformed Around the World"

A photo or sketch-based visual layout showing:

- Tibetan monks destroying a sand mandala after days of building it, representing impermanence.

- An altar in Mexico's Día de los Muertos—celebrating continued presence.

- A Sufi dervish spinning—embodying ecstatic surrender and form-shifting.

- Japanese **Kintsugi** pottery—cracks filled with gold to highlight healing, not hide it.

📌 Each image is paired with a quote from Rumi and a caption on how the culture embodies loss-as-return.

☯ Label this section:

"The World Turns, and So Do We: Images of Transformation"

PRACTICE: "Gratitude for What Was Not Meant to Stay"

☐ A more subtle, soulful exercise. Rumi often reminds us that grief comes not from loss alone, but from **attachment to permanence**.

✦ **Journaling Questions:**

- What was once precious to you, but you needed to leave?

- What longing still lives in your body when you think of it?

- Can you thank it for shaping who you are, even if it broke you?

📌 Frame this as an advanced reflection: not for when grief is raw, but for when readers feel *ready* to find meaning.

Now, let's continue deepening "Don't grieve. Anything you lose comes round in another form" with *even more immersive forms of soul-level engagement.* These tools are designed to engage the *limbic system (emotional processing), right-brain creativity (imagery and symbol), and soul-memory (ancestral and poetic resonance).*

They are ideal for layout integration as experiential inserts, either at the end of the section or scattered throughout as spacious breathers.

RITUAL: "Offering to the Returning Form"

❀ A sacred home ritual for acknowledging loss and inviting its next incarnation.

Materials:

- A candle

- A bowl of water or sand

- A small token representing your grief (e.g., a stone, note, dried flower)

- A Rumi verse (optional: write it on paper)

Steps:

1. **Prepare a sacred space**—Sit quietly, light a candle.

2. Hold your token and say aloud or silently:

   "I offer this as witness to what was lost."

3. Drop it into the bowl. Let silence follow.

4. Now speak the invitation:

   "May what I've lost return in a form I can receive."

5. Read or recite Rumi's line:

   "Don't grieve. Anything you lose comes round in another form."

🖐 Close the ritual with a breath and a gesture of gratitude.

📷 *Tip: Include a visual diagram of the altar layout for design enhancement.*

✦ GUIDED SOUNDSCAPE: "Return of Form" (Imaginal Meditation)

🜁 A deeply calming **imaginal journey** using breath, archetypal symbols, and gentle sound.

For audiobook, website companion, or QR-code access:

Voiceover Script Excerpt:

"Breathe slowly. Imagine you are in a vast field of golden grass. Something you've lost appears in the distance—not as it was, but in a different form. Perhaps a bird. A star. A whisper. It is not what it used to be, and yet you recognize it with your whole heart…"

💡 *Include embedded sound: Ney flute, ocean waves, or faint chanting of Rumi in Farsi or Persian calligraphy brushstrokes appearing visually.*

☐ Can be titled **"Meditation: The Shape of What Remains."**

✦ VISUAL ART CARD: "Transfiguration Mandala"

🎨 A one-page **transformational mandala** centered around Rumi's line.

Design suggestion:

- Concentric circles that evolve from dark inner rings (loss) to glowing outer petals (return).

- Embedded in the outer edges: words like *"Memory, Change, Renewal, Becoming"*

- Center quote:

"Anything you lose comes round in another form."

⬛ *Can be printed in greyscale for reader coloring.*

✎ Include guidance: "Color this mandala in silence while asking: What is ready to return to me in a new form?"

MINI PRACTICE DECK: "Forms of Return" Oracle

♠ Create 5–7 oracle-style "mini cards" at the back of the chapter (or printed detachable insert) with one symbolic archetype per card and its meaning.

Examples:

Card	Symbol	Message
The Bird	Wings	"Freedom now lives where loss once perched."
The Mirror	Reflection	"You're seeing yourself more clearly through what was taken."
The Flame	Candle	"What you burned for still lights your path."
The Stone	Foundation	"Even grief builds strength beneath you."
The River	Flowing water	"You can't return to the old banks—your soul has widened."

✦ These can be digital or printable. Use subtle textures like sand, calligraphy flourishes, or Sufi-inspired iconography.

POETIC CORRESPONDENCE: "Letter to the Form Beyond the Form"

✉ Invite readers to write a letter **to what they lost**, not as it once was, but as it *might exist now*.

Prompt:

"Dear one, I sense you are not gone, just changed. If you can hear me from where you are now, this is what I want to tell you…"

Use Rumi's quote as an epigraph. After the writing, have them fold the letter, place it in an envelope, and **burn, bury, or keep it in a sacred place.**

☐ Suggest they repeat the ritual when new insight arrives—like a message returning "in another form."

STORY-SHARING CIRCLE: "Forms That Returned" *(Optional Group Exercise)*

👥 For workshops or companion groups, encourage a **storytelling session** where participants describe:

- Something they lost

- What eventually returned (in a new shape, role, or awareness)

- What it taught them about soul growth

🎙 Example:

"I lost my father in my twenties. Years later, I started carving wooden birds. I realized I was trying to shape something that could still fly."

🖊 *This can also be a podcast series, or part of a digital community around the book.*

◈ Call this experience: **"Soul Echoes: The Shape of Returning"**

RUMI'S ALCHEMY: Design Integration for Layout

Suggested graphic motifs to include throughout this chapter section:

- A Phoenix in silhouette form

- A rose petal becoming a flame

- Circular calligraphy spirals, echoing the whirling dervish

- Night turning into dawn across the bottom border of a spread

Use these subtly at page corners or as section breaks to keep a **visual thread of metamorphosis** alive across all experiential tools.

Now, let's deepen this section even more by integrating powerful *reader-submitted stories* and new *layered ritual pathways* that embody the essence of this quote.

We will illuminate how loss doesn't vanish but transforms. Through ritual, memory, and soulful interpretation, readers can see the reappearance of their grief in new forms: as wisdom, presence, lineage, or creative expression. These real-life voices and practices help translate Rumi's metaphor into lived experience.

"Don't Grieve. Anything You Lose Comes Round in Another Form."

Expanded with Voices & Rituals of Return

This is not just poetic sentiment—it is a lived truth for many across time and culture. What is lost may not return in its old shape, but it often returns as **a shift in perception, a sacred role, a dream, a ritual, a strange peace**.

Let us now hear the voices of grievers who have witnessed this metamorphosis, and explore **layered rituals** that bring this quote from metaphor into embodied experience.

VOICES OF GRIEF & TRANSFORMATION

Real Stories of What Returned in "Another Form"

Rosa, 47 (Mexico/California):

"When my abuela[1] died, I felt a silence in my chest. For months, I couldn't eat her favorite foods, tamales, café con canela, without sobbing. But one day, I made her recipe for my daughter's birthday. And as we sat together, I realized: my abuela had returned in our hands, our tongues, the joy of cooking. She was still feeding us."

Leila, 35 (Iran):

"After losing my child in a miscarriage, I created a small garden in her name. I planted tulips and jasmine. The first bloom came exactly on her due date. It wasn't my daughter—but it was her echo. It reminded me that beauty returns, and nothing truly vanishes."

---

1. In Spanish-speaking areas, it refers to a person's grandmother.

David, 62 (UK):

"When my husband passed, I kept hearing his favorite jazz song—on radios, in cafés, once in a stranger's ringtone. I started writing letters to him again, and in the music, I felt him nodding. Not here. But not gone."

These stories help us answer the question:

What has your grief become now?

LAYERED RITUAL PATHWAYS: Inviting Grief's Return in New Form

The following are **multi-phase rituals** that unfold slowly, like seasons. They allow readers to move beyond mourning as an end toward the sacred work of **noticing return**.

✦ **Ritual Pathway 1: "Tracing the Return"**

Theme: Finding the shape-shifted presence of the one you lost.

Tools: Journal, object with personal meaning, candle

Steps:

1. **Name What Was Lost.**

   Begin by writing down what (or who) you lost: a person, a role, a home, a dream.

2. **Identify Its Qualities.**

   What energy did this bring into your life? (e.g., laughter, grounding, safety, challenge, innocence)

3. **Notice Where It Shows Up Now.**

   Is there a moment, place, person, or practice where that energy returns?

   Look not for the same form, but for the same **feeling**.

4. **Light a Candle.**

   In silence, light a candle and say aloud:

   "You've come back, not as you were—but as you are."

Optional: Create an altar space where each returned "form" is honored—a feather, a note, a scent, a photograph.

✦ Ritual Pathway 2: "The Other Form"

Theme: Creating artistic expression of transformation

Tools: Art materials, photos, poetry lines, dried flowers, fabric

Steps:

1. **Collect symbols** of what was lost (a scarf, handwriting, a stone from a shared place).

2. Choose a medium to transform them (collage, embroidery, clay, audio).

3. While creating, speak or write this mantra:

   "This is not the end. This is a turning."

4. Complete the ritual by placing the object in a visible place for 40 days—a symbolic cycle of soul transition in many cultures.

✦ Ritual Pathway 3: "Dream Correspondence"

Theme: Receiving messages through dreams and symbols

Steps:

1. Before bed, write a letter to the one you lost.

2. Place it under your pillow.

3. Ask gently:

"May you come back in another form—a dream, a word, a whisper."

4. Upon waking, record your dreams or impressions, not to analyze, but to honor the **emergent presence** of memory.

Repeat this over seven nights, allowing your unconscious mind to join the ritual.

JOURNAL PROMPTS: Tracing the Hidden Return

- What part of my grief is beginning to transform?

- What echoes of my loss have reappeared in surprising ways?

- What might my grief want to become?

- If I imagine my beloved returning in a different form, what do I see?

- How would Rumi speak to my sorrow if he were beside me right now?

READER INVITATION: Share Your "Other Form" Story

At the end of this section, we would like to call for reader submissions:

"Have you seen your grief return in another form? A sign, a ritual, a conversation, a whisper from the world? We invite you to share your story. Let others know: you were not alone in your sorrow—and you are not alone in your rebirth."

The Concept of the Beloved and Eternal Unity

At the center of Rumi's cosmology, his poetry, theology, and mystical experience is the **Beloved**. This is not a romantic partner, nor solely God in the traditional sense, but a deeply personal yet universal presence: the source of all beauty, longing, love, and grief. To understand Rumi's teachings on loss, one must first understand this archetype of the Beloved and what it means for the soul's relationship with unity and separation.

In Rumi's world, all sorrow stems from separation from the Beloved. And all healing arises from reuniting with it—whether in this life or beyond.

This profound view reframes grief not merely as personal pain, but as a **cosmic homesickness**, an echo of a deeper longing that underlies all human love and loss.

Who or What Is the Beloved?

Rumi uses many names and metaphors to describe the Beloved: the Friend, the Flame, the Mirror, the Moon, the Ocean. The Beloved may be:

- **Divine source** or the ultimate reality (God, in Sufi cosmology)

- **A human being** who serves as a mirror to the soul (e.g., Shams of Tabriz)

- **The inner soul** itself, in its pure, original form

- **The unnameable longing** that draws us toward connection, truth, and transcendence

This versatility is what makes Rumi so psychologically rich. To someone grieving the death of a loved one, the Beloved may *be* that person. To someone mourning a life not lived, the Beloved may represent the soul's unlived destiny. And to the spiritual seeker, the Beloved is the Divine they've always yearned for.

"The minute I heard my first love story, I started looking for you, not knowing how blind that was. Lovers don't finally meet somewhere. They're in each other all along."

— **Rumi**, *Divan-e Shams*

Love as Soul Recognition

Psychologically, Rumi's concept of the Beloved aligns with Carl Jung's idea of the **anima/animus**—the inner soul-part that calls us toward wholeness. When we fall in love or bond deeply with someone, it may be that we are seeing a reflection of the **eternal part of ourselves** in them.

That's why loss cuts so deeply. The person we lost wasn't just a companion; they were **a gateway to the Beloved**. They showed us something eternal inside us, and now they are gone. But Rumi would say that glimpse was real, and it lives on inside you.

"You are not a drop in the ocean. You are the entire ocean in a drop."

— **Rumi**

Modern Psychology & the Internalized Beloved

Contemporary grief therapy recognizes that one of the most healing processes in mourning is **continuing bonds**—the idea that we don't sever connections with the dead, but integrate them internally. Therapists encourage clients to:

- Speak to their loved ones in an inner dialogue

- Keep meaningful rituals or touchstones

- Reflect on how their values live on through their own choices

This echoes Rumi's teachings:

"Goodbyes are only for those who love with their eyes.
Because for those who love with heart and soul, there is no such thing as separation."

— Rumi

The Beloved is not something we lose; it is something we remember.

Grief as a Path to Eternal Unity

Rumi's grief for Shams, for the Divine, for the transience of the world was not something he sought to overcome. It was the **fuel of transformation**. The ache of separation, when embraced rather than resisted, became **alchemy**. Through it, he discovered a love that could not be destroyed by death, time, or distance.

"I died as a mineral and became a plant,

I died as a plant and rose to animal,

I died as animal and I was man.

Why should I fear? When was I less by dying?"

— Rumi

INTEGRATION TOOL: "Meeting the Beloved Within"

☐ **Purpose:** Deepen your internal connection to the Beloved archetype and reframe your relationship to loss.

Guided Visualization (Audio or Script)

1. Sit comfortably, close your eyes, and breathe deeply.

2. Imagine yourself in a place that feels sacred to you.

3. Before you, the figure of the Beloved begins to appear. This may be a person you loved and lost, a spiritual image, or a radiant light.

4. Hear them say:

   "You have never lost me. I live in you now."

5. Allow a dialogue to unfold. What do they want you to know?

6. Let them place a symbol in your hands before they fade—a stone, a flame, a rose.

This is your **grief talisman**—a reminder of the love that never left.

🔲 *Journal afterward: Who appeared as the Beloved? What did they say or offer?*

"RUMI'S CIRCLE": Reader Story

✳ *Nadia, 37 (Iran/U.S.):*

"After my sister died, I began reading Rumi every night. One verse stayed with me: 'Your task is not to seek for love, but to find all the barriers within yourself that you have built against it.' I realized I was still looking for her outside. Now I carry her in my work,

in the way I light candles for my students, in the stories I share. She's not gone. She's just behind the veil."

🌀 *Prompt for You:*

Write a letter from your loved one, as if they are the Beloved speaking through time and silence. What would they say to comfort you?

RITUAL PRACTICE: "Creating a Shrine to the Beloved"

🌒 **Materials:**

- A candle

- A photo or object tied to your loved one

- A symbol of the Divine (open to your belief system)

- A poem or verse that reminds you of eternal love

🖼 **Steps:**

1. Arrange these items on a shelf or cloth as an altar.

2. Light the candle and sit quietly.

3. Recite aloud:

"Even in loss, I return to love. Even in death, I return to the Beloved."

4. Spend a few minutes in silent reflection or prayer.

This ritual invites grief to coexist with reverence. It is a space where tears and soul memory can mingle.

DESIGN SUGGESTIONS FOR THIS SECTION

To visually integrate the sacred tone of this section:

- Use **rose gold or soft indigo hues** for text callouts or headers.

- Include **spiraling vine motifs**, suggesting soul-growth.

- Add **watercolor silhouettes** of dervishes or stars falling into hearts.

- Use **a half-open door motif** as a section divider—symbolizing the veil between worlds.

Reframing loss through the lens of the soul

Loss, in its rawest form, often arrives as an experience of rupture, a violent disruption in the narrative of one's life. We feel as if we have been cut off from something essential, from love, from meaning, from safety. But Rumi invites us to see loss not through the lens of ego or material finality, but through the timeless eye of the **soul**.

This shift, from personality to essence, from grief as collapse to grief as metamorphosis, is one of the most powerful transformations a human being can undergo.

"The wound is the place where the Light enters you."

— Rumi

This now-famous line is more than a poetic flourish; it is a profound psychological and spiritual truth. Modern grief work is increasingly recognizing what Rumi knew centuries ago: that **trauma, when held with compassion and insight, becomes initiation.**

Let us now explore how the soul, not the persona, but the eternal part of us can reinterpret the meaning of loss, and how doing so reshapes the very nature of our suffering.

The Soul's View: Beyond Linear Time

In contemporary psychology, we often process grief through models rooted in time: stages, tasks, timelines. These are immensely helpful for the mind. But the soul does not experience time in the same way.

The **soul speaks in symbols, archetypes, synchronicities, and timeless patterns**. For the soul, grief is not about the past or future—it is a **sacred now** in which love, memory, pain, and transformation coexist.

"Don't get lost in your pain. Know that one day your pain will become your cure."

— Rumi

From this perspective:

- A death is not an ending, but an invitation inward.

- A broken heart is not a failure, but a cracking open of the shell around the soul.

- A goodbye is not closure, but an opening to deeper presence.

Psychologist and theologian James Hillman, founder of Archetypal Psychology, speaks of "soul-making" as the process by which loss and hardship deepen our mythic, poetic inner life. Rumi's work aligns beautifully with this: he urges us not to escape pain but to **be ripened by it**.

Practices of Reframing

To reframe grief through the lens of the soul means to step out of the limited identity of "the bereaved" and step into the role of **the sacred witness**, one who holds space for grief as a process of transformation.

Here are key soul-based reframing practices:

1. Symbolic Listening

Ask: "What is this loss asking of me?" Instead of only asking "Why did this happen?", the soul asks, "What new story is being born through this pain?"

2. Mythic Mapping

See your loss as part of a larger journey. You are not broken, you are being called. Like Inanna descending into the underworld, or the Phoenix burning to rise, your grief may be part of a sacred arc.

3. Invoking the Soul's Language

The soul speaks through dreams, images, metaphor, poetry, music, and synchronicity. Begin to **listen to your grief symbolically,** not just literally. What animals appear in your dreams? What lines of poetry arrive unbidden?

"You were born with wings, why prefer to crawl through life?"

— Rumi

VISUAL TOOL: The Spiral of Soul Transformation

⟳ Create a circular graphic that maps the following phases:

   1. **The Shattering (Loss)**

2. **The Descent (Grief)**

3. **The Listening (Inner Work)**

4. **The Meaning (Soul Insight)**

5. **The Offering (Giving Forward)**

Use this spiral to revisit where you are in your process—not to judge yourself, but to locate your place in a living map of soul-growth.

EXPERIENTIAL EXERCISE: Soul Reframing Journal

▪ Choose one meaningful loss in your life. Reflect on the following prompts:

- What was taken from me?

- What part of me died with them—or through this experience?

- What deeper truth about life did this reveal?

- What strengths or sensitivities awakened in me through grief?

- What offering can I now give the world as a result?

✦ End by writing a blessing to your former self who did not yet understand this grief.

"RUMI'S CIRCLE": Reader Submission

✳ *Raúl, 53 (Mexico):*

"When my father died, I felt like my anchor to the world was gone. But after a while, I started remembering the way he danced, the way he hummed to the radio. I started dancing more. I picked up a guitar. I realized I hadn't lost him—I had become more like him. The grief dissolved, but the music stayed."

This is what Rumi meant by the **form changing**. The love doesn't leave. It evolves.

LAYERED RITUAL PATHWAY: "Offering to the Soul's Flame"

🕯 **Purpose:** To transform grief from fixation to flow.

Materials Needed:

- A candle or small fire
- Strips of paper
- A pen
- A bowl of rose water or sacred oil

Steps:

1. Sit in quiet with your candle.

2. On each strip of paper, write:

   o A memory you grieve

   o A strength you gained through that loss

   o A hope you have for your continued life

3. Burn each slip slowly, saying:

   "This pain has shaped me. I offer it now to the flame of becoming."

4. When complete, anoint your wrists or forehead with rose water.

5. Sit in silence and ask your soul:

"What do you want me to know now?"

☞ You may record your insights in a special "Soul Book"—a dedicated journal just for wisdom gained through sorrow.

DESIGN NOTES FOR THIS SECTION

To evoke the soul's vision in your design layout:

- Use **circular elements** and spirals throughout the page margins.

- Include subtle **gold-inked feathers**, referencing Rumi's idea of the soul having wings.

- Overlay quotes in a **veil-like transparency**—suggesting mystery and depth.

- Include **faint celestial motifs** (stars, moon phases) to mark this section's dreamlike tone.

Chapter Closing: Integration and Summary

"Try not to resist the changes that come your way. Instead, let life live through you."

— Rumi

As we close this chapter, we are invited to pause not to conclude our grief, but to walk with it differently.

In the pages above, we've explored loss not as a rupture in life's meaning, but as a threshold into something vaster. Rumi teaches us that death, heartbreak, and impermanence are not failures of the human condition—they are **necessary initiations of the soul**. Through poetic insight and deep mysticism, he shows us that what feels like disappearance is often the beginning of **transmutation**.

We examined:

- The profound teaching that *"Don't grieve. Anything you lose comes round in another form,"* reframes grief not as disappearance but as **reappearance in a new form**.

- Rumi's concept of the **Beloved**, helping us reimagine who or what we have truly lost—and where that presence now lives inside us.

- A soulful psychology of **impermanence**, offering practices that see grief not as pathology, but as a portal to **inner unity**.

What emerges is a new lens—one that sees sorrow as sacred, love as indestructible, and the self as part of a larger soul-story still unfolding.

Integration Tools for the Reader's Journey

To help metabolize the themes in this chapter, we now offer a set of **experiential tools**—rituals, reflections, and visual meditations—that continue the journey of transformation through creative, cross-cultural, and embodied practices.

☐ 1. JOURNALING RITUAL: "Three Forms of Return"

In Rumi's world, nothing is ever lost but only changed. Use this journaling practice to trace the **three forms** in which your grief may be evolving.

Prompt 1:

What did I lose that I cannot get back in physical form?

Prompt 2:

What new form has this person/love/presence taken in my life now? (e.g., a value, an insight, a creative urge)

Prompt 3:

What third form is still unfolding—something I feel approaching, but don't yet fully understand?

◈ Optional: Write your answers on three leaves or stones, and keep them at your altar to symbolize the metamorphosis.

☐ 2. CROSS-CULTURAL WISDOM CALL-OUT

From the Field: Voices on Loss and Metamorphosis

✳ *Ainu Elder (Japan):*

"When someone dies, we wear their scent around our necks and sing their name into the trees for thirteen nights. This way, the soul knows it is still loved and not forgotten."

✳ *Zulu Healer (South Africa):*

"The ancestors come back through our dreams, our fears, and even our sickness. We don't fear loss—we make room for the return."

🌀 Reflection Prompt:

How do your cultural roots understand return, presence, and transformation after death? What practices might you reclaim or recreate?

☐ 3. VISUAL MEDITATION: "The Flame Returns as Light"

Create or reflect on the following image (suggested to include in layout):

- A candle melting into flame

- That flame turning into a phoenix

- The phoenix dissolving into stars

- The stars becoming the eyes of the mourner

This mandala of transformation reminds us: **we do not lose light; we become it.**

▬◖ *Reader Prompt*: Draw or trace your own version of this image. Place your current grief within it—where are you in this cycle of becoming?

☐ 4. MINI-RITUAL: "The Whisper of the Beloved"

Before sleep tonight:

1. Light a candle and sit in silence.

2. Whisper the name of the one you grieve.

3. Say out loud:

"I welcome you in the new form you now take in my life."

4. Journal any dreams or emotions that arise the next day.

🌀 Optional addition: Use an essential oil like frankincense or rose during this ritual to awaken scent-memory and anchor the soul's presence.

✦ Suggested Graphic Motifs for Chapter Closure

To visually reinforce the integration theme and Rumi's alchemy of transformation:

- A **circle of rose petals** gradually shifting into flame

- A **silhouette of a figure walking into a spiral doorway**, suggesting inward travel

- Thin, gold calligraphic rings echoing the **whirling dervish**, as a symbol of inner turning

- A **sunrise horizon** along the bottom of the page, signaling return and renewal

Closing Blessing from Rumi

"With life as short as a half-taken breath, don't plant anything but love."

This chapter asks us not to rush our way out of grief—but to lean more deeply into its mysteries. To trust that what breaks us may also bless us. That what disappears may reappear. That **what we lose is not gone, it is being reshaped by love**.

As we've journeyed through Rumi's mystical lens of loss, where impermanence becomes beauty, and absence reveals the soul, we now turn toward the deeply embodied terrain of grief itself.

In **Chapter 4: The Emotions of Grief – How to Feel Without Drowning**, we will explore the raw, often overwhelming emotions that accompany loss: sadness, anger, guilt, numbness, and yearning. Drawing from modern psychological insights and the spiritual companionship of Rumi's poetry, we'll learn how to meet these emotions not as enemies to escape, but as sacred messengers from within.

Chapter 3 Summary: Rumi and the Soul's Perspective on Loss

In this chapter, we shifted from the emotional lens of grief to the soul's view, one that sees death not as annihilation, but transformation. Rumi's poetry offered a radical reframing of loss: *"Don't grieve. Anything you lose comes round in another form."*

Through meditations on mortality, impermanence, and the Beloved, we explored what it means to love beyond the physical and to recognize pain as a doorway to divine intimacy.

From soul teachings to ritual pathways, this chapter invited us into a more expansive, luminous conversation with loss.

Part II:
Walking Through the Fire

Chapter 4:
The Emotions of Grief – How to Feel Without Drowning

Grief is not a single emotion. It is a *symphony of feelings* that rise and fall, often discordantly, within the human heart. While sadness may seem to be the dominant note, anger, guilt, relief, numbness, longing, and even joy can play their roles. In this chapter, we will explore each of these emotions, not as obstacles to recovery, but as vital expressions of love, attachment, and transformation. We will also draw on modern psychology's most effective tools for emotional regulation—tools that do not suppress feeling but create a safe space for it. Throughout, Rumi will be our guide, reminding us that our emotions are not problems to solve but *guests to welcome*.

"Try not to resist the changes that come your way. Instead, let life live through you."

— **Rumi**

Feeling the Storm: Sadness, Anger, Guilt, Relief, Numbness

Grief doesn't arrive as one feeling—it's a whole weather system. A storm that moves through the inner landscape, changing direction without warning. One moment, you're weeping with sadness. Next, you're filled with rage. Then, silence. Relief. Even guilt for feeling anything at all.

This emotional volatility is normal. It's not a sign that something is wrong with you. In fact, according to both **modern psychology** and the **wisdom of Rumi**, it's a sign that you're alive and deeply engaged with your loss.

Let's walk through five of the most common—and most misunderstood—emotional waves in grief.

Sadness: The Sacred Ache of Love

Sadness in grief is not just a mood—it's a profound expression of the love we had, and perhaps still have, for the person or thing we've lost. It can feel like a heavy fog or a piercing ache. It may come in steady tears or quiet numbness.

From an attachment perspective (Bowlby[1], 1980), sadness is the heart's natural response to separation. You feel it because your bond was meaningful. There is nothing pathological about sorrow; in fact, it often carries profound beauty.

"Sorrow prepares you for joy. It violently sweeps everything out of your house, so that new joy can find space to enter."

— Rumi

Rather than trying to "cheer up," we can learn to sit with sadness as a sacred teacher—a way for the heart to stay open even in pain.

Tool: Try placing your hand over your heart and saying aloud:

"This sadness is love with nowhere to go. I welcome it."

Anger: The Fire That Protects

---

1. **Edward John Mostyn Bowlby** was a British psychiatrist and psychoanalyst, notable for his interest in child development and for his pioneering work in attachment theory. A Review of General Psychology survey, published in 2002, ranked Bowlby as the 49th most cited psychologist of the 20th century.

Grief often brings anger—fierce, unpredictable, even frightening. You may feel angry at doctors, at God, at family, at yourself, or even at the one who died. This can feel taboo, but it is completely valid.

In modern trauma research, **anger is understood as a protective response** (van der Kolk[1], 2014). It rises when we feel helpless or violated. It tells us:

Something mattered. Something was not okay.

"Don't get lost in your pain. Know that one day, your pain will become your cure."

— Rumi

Anger is not an enemy. It's a fire that, if honored safely, can burn through numbness and bring us back to our aliveness.

Tool: Write a letter that says everything you wish you could scream. You don't need to send it—the point is to give the emotion space to be heard.

Guilt: The Weight of What-Ifs

Guilt is common in grief—and incredibly heavy. You might replay moments in your mind, wondering if you could have done more, said something different, prevented the outcome. This is especially true for caregivers or survivors of traumatic loss.

---

1. **Bessel van der Kolk** is a Boston-based Dutch-American psychiatrist, author, researcher and educator. Since the 1970s his research has been in the area of post-traumatic stress.

Psychologically, guilt is often a way we try to find control in chaos. If we believe it's our fault, then maybe—just maybe—we could have prevented it. But guilt doesn't equal truth.

"Don't turn your head. Keep looking at the bandaged place. That's where the light enters you."

— Rumi

From a self-compassion lens (Kristin Neff[1], 2003), the antidote to guilt is not proof of innocence—it's kindness. You were human. You did what you could.

Tool:

Say aloud:

"I forgive myself for being human in an impossible situation."

Write:

"If guilt could speak, what would it say? And what might my heart say back?"

Relief: The Unspoken Truth

Some people feel a sense of **relief** after a death or loss—especially if their loved one suffered, or if the relationship was complex, strained, or burdensome.

This can feel shameful. Many people ask, "What kind of person feels *relief* after a loss?"

Answer: A human one.

---

1. **Kristin Neff** is an associate professor in the University of Texas at Austin's department of educational psychology.

Relief is not a sign of disloyalty or lack of love. It's often the body's natural way of exhaling after prolonged stress or emotional holding. It's the nervous system saying, *We survived.*

"Try not to resist the changes that come your way."

— **Rumi**

In truth, relief and grief often coexist. You can grieve someone deeply, and also feel grateful that their pain—or yours—has ended.

Tool:

Ask yourself:

"Is it possible I'm feeling more than one thing at once?"

Then write what all those feelings are—even the ones you're afraid to name.

Numbness: When Feeling Disappears

Sometimes, grief doesn't feel like anything. You go blank. Numb. Disconnected from your body or emotions. This can feel disorienting or even frightening.

But numbness, in psychology, is not the absence of emotion, it's the mind and body **protecting themselves** from overload. In trauma science (Dan Siegel[1], 2020), we call this hypoarousal[2]: a state of shutdown.

---

1. **Daniel J. Siegel** is a clinical professor of psychiatry at the UCLA School of Medicine and executive director of the Mindsight Institute. He mainly works on interpersonal neurobiology to enhance mental health, relationships, and mindful awareness for a well-rounded life.
2. Hypoarousal is a "shut down" or "freeze" response where the nervous system slows down in response to overwhelming stress or trauma, leading to feelings of numbness, disconnection, low energy, and an inability to act

"Don't think the garden loses its ecstasy in winter. It's quiet, but the roots are down there working."

— Rumi

Numbness is part of the process. It may mean you need gentleness, slowness, rest—not more effort.

Tool:

- Sit in silence for 5 minutes.

- Instead of trying to "feel," just notice what *is* present. Breath? Temperature? Body sensations?

Over time, presence invites feeling back when it's safe.

Summary: All Feelings Welcome

These five emotions—sadness, anger, guilt, relief, numbness—are not enemies. They are messengers. Signals that love, attachment, and loss have passed through you.

Grief does not follow a straight path. You may feel one, then another, then loop back again. What matters most is that you let the storm move through—and trust that you won't drown in it.

As Rumi teaches, the heart is vast enough to hold every emotion—and still, somehow, grow.

Now, let's deepen the section by interweaving *reader-submitted stories* and *visual/exploratory tools* that bring the emotional landscape of grief alive in layered, sensory ways. These elements can be formatted as *callouts or sidebars* in the layout, under headings like *Voices of Grief*, *Grief Studio*, or *Emotion Lab*. Here's how they might look:

VOICES OF GRIEF: Real Letters from the Heart

"Anger Was the Only Language My Grief Knew"

— Noura, 36, Jordan

"I felt like a terrible daughter. My father died after years of tension between us, and all I could feel was this simmering rage. I didn't cry for weeks—just snapped at everyone, even my children. A therapist told me that anger was the part of me that wanted justice, that still hoped I could make it right somehow. That helped. Later, I started writing letters to my dad—angry ones at first, then soft ones. They let me grieve the relationship we never had. I'm still grieving it."

Reflection Prompt (in margin):

What part of your grief is asking to speak loudest right now? Is it sadness, rage, confusion, exhaustion, numbness? Write a letter from that part of you.

GRIEF STUDIO: Illustrated Emotion Wheel

Create a **custom grief emotion wheel** that expands beyond basic feelings to reflect the complexity of your emotional terrain. You can draw this by hand or use a digital template.

Instructions:

1. In the center, write: *"My Grief Today"*.

2. Create concentric circles around the center with 5–7 rings.

3. Fill each layer with emotions you've experienced—don't be afraid to include opposites like *love and fury, peace and terror.*

4. Use **colors** intuitively: warm for intensity, cool for silence, greys for numbness.

5. Include tiny drawings or symbols that resonate (e.g., broken clock, moon phases, birds).

"With life as short as a half-taken breath, don't plant anything but love."

— Rumi

Design Note: This can appear as a full-page sidebar with a blank version of the wheel lightly illustrated for reader interaction.

EMOTION LAB: Collage Therapy

Create a Soul Collage for Each Emotion

Collaging allows the unconscious to speak—textures, images, and colors, often expressing what words cannot.

Materials: Old magazines, scissors, glue, a large notebook or poster board

Instructions:

1. Choose one emotion (e.g., Guilt).

2. Flip through magazines or search online and **cut/paste anything** that *feels* like that emotion—even if it doesn't "make sense."

3. Don't censor. Let it be abstract.

4. After assembling it, sit quietly and ask:

"What is this emotion trying to teach me?"

Reflection Prompt (printed beneath collage space):

"If this emotion were a weather pattern, what would it be? How would I shelter within it without denying it?"

Design Element Suggestion: Include a semi-transparent image of a **rose petal becoming a flame** along the border of the collage page, tying back to Chapter 3's motifs.

RUMI'S CIRCLE: Embodied Practice for Numbness

"Don't get lost in your pain. Know that one day, your pain will become your cure."

— Rumi

Body Awakening Ritual: The Five-Minute Touchstone

This gentle practice helps reconnect with feeling when numbness dominates.

1. Find a quiet space. Light a candle if you wish.

2. Touch five different textures around you: something rough, soft, cool, warm, smooth.

3. Place your palm on your chest and say:

"Even when I feel nothing, I am still here."

4. Inhale deeply through your nose for four counts, hold for four, and exhale for six. Repeat three times.

5. Listen to a soundscape that reminds you of rain, wind, or heartbeat. (Link to audio download or Spotify playlist.)

Optional Visual Integration:

Use **calligraphic spirals** or **whirling motifs** in the background to evoke inner movement. This can accompany a downloadable **sound meditation card** with a QR code.

Now it's time to expand this section with a deeper tapestry of *reader-submitted stories* and *cultural grief rituals* related to the emotional dimensions of loss. These will offer intimate, global perspectives that validate and broaden the emotional scope of grief. These stories can be framed as immersive callout features, styled for print/digital layout under thematic headings. I've also included *ritual ideas* drawn from global traditions, all interwoven with Rumi's soul-centered reflections.

VOICES OF GRIEF: Stories from Around the World

"Grief Has No Accent" — Aya, 29, Palestine

"After my sister was killed, my family went silent. Our grief was not allowed to be loud. But in the privacy of the kitchen, we made ma'amoul cookies from our grandmother's recipe—cardamom, dates, dusted sugar like soft snow. We would cry into the dough. That was our ritual. The baking reminded us we were still human, still loving, still alive."

🕊 Reflection Prompt:

What scents, foods, or textures connect you to the love you've lost? Could recreating them be a form of grief ritual?

RITUAL PATHWAYS: Cross-Cultural Practices for Feeling Emotions Fully

Grief rituals help emotions move through the body and psyche without stagnating. They are tools not to erase pain, but to *accompany* it, giving it shape, time, and voice. Below are selected cultural rituals specifically addressing core emotions in grief, sadness, anger, guilt, numbness, and even relief.

◊ Anger & Fire Rituals — Japan & African Diaspora

In many Shinto-aligned Japanese traditions, anger and unresolved energy are seen as spiritual imbalances. To reset this energy, people may **burn written messages to ancestors** during the Obon Festival. Similarly, Afro-Caribbean traditions like Yoruba often incorporate **drumming, dance, and fire** to let grief move, especially anger that feels "unacceptable."

♦ Try This:

Write your anger as a letter to the deceased, or even to God. Burn it (safely) in a fireproof bowl while drumming or playing rhythmic music. Say:

"This fire is not destruction. It is a transformation."

● Sadness & Water Rituals — Ireland & India

In old Irish keening traditions, women gathered to **wail and sing** over the body of the deceased. These laments allowed sorrow to *flood* outward. Similarly, in parts of India, grief is expressed through **ritual bathing or river immersions** as a release of tears into sacred waters.

149

● Try This:

Take a "grief bath." Light a candle, play soft music, and pour a handful of salt into the water. Let your tears fall into the tub as a prayer. Imagine Rumi whispering:

"You were born with wings. Why prefer to crawl through life?"

♡ *"I Felt Relief, and Then Shame" — Daniel, 52, Brazil/US*

"When my mother passed after years of dementia, I felt... relief. And then overwhelming guilt. I thought, 'What kind of son feels lighter when she dies?' But my therapist said: Relief is still love. I was exhausted. I missed her, yes. But I also missed myself. Learning to forgive that emotion was the real grief work."

⸙ Reflection Prompt:

Have you felt something that didn't "match" what society expects of a mourner: relief, indifference, calm? Write a forgiveness letter to yourself.

⚶ Numbness & Light Rituals — Jewish Shiva & Tibetan Butter Lamps

In Judaism, the seven-day mourning period of *Shiva* includes quiet prayer, sitting low to the ground, and **lighting candles** for the departed—allowing space for stillness. In Tibetan Buddhist traditions, **butter lamps** are lit to symbolize consciousness continuing after death.

⚶ Try This Light Ritual:

Each night for seven nights, light a single candle for your grief. Sit in silence for just three minutes. Watch the flame. Say aloud:

"Even when I feel nothing, I still hold love."

RUMI'S CIRCLE: Universal Emotions, Universal Soul

Grief is always particular. It is also always universal. Rumi reminds us that emotion is not separate from the divine, it is a channel.

"Sorrow prepares you for joy. It violently sweeps everything out of your house, so that new joy can find space to enter."

Suggested Layout Design:

- Place this quote in a **circular calligraphy spiral**, with a faint phoenix silhouette in the background.

- Use **soft watercolor borders** around each cultural story to create emotional tone and visual warmth.

Deepening emotional work through *sensory rituals* and *creative art pathways* allows grievers to engage the body, imagination, and soul, not just the mind. These practices offer a container to express what language cannot, especially when emotions like sadness, anger, or numbness become too large, subtle, or tangled.

Below is an expanded series of *multi-sensory, cross-cultural experiential tools*, designed to move grief through the body's sensory channels touch, sound, scent, image, and movement—all interwoven with Rumi's mystical psychology.

MULTISENSORY RITUALS FOR EMOTIONAL ALCHEMY

These rituals can be placed as callouts or interactive spreads throughout the chapter. Each includes:

- *Title & Intention*

- *Materials or Setup*

- *Instructions*

- *Quote from Rumi*

- *Psychological Insight*

🔥 RITUAL 1: *"Hands of Ash and Rose"* – *Touch & Texture for Anger + Longing*

Intention: Transmute anger and yearning into grounding physical sensation.

Materials:

- Clay or raw earth

- Dried rose petals or essential oil

- A flat stone or slab

- A journal nearby

Instructions:

Mix petals or a few drops of rose oil into a ball of clay. Mold the clay as if you were shaping your grief: press, knead, strike, smooth. Let your hands express everything your mouth cannot.

After 15 minutes, place the shaped clay on the stone. Write what emotions showed up.

"Don't get lost in your pain. Know that one day, your pain will become your cure."

— Rumi

⊙ **Psych Insight:** Touch-based rituals engage the sensorimotor system, allowing grief to exit the body somatically (van der Kolk, 2014). The tension of anger can be redirected toward creativity rather than collapse.

♪ **RITUAL 2:** *"The Sound Beneath Silence" – Soundscape Grief Meditation*

Intention: Tune in to what emotions sound like and what silence reveals beneath them.

Materials:

- Headphones and an audio player

- Optional playlist: Tibetan bowls, frame drums, mourning songs from your heritage, Rumi poetry recitations, ocean or wind sounds

- A quiet room and a blindfold

Instructions:

Choose a 15-minute soundscape. As you listen, lie down or sit. Let your breath match the rhythm of the sound. When the sound ends, remain in stillness. Then write: *What feelings emerged? What did the silence hold?*

"There is a voice that doesn't use words. Listen."

— Rumi

⊙ **Psych Insight:** Sound bypasses intellectual filters and helps re-regulate the limbic system, where trauma often resides. Music therapy research shows it supports emotional access and nervous system balance.

❀ RITUAL 3: *"The Collage of What Remains"* – *Image Integration for Numbness + Guilt*

Intention: Discover what's still alive and sacred within your grief story.

Materials:

- Magazines, scissors, glue

- 1 large piece of paper

- Optional: photos, fabric, dried flowers, handwriting samples

Instructions:

Without overthinking, cut out images that "pull" at you. Don't search, just respond. Arrange them into a layered visual story. What does this collage know that you don't yet?

"Try not to resist the changes that come your way. Instead, let life live through you."

— Rumi

⊚ **Psych Insight:** Visual storytelling helps the right brain integrate unspoken experiences and helps develop a coherent grief narrative (Neimeyer, 2001). This process mirrors meaning-making, a key stage in long-term adjustment.

FROM THE FIELD: READER ART SUBMISSIONS

These submissions can be used in layout as full-page or sidebar spreads, offering diversity and resonance:

🖼 *"My Grief Altarpiece" – Sarita, 41, Nepal/Canada*

"I built an altar with photos of my brother, a candle, a white scarf, a piece of driftwood, and a print of Rumi's quote: 'Try not to resist the changes that come your way...' I add one item each full moon. It's not religious—just sacred."

Suggested Design Element: Photograph of Sarita's altar or artist rendering, alongside a quote from her journal.

◢ WRITING PROMPT: *"Draw Your Emotion Landscape"*

Instead of writing, take a pen or crayon and draw what your internal emotional landscape looks like today. Is it a stormy sea? A burnt forest? A cracked bowl? A hidden cave? Then write: *What does this place need from me?*

"This moment is a monument."

◐ RITUAL 4: *"Movement Mandala" – Body-Based Integration Practice*

Intention: Move grief through and out of the body using symbolic gesture.

Materials:

- Large paper taped to the floor

- Chalk or soft crayons

- Music (drumming, flute, ambient)

- Bare feet

Instructions:

Stand on the paper and begin moving slowly in a spiral, letting your body draw shapes with the chalk. Let emotion shape your motion. When finished, sit at the center. Trace the spiral with your fingers.

"Be like a tree and let the dead leaves drop."

— **Rumi**

🧠 **Psych Insight:** Movement-based expressive therapies (like Authentic Movement or DMT) support trauma integration by engaging the motor and sensory pathways in healing rhythm.

CLOSING REFLECTION: "You Are the Vessel"

As you engage these sensory practices, remember: emotion is not a threat. It is sacred material. Rumi reminds us:

"You were born with wings. Why prefer to crawl?"

These rituals are your wings.

They do not fix your pain, they give it flight.

COLLECTIVE GRIEF SOUND & POETRY RITUALS

🔊 **Ritual 5:** *"Echoes of the Soul" – Collective Grief Soundscape & Vocalization*

Intention: Create shared emotional resonance and transform isolation into connection through sound.

Materials:

- Group or solo setting

- Simple instruments (hand drums, rattles, singing bowls, shakers) or recorded nature sounds

- Optional: space for chanting or vocal improvisation

Instructions:

In a quiet circle or private space, begin by listening to a soundscape of natural elements (wind, rain, river) for 5 minutes. Then invite participants to vocalize what grief sounds like for them—a sigh, a hum, a wordless wail, or a song fragment. Layer these sounds, letting each voice weave into the other, creating a tapestry of collective sorrow and hope. End with silence or a soft chant.

"The wound is the place where the Light enters you."

— Rumi

☯ **Psych Insight:** Group sound-making activates mirror neurons and social bonding systems, reducing feelings of alienation common in grief (Porges, 2011).

🎨 **Ritual 6:** *"Visual Poetry Collage: Letters to the Beloved"*

Intention: Externalize grief and love through art and the written word—a letter to what is lost or left unsaid.

Materials:

- Transparent acetate sheets or tracing paper
- Watercolors, ink pens, or colored pencils
- Old letters, poems, or song lyrics (optional)
- Glue or tape

Instructions:

Write a letter to your lost loved one or to grief itself on acetate. Overlay with watercolor washes or abstract patterns representing your emotional landscape. Layer multiple sheets to create depth, holding these translucent "pages" up to the light to reveal how loss and love intertwine.

"Love is the bridge between you and everything."

— Rumi

⟨☺⟩ **Psych Insight:** Expressive writing combined with visual art enhances emotional processing and memory reconsolidation (Pennebaker & Seagal, 1999).

☽ Ritual 7: *"Dream Weaving: Nighttime Grief Journal & Intention"*

Intention: Use dreams as a gateway to subconscious healing and guidance from the soul.

Materials:

- Dream journal or notebook by the bedside

- Pen or colored pencils

- Quiet, meditative space before sleep

Instructions:

Before sleep, write an intention such as: *"May I receive insight and healing through my dreams tonight."* Upon waking, immediately jot down any dream fragments or emotions. Over time, notice recurring symbols or messages. Use Rumi's poetry as dream seeds:

158

"When the soul lies down in that grass, the world is too full to talk about."

Optionally, create a dream collage or mandala based on dream imagery.

⊗ **Psych Insight:** Dream journaling facilitates emotional integration and problem-solving by accessing the unconscious mind (Hill, 1996).

VISUAL & LAYOUT DESIGN FOR THESE RITUALS

- Use **soft, translucent overlays** in page design to echo the layered acetate poetry sheets.

- Include **ethereal background gradients** from deep indigo (night) to dawn gold, connecting soundscape and dream themes.

- Frame poetry excerpts with delicate **floral or flame motifs** to symbolize transformation.

- Sidebars labeled "**Rumi's Circle**" can include short reflective quotes to invite quiet contemplation.

Guided Audio Script: Echoes of the Soul — Collective Grief Soundscape

Opening - Soft ambient music or nature sounds fade in

Welcome, and thank you for joining this sacred space of shared grief and healing. Today, we gather—whether together in person or in spirit—to give voice to our sorrow, to honor our losses, and to find connection through sound.

Pause, soft wind or gentle rain sound for 10 seconds

Begin by settling into your body. Close your eyes if you feel safe to do so. Take a slow, deep breath in through your nose and exhale fully through your mouth. Again, breathe in and out. Feel the rhythm of your breath grounding you here, now.

Pause, 15 seconds with gentle flowing water sounds

Allow your mind to drift to the one or the ones you have lost. Feel the presence of your grief—the weight, the ache, the memories. Notice how your body responds. There is no right or wrong way to feel here.

Pause, 20 seconds

Now, bring your attention to sound. Listen deeply to the ambient sounds around you—the earth breathing, the rustle of leaves, the whisper of wind.

If you feel called, gently begin to vocalize what grief sounds like for you. It may be a sigh, a hum, a whisper, a cry, or simply a breath. There is no need to form words unless you wish. Let your voice emerge naturally, like a wave.

Pause, 30 seconds to allow vocalization

If you are in a group, listen with compassion as others join you. Hear the tapestry of voices—each unique, each real—weaving together the shared experience of loss.

If you are alone, imagine your voice reaching out and joining with others across time and space—a chorus of souls bearing witness.

Soft drum or rattle begins slowly

Feel the vibration of sound supporting you, holding you. Let yourself be carried on this wave, knowing you are not alone.

Pause, 20 seconds

As the sounds slowly fade, bring your focus back to your breath—steady, calm, present.

In your heart, whisper these words:

"The wound is the place where the Light enters you."

Take one last deep breath in and exhale fully.

Soft music fades out

When you are ready, gently open your eyes. Carry this resonance of connection and healing with you as you move through your day.

Emotional Regulation Tools from Modern Psychology

Grief is an emotional tempest—powerful waves of sorrow, anger, guilt, relief, and numbness rise and crash unpredictably. To navigate these intense currents without capsizing, modern psychology offers a rich arsenal of emotional regulation tools. These tools do not aim to erase or suppress feelings but to help us engage with them wisely—acknowledging their presence while preventing overwhelm.

Understanding Emotional Regulation

At its core, **emotional regulation** is the process by which we influence which emotions we have, when we have them, and how we experience and express these emotions. This skill is crucial in grief, where emotions are raw, intense, and often confusing.

The inability to regulate emotions during grief can result in feelings becoming overwhelming, leading to shutdown (numbness) or dysregulation (rage, panic). Conversely, effective regulation supports resilience, enabling mourners to **feel deeply yet remain grounded**.

Foundational Emotional Regulation Strategies

"You were born with wings. Why prefer to crawl through life?"

— Rumi

When grief washes over us like a storm tide, it can feel impossible to stand upright. Emotions surge in unexpected moments—overwhelm, despair, anger, numbness—and we may wonder whether we'll ever return to solid ground.

Emotional regulation is not about controlling or muting these feelings. It's about cultivating *resilience through presence*—learning how to hold our pain without being consumed by it. These foundational strategies offer safe anchoring practices drawn from modern psychology, somatic therapies, and contemplative wisdom. Each technique invites you to remain rooted in your body, grounded in the present, and softened by compassion.

These are wings you can grow—again and again.

In this section, we explore simple yet profound strategies drawn from modern psychology that help us hold space for pain while gently cultivating balance. These are not cures, but tools for anchoring—ways to return to ourselves when the chaos of loss feels too vast.

As Rumi reminds us:

"You were born with wings, why prefer to crawl through life?"

— Rumi

These strategies invite us to stretch those wings—slowly, tenderly—even when grief makes us forget we ever had them.

Mindfulness and Present Awareness

Mindfulness, a practice derived from ancient meditative traditions and now widely validated by modern psychology, invites us to gently observe our emotions without judgment. Instead of resisting or avoiding painful feelings, we learn to "be with" them—witnessing their ebb and flow like clouds passing through the sky.

- **Why it helps:** Mindfulness interrupts the vicious cycle of rumination and avoidance, both common in grief. It enhances emotional clarity and reduces distress.

- **Rumi's parallel:** "Try not to resist the changes that come your way. Instead, let life live through you." Mindfulness embodies this surrender, allowing feelings to arise and pass naturally.

Exercise: Spend five minutes daily sitting quietly, focusing on the breath. When grief arises, acknowledge it by naming it silently ("This is sadness," or "Here is anger"), then gently return to the breath.

Cognitive Reappraisal

This strategy involves changing the way we interpret or think about a situation to alter its emotional impact. It does not mean denying pain but reframing it in a way that reduces suffering or promotes hope.

- **Modern example:** Instead of "I am broken beyond repair," try "I am broken, and healing is possible."

- **Rumi's insight:** His poetry constantly shifts perspective—loss becomes a form of gain, death a threshold to eternal life.

Exercise: Write down a painful thought about your loss, then actively rewrite it with a more compassionate or hopeful framing.

☛ Grounding Techniques

Grief can cause dissociation or overwhelming emotional flooding. Grounding techniques anchor us in the present moment and our physical bodies.

- *Examples include:*
  - Naming five things you see, four you hear, three you feel, two you smell, and one you taste.
  - Holding a comforting object, such as a smooth stone or a piece of fabric.
  - Focused deep breathing or progressive muscle relaxation.

When grief floods the nervous system, we can become untethered—either overwhelmed (hyperarousal) or numb (hypoarousal). Grounding techniques reconnect us to the body and environment, helping restore balance and safety.

Practice: Feet like Roots

- Sit or stand with both feet planted firmly on the ground.
- Inhale slowly, imagining roots extending from the soles of your feet deep into the earth.
- Exhale fully, feeling the weight of your body supported by gravity.

Breathing Cue:

Inhale for 4 counts → Hold for 2 → Exhale for 6. Repeat 5 times.

With each exhale, silently say: *Here. Now.*

Rumi's Mirror:

"Be like a tree and let the dead leaves drop."

— Rumi

Let grief fall gently, leaf by leaf. Let your breath be the wind that clears.

☝ Self-Compassion

Grief can provoke harsh self-judgment, as when guilt or anger toward oneself arises. Cultivating **self-compassion**—treating ourselves with kindness and understanding as we would a dear friend—softens this inner critic.

- **Research evidence:** Self-compassion correlates with reduced anxiety, depression, and improved emotional resilience.

- **Rumi's voice:** "Be like melting snow—wash yourself of yourself."

Exercise: Practice the self-compassion break by silently saying:

"This is a moment of suffering. Suffering is part of life. May I be kind to myself in this moment."

☝ Labeling Emotions with Kindness

Psychological Insight:

Neuroscience shows that naming an emotion—called *affect labeling*—activates the brain's prefrontal cortex, helping to regulate overwhelming feelings. Simply put: *naming helps taming.*

Practice: Name It to Tame It

- Pause and ask yourself: *What am I feeling right now?*

- Choose specific words: sadness, guilt, loneliness, confusion, yearning.

- Speak it aloud or write it down without judgment.

Supportive Phrase:

"This is sadness. This is part of loving. This belongs."

Rumi's Mirror:

"This moment is all there is. Don't wait for the next one to arrive."

— **Rumi**

Each feeling is a guest. Let it come. Let it be known.

↻ The Window of Tolerance

Psychological Insight:

Coined by Dr. Dan Siegel, the "Window of Tolerance" describes the emotional zone where we can function with stability. Too much stress pushes us out—into panic or shutdown. Grief frequently narrows this window, making regulation tools essential.

Practice: The Lantern Within

- Close your eyes and imagine a soft lantern glowing inside your chest.

- This is your inner steadiness, your witness light.

- Check in: Am I overwhelmed? Numb? Present?

Breathing Cue:

Try *box breathing*:

Inhale for 4 → Hold for 4 → Exhale for 4 → Hold for 4. Repeat 4 rounds.

Rumi's Mirror:

"With life as short as a half-taken breath, don't plant anything but love."

— Rumi

Return to your breath. Your breath is love.

◐ Reframing Self-Talk

Psychological Insight:

Grief often stirs harsh inner voices: *"I should be over this." "I'm weak."* Cognitive Behavioral Therapy (CBT) encourages us to notice and gently reframe these narratives.

Practice: Grief Reframing Cards

- Write down a recurring self-judgment. Example: *"I'm falling apart."*

- On the back, write a truth in your own voice:
  "I'm feeling pain, and that's human. I'm still here."

- Keep this "deck" near your journal as a practice of loving truth-telling.

Supportive Mantra:

"Grief is not a weakness. It's the echo of deep connection."

Rumi's Mirror:

"You were not meant for crawling, so don't."

— Rumi

Let words lift you. Speak to yourself as you would to a beloved.

☾ Touchstones of Safety

Psychological Insight:

Regulation anchors are tangible objects or sensory tools that bring calm during distress. These "grief comfort kits" activate the parasympathetic nervous system and remind us that safety is possible, even in sorrow.

Practice: Create a Grief Comfort Kit

Include:

- A soft scarf or textured object
- A calming scent (lavender, cedar, rose)
- A quote or photo that feels sacred
- A small stone, token, or symbolic item
- A handwritten Rumi poem
- A memory object from your loved one

Sensory Cue:

When overwhelmed, hold one item. Breathe slowly. Let the sensation guide you back to the now.

Rumi's Mirror:

"The wound is the place where the Light enters you."

Let the smallest comfort become a beam of light.

— Rumi

Integration Reflection:

Before moving on, take a moment to reflect or journal:

- Which of these practices feels most natural to me?

- Which feels new or difficult?

- How might I create a daily rhythm that includes at least one of these?

"Don't turn away. Keep your gaze on the bandaged place. That's where the light enters."

— Rumi

Emotional regulation is not about achieving perfection or removing pain. It's about creating small portals of safety—lighted spaces where grief can exhale and the soul can stretch.

Psychotherapeutic Approaches Enhancing Emotional Regulation in Grief

Modern therapy has developed several evidence-based models that emphasize emotional regulation as a core skill during grief:

- **Dialectical Behavior Therapy (DBT):** Originally designed for emotional dysregulation, DBT teaches skills like distress tolerance, emotional modulation, and interpersonal effectiveness. Techniques such as **'TIP'** (**Temperature, Intense Exercise, Paced breathing**) can rapidly reduce overwhelming emotions.

- **Acceptance and Commitment Therapy (ACT):** We touched on ACT previously. It integrates acceptance of emotional pain with committed action towards valued life directions, fostering psychological flexibility.

- **Complicated Grief Therapy (CGT):** A targeted therapy for prolonged grief disorder, CGT includes techniques to process painful emotions without avoidance, balancing acceptance and re-engagement with life.

Psychotherapeutic Approaches Enhancing Emotional Regulation in Grief

"When the soul lies down in that grass, the world is too full to talk about."

— Rumi

While foundational strategies ground us in daily resilience, many grievers also seek deeper, structured healing pathways. Psychotherapy offers not just a place to speak our truth, but evidence-based methods for navigating intense emotional landscapes with support and skill.

Grief is not a problem to solve; it is a terrain to move through. In this section, we explore how specific therapeutic modalities enhance emotional regulation by teaching us to stay with discomfort, make meaning from sorrow, and re-engage with life in alignment with our inner compass.

These approaches do not silence pain—they help us befriend it.

Let us now explore how grief meets the therapy room: gently, courageously, and often with the soul whispering in the background, "You are not broken. You are becoming."

Modern therapy has developed several evidence-based models that emphasize emotional regulation as a core skill during grief:

- **Dialectical Behavior Therapy (DBT):** Originally designed for emotional dysregulation, DBT teaches skills like distress tolerance, emotional modulation, and interpersonal effectiveness. Techniques such as **'TIP' (Temperature, Intense Exercise, Paced breathing)** can rapidly reduce overwhelming emotions.

- **Acceptance and Commitment Therapy (ACT):** We touched on ACT previously. It integrates acceptance of emotional pain with committed action towards valued life directions, fostering psychological flexibility.

- **Complicated Grief Therapy (CGT):** A targeted therapy for prolonged grief disorder, CGT includes techniques to process painful emotions without avoidance, balancing acceptance and re-engagement with life.

Bridging Rumi's Wisdom and Modern Psychology

"Don't turn away. Keep your gaze on the bandaged place. That's where the light enters you."

— Rumi

In the field of grief work, there has long been a yearning to bridge the rational and the soulful, the clinical and the poetic. Where psychology provides language for the mind, Rumi's poetry gives language to the heart. Together, they form a powerful dyad—one offering tools, the other offering meaning.

The modern psychology of grief emphasizes emotional regulation, self-awareness, and behavioral flexibility. It asks us to observe our internal states, create safe containers for emotion, and foster post-traumatic growth through values-driven action. These are deeply important and practical goals.

Yet, there remains a space that modern psychology often approaches carefully, even hesitantly: the **sacred, the symbolic, the transcendent**. This is where Rumi enters.

☯ The Meeting Point: Soul Meets Science

Rumi was not merely a mystic; he was a psychologist of the soul, centuries before the field was formalized. He understood trauma as a breaking open, not a breaking down. He knew that grief could burn through illusion to awaken what is essential.

Modern therapeutic approaches, such as Acceptance and Commitment Therapy (ACT), Internal Family Systems (IFS), and Compassion-Focused Therapy (CFT), increasingly recognize that **healing involves more than emotional regulation—it involves meaning-making, spiritual integration, and identity transformation**. These ideas echo the teachings embedded in Rumi's metaphors: fire as purification, longing as a divine signal, darkness as a prelude to light.

"You were born with wings, why prefer to crawl through life?"

— **Rumi**

ACT would say: you are not your suffering; you are the space that holds it.

IFS might say: Your pain is a part of you, not the whole of you.

Rumi would say: You are the sky—everything else is just weather.

☯ Embracing Inner Multiplicity

Internal Family Systems, a model that sees the self as composed of many "parts" (e.g., the grieving part, the angry part, the protector), finds a mirror in Rumi's verses:

"This being human is a guest house. Every morning a new arrival..."

— **Rumi**

Rather than exiling emotions, IFS invites each one in as a guest, a visitor with a message. Grief, in this frame, is not just pain but communication—your soul speaking through sorrow. Modern psychology now encourages this internal listening, just as Rumi encouraged radical hospitality of the heart.

☯ From Avoidance to Acceptance

Cognitive-behavioral therapies often teach clients to approach, rather than avoid, painful emotions—challenging avoidance patterns that can deepen suffering. Rumi's wisdom makes this same point in spiritual language:

"Why do you stay in prison when the door is so wide open?"

— **Rumi**

Avoidance builds walls around pain. Presence opens doors. ACT and Rumi agree: when we turn toward what hurts, we often find what heals.

☉ The Healing Power of Symbol, Story, and Silence

Where modern therapy uses narrative restructuring or trauma-informed memory work, Rumi brings metaphor, story, and silence. His metaphors often serve as inner visualizations that parallel guided imagery techniques used in somatic or expressive therapies.

- The **caged bird** longing for the open sky

- The **burning candle** losing itself to illuminate the dark

- The **broken reed** whose music is born from separation

These metaphors bypass cognitive defenses and speak directly to the soul. Many therapists today are reintroducing **symbolic storytelling** and **visual journaling** to help clients access emotional truths beneath language—again, reflecting the ancient, imaginal language of mystic poets like Rumi.

☉ Integrative Practice: A Two-Lens View

Try reflecting on your grief experience from both the psychological and poetic perspectives. Use the prompts below to hold both simultaneously:

Journaling Dual Lens Exercise

- What emotion am I feeling right now? (Psychological naming: sadness, anger, guilt)

- What image or metaphor could express it? (Poetic naming: a cracked teacup, a storm at sea, a silent rose)

- What would this emotion say if it had a voice? What is its purpose or message?

- How might I honor both the emotional truth and its symbolic wisdom?

Bridging these two realms isn't just about combining vocabulary—it's about integrating worlds. In doing so, grief becomes not only survivable but alchemical: a space where science guides the nervous system, and poetry nourishes the soul.

The seeming distance between the poetic mysticism of Rumi and the structured clarity of modern psychology is, in truth, a doorway—not a wall. At their essence, both traditions are devoted to **liberating the self from suffering**. While one speaks through metaphor and music, and the other through science and structure, they share common ground in the belief that **healing requires presence, courage, and love**.

Psychology gives us the language of **neurobiology, emotional regulation, and behavior change**. Rumi offers us the language of the **soul, longing, and divine transformation**. Together, they allow us to grieve with both **understanding and mystery**, to feel deeply while staying grounded.

☯ Rumi's Mirror

"Your task is not to seek for love, but merely to seek and find all the barriers within yourself that you have built against it."

— **Rumi**

Interpretation:

Psychology might call these barriers *maladaptive schemas*, *defense mechanisms*, or *cognitive distortions*. Rumi calls them veils between us and the Beloved. Both point to the same truth: healing comes when we **face the parts of ourselves we've hidden**, especially in grief.

Visual Element Suggestion: Include a transparent overlay of a rose over a blurred mirror or glass surface—symbolizing the self-reflected through loss.

☮ In the Therapy Room

In grief therapy—whether through CBT, ACT, or somatic approaches—clients are gently invited to name their feelings, track their bodily sensations, and re-author the story of their loss.

In parallel, Rumi invites us into the *sacred witnessing* of these same experiences—not to fix them, but to **transmute them into deeper forms of love**.

- **CBT** (Cognitive Behavioral Therapy) asks: "What are you believing about your grief?"

- **ACT** asks: "Can you let your grief be here without pushing it away?"

- **IFS** (Internal Family Systems) asks: "What part of you needs your compassion most right now?"

- **Rumi** asks: "Can you welcome your sorrow as a guest from beyond the veil?"

Design Suggestion: Include this comparison in a stylized table or two-column layout:

Psychological Term	Rumi's Equivalent
Core belief	Veil of illusion
Somatic awareness	Listening with the body
Values-based action	Movement toward the Beloved
Mindfulness	Holy presence

☯ SOUL PRACTICE: Unveiling the Griever Within

Try This Practice

Set a timer for 10 minutes. Sit in silence, eyes closed.

Ask inwardly:

"What barrier within me does my grief reveal?"

Let the answers come not as thoughts, but as **images, body sensations, or metaphors**.

Now, write a Rumi-style couplet that begins:

"I thought grief was a wound, but..."

Optional: Draw the image or barrier you saw. Place it on your altar or grief journal page.

☯ Pull Quote

"Grief is not a mistake to fix, but a flame that wants to illuminate the shape of your love."

Use this visually—perhaps etched across a calligraphic spiral or flame motif—spanning a spread as a breath between two dense sections.

Experiential Sidebar: Rumi's Emotional Compass

A poetic-mindful tool for navigating the inner landscape of grief!

The emotional experience of grief is rarely linear. Instead, it unfolds like a spiral—at times dizzying, at times still, often sacred. Rumi's poetry offers us not a roadmap, but a *compass*—one attuned to the winds of longing, sorrow, awe, and joy. This experiential tool invites you to work with your emotions not as problems to be solved, but as sacred messengers to be heard, held, and honored.

Think of this as a **soulful navigation device**, blending contemplative reflection, poetic metaphor, and somatic anchoring practices—rooted in both Rumi's spiritual vision and psychological science.

How to Use Rumi's Emotional Compass

Set aside 20–30 minutes. Create a sacred space: light a candle, sit by a window, or wrap yourself in a blanket. Choose the emotional "direction" you feel most drawn to explore today—or spin randomly and trust what arises.

Then, read the associated Rumi quote, reflect on the psychological insight, and follow the somatic or creative practice suggested.

▼ SOUTH: SADNESS — The Ocean Within

"Sorrow prepares you for joy. It violently sweeps everything out of your house, so that new joy can find space to enter."

— Rumi

Modern Insight:

In psychology, sadness signals a need for slowing down, rest, and inward integration. It can feel heavy, but it deepens our empathy and opens access to memory and meaning.

Practice:

- Place a warm hand over your heart.

- Ask: *What is the name of my sorrow today?*

- Free-write a letter to your sadness as if it were a wise, gentle guest who has come to tea.

▲ NORTH: ANGER — The Sacred Fire

"Don't you know yet? It is your light that lights the world."

— Rumi

Modern Insight:

Anger, especially in grief, often masks pain, powerlessness, or injustice. Modern therapies encourage "befriending" anger as a protective emotion—not suppressing it, but understanding its deeper roots.

Practice:

- Move your body: walk briskly, punch a pillow, stomp your feet.

- Then journal: *What does this anger want to protect? What boundary is it guarding?*

- Rumi says, *"Be like a tree and let the dead leaves drop."*—What are your "dead leaves" now?

◀ WEST: NUMBNESS — The Silent Valley

"You were born with wings, why prefer to crawl through life?"

— Rumi

Modern Insight:

Dissociation or numbness is often the nervous system's way of coping with overwhelm. This doesn't mean you are broken—it means you are trying to survive.

Practice:

- Slowly name five things you can see, hear, and feel in the space around you.

- Gently place your feet on the ground, feeling into the earth.

- Ask: *What would it be like to feel 1% more here?*

▶ EAST: LOVE — The Unbroken Thread

"Try to learn to let what is always moving within you, move you."

— Rumi

Modern Insight:

Love doesn't vanish after death—it changes form. Holding on to love is not the same as refusing to move forward. In ACT therapy, we learn to live **with** pain *and* move **toward** what we value.

Practice:

- Create a small altar or collage of what you loved and still love.

- Whisper their name. Speak your love aloud.

- Sit quietly. Let that love soften your chest and open your breath.

☉ CENTER: THE BELOVED — Stillness Beneath the Storm

"You were never alone in your sorrow."

— Rumi

The center of this compass is not a direction—it is a **reminder** that even as emotions spin and shift, there is a still point of awareness, a sacred place within you that remains unshaken.

Centering Breath Practice:

- Breathe in for four counts, hold for four, exhale for six.

- As you breathe, silently repeat: *"I am here. I am whole. I am held."*

☉ Suggested Printable Layout

The *printable version of Rumi's Emotional Compass* is a visually poetic and contemplative tool designed to help readers navigate the complex emotional terrain of grief. The compass integrates modern emotional awareness frameworks with Rumi's timeless spiritual insight, offering a sacred mirror for self-reflection and emotional regulation.

❀ Design Overview

- **Shape & Layout**:

  The compass takes the form of a circular mandala, symbolizing wholeness and the cyclical nature of emotional experience. The outer ring is segmented into six primary emotional directions: **Sadness,**

Anger, Guilt, Relief, Numbness, and Longing—the core affective states often encountered in grief.

- **Visual Language**:

  Ethereal hues fade into one another like ink in water—blues and purples for sadness and numbness; deep reds and burnt oranges for anger and guilt; soft greens and golden ambers for relief and hope. Faint textures of rose petals, whirling dervishes, and celestial constellations weave subtly in the background

- **Typography**:

  Key emotional words are rendered in hand-lettered Farsi-style calligraphy (in English letters), encircling the inner core of the wheel. Each emotion is paired with a line from Rumi's poetry and a short, reflective question drawn from therapeutic models.

✸ Sections of the Compass

1. **Sadness**

   - *Rumi's Line*: "Don't get lost in your pain, know that one day your pain will become your cure."

   - *Reflective Prompt*: What is your sadness protecting right now?

2. **Anger**

   - *Rumi's Line*: "The wound is the place where the Light enters you."

   - *Reflective Prompt*: What boundary feels crossed? Where do you need to reclaim your voice?

3. **Guilt**

   o *Rumi's Line*: "Why do you stay in prison when the door is so wide open?"

   o *Reflective Prompt*: Are you blaming yourself to make sense of the chaos?

4. **Relief**

   o *Rumi's Line*: "Try not to resist the changes that come your way."

   o *Reflective Prompt*: What does this relief reveal about what was heavy?

5. **Numbness**

   o *Rumi's Line*: "Be like melting snow. Wash yourself of yourself."

   o *Reflective Prompt*: What would your body say if it could speak?

6. **Longing**

   o *Rumi's Line*: "You were born with wings. Why prefer to crawl through life?"

   o *Reflective Prompt*: Who or what are you truly yearning toward?

✦ **Center of the Compass**

At the heart of the wheel is a stylized flame wrapped in a rose—Rumi's emblem for transformation. Around it reads the phrase:

"All emotions are thresholds. Pass through them."

This center invites pause—a reminder that beneath every emotion is the possibility for movement and meaning.

♨ How to Use

- **Print** the compass as a journal insert, wall hanging, or altar card.

- **Choose an emotion** daily or weekly. Use the Rumi line and prompt to journal, meditate, or create art.

- **Color or annotate** the segments with textures, drawings, or new phrases as grief evolves.

- **Pair** with breath work, sound, or dream journaling for deeper introspection.

ॐ Optional Add-On Ritual

Surround your compass with:

- A single candle

- A whisper of incense or scent that evokes memory

- An object from your loved one or ancestral tradition

- Play a short piece of music in a minor key to allow emotional resonance to rise for Bridging Rumi's Wisdom and Modern Psychology, as you already suggested now, style this section with visual elements, pull quotes, or specific callout boxes like "Rumi's Mirror", "In the Therapy Room", or "Soul Practice."

Holding Space for Pain without Being Consumed

"Try not to resist the changes that come your way. Instead, let life live through you."

— **Rumi**

To "hold space" for pain means to welcome your grief with the same gentle awareness a mother offers her child in distress—not rushing to fix, not judging the tears, but remaining fully present. In psychological terms, this is the cultivation of **emotional containment**: the ability to sit with difficult emotions without being overtaken by them. It is not avoidance, nor is it indulgence. Rather, it is the practice of compassionate witnessing—of grief, rage, sorrow, and all their companions.

Grief can often feel like a tidal wave—unrelenting, deep, and unpredictable. And when it hits, many fear drowning in its undertow. But when we learn to hold space for these waves rather than resist or deny them, we discover they can pass through us without destroying us. Holding space is both a psychological strategy and a spiritual act. It is both discipline and devotion.

What It Means to Hold Space

In modern therapeutic language, holding space refers to:

- **Emotional Regulation**: Being able to observe without immediately reacting.

- **Somatic Awareness**: Sensing where grief lives in the body without trying to shut it down.

- **Nonjudgmental Presence**: Allowing whatever arises—rage, guilt, confusion—to be seen and known.

In many spiritual and indigenous traditions, holding space also means:

- **Ritual Containment**: Creating a sacred boundary or structure where grief can move safely.

- **Community Bearing Witness**: Allowing others to be present with you without offering solutions or distractions.

- **Silent Vigil**: Trusting that simply *being* with pain is a meaningful offering.

Rumi's verse offers guidance here. When he says, *"Try not to resist the changes that come your way,"* he's inviting us to soften into the experience, to let the pain move through us like a river through a canyon. The shape of the canyon changes over time—but only because it was willing to be carved.

RUMI'S MIRROR: A Poetic Invitation

"This moment is all there is. If you are waiting for something else, you are missing your life."

Pain, in Rumi's cosmology, is not an error. It is a sacred messenger. When we suppress pain, we delay our encounter with truth. When we allow it, we become initiates in the school of the soul.

In fact, many of Rumi's metaphors about the heart—breaking open, being torn, burned, drowned—are not metaphors of destruction but of **transmutation**. He shows us that pain is the fire through which the soul is annealed.

IN THE THERAPY ROOM: Clinical Techniques for Holding Pain

Therapists often teach clients how to "hold" intense emotions with techniques rooted in **mindfulness-based therapies**, **polyvagal theory**, and **trauma-informed somatic work**. Key strategies include:

1. Window of Tolerance

Coined by Dr. Dan Siegel, this concept refers to the optimal zone of arousal in which one can function effectively. If grief pushes you above (hyperarousal) or below (hypoarousal) this window, emotional flooding or numbness may occur. Holding space means gently **returning to your window,** sometimes with co-regulation (with a therapist or loved one).

2. Somatic Grounding Techniques

- Place a hand on your chest and say, "This is grief. I am here."

- Press feet into the floor while inhaling for 4, holding for 4, exhaling for 6.

- Name 5 things you see, 4 you can touch, 3 you hear, 2 you smell, 1 you taste.

These techniques return awareness to the body, the *anchor* during emotional overwhelm.

3. Container Visualization

A powerful guided imagery tool: imagine placing your grief in a container—a glowing bowl, a sealed jar, a quiet room. You're not discarding it, only choosing to **visit** it with intention. This can be part of a nightly grief ritual.

SOUL PRACTICE: Rumi-Inspired Grief Container Ritual

Materials: A small bowl, a candle, slips of paper, and a quiet space

Steps:

1. Light the candle and recite:

   "The wound is the place where the light enters you."

2. Write your grief feelings on slips of paper (e.g., "rage," "emptiness," "fear").

3. Fold and place each into the bowl.

4. Hold the bowl and whisper: "You are allowed. You are held. You are holy."

5. Sit in silence for 3 minutes, hand over heart. Then extinguish the candle.

Repeat this ritual regularly. Over time, you'll see how holding grief in a sacred space transforms your relationship with it.

EXPERIENTIAL SIDEBAR: "From the Field — Holding Space in Culture"

Maori Tangihanga

In Māori culture of Aotearoa (New Zealand), *tangihanga* is a multi-day mourning process filled with wailing, storytelling, and shared meals. Pain is **not hidden** but fully expressed, as the entire community participates in its ritual container.

Jewish Practice of Sitting Shiva

During the 7-day period of *shiva*, mourners stay home while the community visits, bringing food and comfort. There's no expectation to entertain or speak—*presence* is the medicine.

Reader Submission: Naomi, 58, South Africa

"After my son died, my therapist told me to make a 'grief altar.' At first, I thought it was silly. But adding his photo, a scarf, a poem each week— something changed. I stopped drowning and began relating. I still miss him, but the panic softened into prayer."

In closing, holding space does not mean being strong. It means being honest. Being *with* pain, not *becoming* it. This is where transformation begins—not when we force grief to go away, but when we offer it a seat at the sacred table of our lives.

As Rumi teaches:

"You were born with wings. Why prefer to crawl through life?"

— Rumi

To hold space for pain is to begin spreading those wings not by escaping grief, but by resting fully in its truth.

Rumi: "Try Not to Resist the Changes That Come Your Way…"

Learning to Flow With Grief as a Messenger, Not a Threat.

"Try not to resist the changes that come your way. Instead, let life live through you."

— Rumi

These words from Rumi are not a passive surrender, but a deep spiritual psychology. They invite us to release the futile war against what already *is*— the death, the change, the rupture. Resistance to pain is a natural human reflex. We flinch from loss. We freeze in the face of the unknown. But grief is not the enemy. In Rumi's cosmology, *resistance* is what breeds suffering— not grief itself.

Modern trauma theory echoes this. According to psychologist Dr. Peter Levine, the unresolved energy of trauma—what gets trapped in the body and psyche—is often the *unfelt*, *unfinished*, or *unwelcomed* emotion. The grief that we avoid only festers, shapeshifting into anxiety, depression, or physical illness. But when we **turn toward it**, we create the conditions for grief to evolve into something transformative.

Grief as a Current, Not a Cage

Imagine grief as a river. When we try to dam it up—through denial, avoidance, perfectionism, or emotional numbing—it builds pressure behind the walls. Eventually, it floods. But when we learn to **float** within it, we stop fearing its depth. We become fluent in its language.

Rumi did not just write about this—he *lived* it. The death of his beloved companion Shams shattered his soul, but instead of collapsing or closing off, Rumi danced. He turned his loss into poetry, movement, and presence. He did not bypass his sorrow. He *partnered* with it.

This is the invitation to the modern griever: Let *change you*. Let it open doors in your psyche that you never dared to walk through. Let it compost what no longer serves, and make fertile ground for the next season of your life.

PSYCHOLOGICAL FLEXIBILITY: A Modern Mirror of Rumi's Flow

In Acceptance and Commitment Therapy (ACT), a core principle is **psychological flexibility**—the ability to contact the present moment fully and change or persist in behavior aligned with values. This mirrors Rumi's call to "let life live through you."

When we resist change, we become rigid. When we embrace it, we grow more *flexible*, more adaptive. We move from fear to freedom.

🔍 Therapeutic Insight:

According to Dr. Steven Hayes (ACT founder), people with higher psychological flexibility report lower rates of depression and anxiety after major loss. They do not avoid their pain—they engage with it meaningfully, through mindfulness, values, and committed action.

RUMI'S MIRROR — Poetic Medicine for Change

"Don't get lost in your pain. Know that one day your pain will become your cure."

"Why do you stay in prison when the door is so wide open?"

"Don't grieve. Anything you lose comes round in another form."

These verses are not motivational slogans. They are soul-maps for moving through disorientation. They remind us that grief doesn't erase life's meaning—it *sharpens* it.

SOUL PRACTICE: The Grief Flow Meditation

Duration: 10–15 minutes

Purpose: To soften resistance and reconnect to the movement of change within

Instructions:

1. Sit comfortably with your feet grounded. Breathe slowly and deeply.

2. Visualize a river flowing through you—beginning at the crown of your head and pouring through your chest, belly, and legs.

3. Say silently:

   o   *"I don't have to fix this. I only have to feel it."*

   o   *"Let it move through."*

   o   *"Change is not my enemy."*

4. If tears come, let them. If numbness comes, welcome that too.

5. End with Rumi's whisper: *"Try not to resist the changes that come your way."*

Repeat this practice weekly during seasons of grief or transition.

EXPERIENTIAL SIDEBAR: "Grief Letters to the Self"

Many readers have found healing in writing letters not just to lost loved ones, but to their *future* selves—the self who has survived, integrated, and alchemized grief into wisdom.

Try this prompt:

"Dear Future Me, I'm writing from the heart of my grief. Here's what I hope for you..."

Pair it with a visual ritual: fold the letter, seal it in an envelope with rose petals or dried leaves. Mark it with a future date and keep it on your altar or in your journal.

COLLECTIVE RITUAL: Resistance-to-Surrender Burning Bowl

Materials: Paper strips, fire-safe bowl, matches

Steps:

1. Write down what you're resisting: "I don't want to feel alone," "I wish it didn't change," "Why did they leave?"

2. Fold each slip and say: *"You had a place. But now I release you."*

3. Burn each paper safely in the bowl.

4. As the smoke rises, speak:

"I do not need to understand to trust the river."

This ritual echoes Rumi's flame imagery—that transformation begins with surrender.

Closing Reflection

To resist change is to resist life. But to welcome grief as a messenger—however painful—is to begin healing in the soul's native tongue. As Rumi teaches us, every wound has its own path to light. The wave that crashes can also carry us.

When we stop fighting the tide, we discover something radical: **grief is not just a response to loss — it is an opening into wholeness**.

Chapter 4 Summary: The Emotions of Grief — How to Feel Without Drowning

Grief brings waves—sadness, rage, guilt, numbness, even relief—all valid, all holy. This chapter helped us normalize the emotional terrain of loss, using both psychological insight and Rumi's poetic language as tools for navigating the storm. We explored emotional regulation strategies, cultural emotion rituals, and creative expression to keep us afloat. Most importantly, we learned how to hold space for pain without being consumed by it. Emotions, like guests, are passing through—and we are the home that can hold them with grace.

Chapter 5:
Embracing Pain with Compassion

"The wound is the place where the Light enters you."

— Rumi

Grief's agony is often sharpened not only by the loss itself but by how we treat ourselves in its aftermath. While our outer world collapses, our **inner world** often turns hostile. We question our strength. We critique our sadness. We compare our progress to others, and perhaps most painfully, we **judge** ourselves for still hurting.

Yet there is another path—one illuminated by the teachings of Rumi and mirrored in modern psychological frameworks: the path of **self-compassion**. This chapter gently leads the reader toward this internal sanctuary, where the heart can begin to cradle its pain, not exile it. Here, we explore how grief heals when the self becomes less of a battlefield and more of a balm.

Grief does not unfold in isolation—it unfolds within us, and how we relate to ourselves profoundly shapes our experience of loss. It's not only the external rupture—the absence of a person, a role, a future—that hurts. It's often what comes *after* that loss, internally: the inner blaming, the subtle shame, the relentless *shoulds*.

"I should be stronger by now."

"I shouldn't cry so much."

"Other people seem to move on faster."

"I keep failing at healing."

These whispers of self-judgment can become louder than the grief itself, turning natural pain into prolonged suffering. In this state, grief becomes entangled with emotional self-abuse—what psychologist Kristin Neff and Buddhist teachers describe as the "second arrow": the pain we inflict on ourselves *about* our pain.

This chapter offers another way—what both Rumi and contemporary psychology recognize as a path of internal mercy. It is a *counter-cultural softness*, a turning inward with the same kindness we might offer a grieving friend. It is the radical notion that the way we speak to ourselves—especially in moments of despair—*can change the arc of our healing*.

The Ancient and the Clinical Agree: Compassion is Medicine

Rumi, the 13th-century mystic, lived through the death of his beloved companion Shams, the forced migrations of war, and the continual severing of his attachments. And yet, his poetry glows with a fierce tenderness—not one of denial, but of deep spiritual embrace. He teaches that pain is not to be banished, but welcomed.

"This being human is a guest house.

Every morning a new arrival...

Welcome and entertain them all!"

— **Rumi**, *The Guest House*

The Wound is the Place Where the Light Enters You

This oft-quoted line by Rumi is not spiritual bypass. It does not mean "your pain is good," or "don't worry, it's all divine." Instead, it's an invitation to *reframe* our relationship with pain. The wound is not the punishment—it's the *portal*. It's where our old identities crack, where our masks fall, where something essential and luminous begins to stir.

In Masnavi I:112, Rumi writes:

"Don't turn your head. Keep looking

at the bandaged place.

That's where the Light enters you."

— Rumi

This idea resonates with the clinical principle of **post-traumatic growth**, introduced by psychologists Tedeschi and Calhoun (2004). While not all suffering leads to growth, the *potential* exists when individuals are supported in meaningful ways—particularly when they feel safe to grieve, reflect, and reconstruct their inner world. Self-compassion, according to Neff and Knox[1] (2017), is a *predictor* of post-traumatic growth because it reduces resistance and fosters emotional openness.

✦ In Buddhist psychology, this is called **"tender sorrow."**

✦ In grief therapy, it's known as **holding the pain with presence.**

✦ In Rumi's language, it is **letting the light enter where we break.**

❖ Sidebar: *Rumi's Mirror*

"Don't get lost in your pain. Know that one day your pain will become your cure."

— Rumi

---

1. **Michael D. Knox** is an American educator, psychologist, author, and anti-war activist. He is a distinguished university professor emeritus in the Department of Mental Health Law and Policy, etc.

Therapeutic Reflection Prompt

Take a quiet moment. Write a letter to the part of you that is most wounded. Instead of fixing or analyzing, simply speak to it like you would to a child or beloved friend. What would your wisest, kindest self say?

- *"I see how much you've endured…"*

- *"You're not weak for still aching…"*

- *"You belong here, even in your sorrow…"*

Repeat this as a weekly practice. Watch how the voice inside begins to soften.

◆ Self-Compassion as Grief's Companion, Not a Cure

Let us be clear: **self-compassion is not about "fixing" grief.** It is not a tool for speeding up the mourning process or a clever trick for bypassing pain. Rather, it is the **tone** of our inner relationship *during* the process. It is how we speak to ourselves when we can't stop crying, when we forget something important, when we isolate from others, when we think we're doing grief "wrong."

It says: "Of course it hurts. You're grieving."

It asks: "Can I sit with you in this?"

It assures: "You don't have to be perfect to be lovable."

Rumi offers the same radical kindness:

"Don't you know yet? It is your Light that lights the world."

— Rumi

In choosing compassion over criticism, we create an internal sanctuary—a sacred room inside the storm. From there, we can begin to listen, to breathe, to rest. Not because the grief is gone. But because, in that space, we are finally not alone with it.

Modern psychology echoes this wisdom. Dr. Kristin Neff, one of the leading researchers on self-compassion, defines it not as self-indulgence, but as a **courageous presence** to one's own suffering. Her empirical research shows that self-compassion is correlated with:

- **Lower levels of depression and anxiety** (Neff & Germer, 2013)

- **Reduced PTSD symptoms** in trauma survivors (Hiraoka et al., 2015)

- **Greater emotional resilience** and **healthier coping** in bereavement (Wakeman & Fincham, 2011)

Similarly, Dr. Paul Gilbert, founder of **Compassion-Focused Therapy (CFT)**, notes that many people—especially those with histories of trauma or cultural shame—find it difficult to turn toward themselves with kindness. In grief, this difficulty is often intensified: when the world falls apart, many of us instinctively turn the blame inward.

Yet from a neurological perspective, **compassion activates the caregiving system** of the brain—particularly the *ventral vagal complex*, which fosters emotional safety, and the *oxytocin system*, associated with bonding and trust (Porges, 2011; Longe et al., 2010). In short, kindness toward ourselves helps us *feel safe enough* to grieve fully. Without that safety, we may fragment, numb out, or stay stuck in cycles of shame or rumination.

Self-Compassion (Dr. Kristin Neff's Model)

Grief, for many, opens not just a wound of loss, but a floodgate of self-condemnation. We judge our tears. We question our memories. We compare our pain. We wonder, *"Why am I not handling this better?"*

And yet, as modern science and ancient wisdom both insist, **healing cannot occur in the presence of hostility toward the self.** The wounded heart does not mend when met with more wounding. It begins to mend when met with **compassion**—not as a vague concept, but as an actionable, embodied practice.

Dr. Kristin Neff, a pioneering psychologist and researcher at the University of Texas at Austin, has devoted the last two decades to studying **self-compassion**. Her model, which integrates Buddhist psychology and empirical clinical research, provides a powerful tool for grieving individuals to tend to their emotional landscape with *presence, tenderness,* and *humanity.*

The Three Pillars of Self-Compassion

Dr. Neff's self-compassion framework consists of three key components, each one vitally relevant to the grief experience:

1. Self-Kindness vs. Self-Judgment

This is the core of compassionate grief work: **responding to our suffering with gentleness instead of attack.** Rather than criticize ourselves for "not moving on," we ask:

"What do I need right now?"

"How can I comfort myself?"

Self-kindness doesn't mean indulgence or denial. It means we recognize our emotional wounds and choose care over cruelty.

Clinical Insight

Research shows that high levels of self-criticism during grief are strongly associated with **complicated grief**, depression, and anxiety (Field & Bega, 2011). In contrast, self-kindness supports emotional regulation, stress resilience, and adaptive coping (Neff, 2003).

Rumi's Reflection

"Don't grieve. Anything you lose comes round in another form."

— Rumi

The call here is not to *stop grieving*, but to stop grieving with cruelty. What if we could offer our pain the same kindness Rumi offers to his broken-hearted reader?

2. Common Humanity vs. Isolation

In grief, we often feel exiled from the living. The world rushes past while we move in slow motion. Friends, stop calling, and smiles sting. We scroll through photos or memories and feel utterly, cosmically alone.

Self-compassion reminds us: *you are not alone.* Your sorrow is not unique in its presence—though it is unique in its form. Every human being will know loss. Every heart will break. You belong to this shared human condition, and in that truth is comfort.

Psychological Insight

Dr. Neff's research emphasizes that people who view their suffering as part of the human experience are less likely to experience self-loathing or emotional avoidance. Instead of saying "What's wrong with me?", they say, "This is hard... and it's human."

Rumi's Echo

"Sorrow prepares you for joy. It violently sweeps everything out of your house... so that new joy can find space to enter."

— Rumi

Here, Rumi aligns with Neff: grief is not personal punishment—it is the path walked by every soul eventually. Knowing this does not minimize our pain. It gives it context.

3. Mindfulness vs. Over-Identification

This component is especially important in grief, when emotions can flood the system. Mindfulness in Neff's model means we **allow our grief to exist without either ignoring it or being consumed by it**.

It means we say:

- "This is grief. It is painful."
- "I am aware of this sadness."
- "It is here, but it is not all of me."

Therapeutic Perspective

Over-identifying with grief ("I'll always feel this way," "I am my pain") can lead to emotional entrapment or avoidance behaviors. Mindfulness helps us observe our emotions *without fusing with them*, creating space for choice and healing.

Rumi's Companion Line

"Try not to resist the changes that come your way."

— Rumi

Mindfulness helps us ride the wave of change rather than fight against its tide. It is the art of witnessing without drowning.

Compassion Practice: The 3-Step Self-Compassion Break

(Developed by Dr. Kristin Neff)

In moments of overwhelm or despair, pause and place a hand on your heart (or any comforting gesture). Then say to yourself:

1. **Mindfulness**: "This is a moment of suffering."

   (Noticing what is here.)

2. **Common Humanity**: "Suffering is part of life."

   (I am not alone.)

3. **Self-Kindness**: "May I be kind to myself in this moment."

   (Offering what is needed.)

Repeat as needed—at bedtime, during grief waves, or in the middle of the grocery store aisle when tears come unexpectedly.

Optional Rumi Add-On:

"The wound is the place where the Light enters you."

— Rumi

Whisper it softly. Let it be an anchor in the storm.

➥ Journaling Prompt: The Compassionate Mirror

Write a letter from your **compassionate inner self** to the part of you that is grieving. Let it speak in the voice of Dr. Neff's framework and Rumi's tenderness.

Begin with:

"Dear grieving heart, I see you. I know this hurts. I want you to know that…"

Let the words come gently. Do not edit. Read it aloud to yourself afterward as if from a friend.

❋ Self-Compassion is Not Optional in Grief—It Is Essential

Many of us, especially in performance-driven or emotionally suppressed cultures, are conditioned to **toughen up** when grief strikes. We are told to be strong, move on, and smile through the tears. But what we truly need is not toughness—it is **tenderness**. Not bravado, but **belonging**.

Dr. Kristin Neff's model provides an evidence-based map for doing just that: treating ourselves as someone worthy of love and mercy, even in our darkest hour.

❆ And Rumi reminds us

"With life as short as a half-taken breath, don't plant anything but love."

— Rumi

Self-compassion is a form of planting love in the soil of the soul that has been scorched by grief.

The Inner Critic Vs. The Compassionate Inner Voice

In the aftermath of loss, we often assume grief will come from the outside—from the empty chair, the canceled plans, the quiet house. But for many, the most piercing pain is **internal**, born from the *inner critic* who whispers blame, shame, and judgment.

This voice might sound like:

- *"You should've done more."*

- *"You're too sensitive."*

- *"It's been months. Why are you still like this?"*

- *"You're not grieving the right way."*

This is the voice of the *Inner Critic*—a psychological construct well-documented in therapeutic modalities such as Internal Family Systems (IFS), Compassion-Focused Therapy (CFT), and Schema Therapy. The critic may have been shaped by childhood conditioning, cultural expectations, or trauma. Its mission is often protection: by shaming us, it believes it's motivating us, shielding us from future harm or deeper pain.

But in grief, this strategy backfires. Instead of resilience, it fosters **despair**. Instead of growth, it tightens the grip of **emotional paralysis**.

Modern psychology offers an antidote: **The Compassionate Inner Voice**—a part of the self that speaks with kindness, wisdom, and grounded presence. This is not the same as positive self-talk or empty affirmations. It is a **deliberate and practiced shift** in how we relate to ourselves in pain.

PSYCHOLOGICAL INSIGHT: The Science of the Inner Voice

Neuroscience has shown that harsh self-talk activates the **threat-defense system** in the brain, leading to cortisol release, increased heart rate, and narrowed attention. This heightens anxiety and reduces the capacity for creative coping.

In contrast, **self-compassion activates the care system**, increasing oxytocin and soothing emotional circuits (Klimecki[1] et al., 2013; Neff & Germer[2], 2013). The compassionate voice actually calms the nervous system, expanding our emotional bandwidth to grieve with more safety and less self-punishment.

RUMI'S WISDOM: Making Friends With the Voice Within

Rumi often personifies conflicting parts of the self—from grief to joy, longing to wisdom. His work invites not repression, but *intimacy with the self:*

"There is a voice that doesn't use words. Listen."

"Don't get lost in your pain. Know that one day your pain will become your cure."

— Rumi

---

1. **Olga Klimecki**, PhD, is a neuroscientist and psychologist. She is currently interim chair of *SocialPsychology* at the Universität der Bundeswehr Hamburg, Germany.
2. **Christopher Germer**, PhD, is a clinical psychologist and Lecturer on Psychiatry (part-time) at Harvard Medical School.

What if we could see the inner critic not as the enemy, but as a part of ourselves in pain, needing transformation? What if, as Rumi teaches, our darkest voices are also **teachers in disguise**?

IN THE THERAPY ROOM: Dialogue with the Inner Critic

(Adapted from Internal Family Systems and Gestalt Techniques)

1. **Name the Critic.**

Give it a form, a tone, even a backstory. Is it your high school coach? A parent's voice? A cultural archetype?

2. **Dialogue with It.**

Ask:

- o "What are you trying to protect me from?"
- o "How long have you been speaking to me this way?"
- o "What would happen if you softened?"

3. **Introduce the Compassionate Inner Voice.**

Imagine this voice as a mentor, soul friend, or even Rumi himself. What would *that* voice say to you now?

4. **Write a Compassionate Reframe.**

Example:

- o Critic: "You're weak for crying again."
- o Reframe: "You are human. Your tears are not weakness—they're proof of your depth."

SOUL PRACTICE: Rumi's Mirror

Use this as a journaling or mirror practice.

- Stand before a mirror. Breathe deeply.

- Imagine Rumi standing behind you, whispering this line:

    "You were born with wings, why prefer to crawl through life?"

- Say aloud:

    "Even in grief, I am enough."

    "I speak to myself with the voice of mercy."

    "I am not my critic. I am my soul's companion."

Repeat daily for 7 days.

READER STORY: Noura's Voice Shift

Noura, at age of 38 lost her partner to cancer after a long caregiving journey. In the first months, her internal narrative was dominated by shame:

"I should've seen the signs sooner."

"I let him down at the end."

Through working with a grief counselor trained in CFT, she began writing letters from her *inner critic*, followed by responses from her *compassionate self*. Eventually, her inner voice began to change. She created a mantra from a Rumi line that helped her reframe:

"Don't you know yet? It is your light that lights the world."

— Rumi

This became a morning practice—speaking to herself not as the failed caregiver, but as a soul who loved deeply.

CREATIVE PRACTICE: Voice Collage

Materials: Old magazines, scissors, glue, paper.

1. Create two sides:

   o **The Inner Critic's Voice**: Use harsh colors, critical phrases, strict imagery.

   o **The Compassionate Inner Voice**: Use warm tones, gentle words, nurturing symbols.

2. Reflect: How does each voice feel in your body?

3. Display the compassionate side somewhere visible. Let it become the louder voice.

🔔 Optional Audio Companion

Consider recording two versions of your internal dialogue—one from the critic, one from the compassionate self—and listening with headphones. Notice the somatic response each creates. Rewrite and re-record until the *compassionate voice feels embodied.*

☽ DREAM RITUAL: Inviting the Compassionate Voice

Before sleep, whisper this to yourself:

"Tonight, may I dream in the voice of mercy."

"May the Beloved remind me I am lovable even in sorrow."

"May Rumi's soul sit with me in the silence of night."

Record dreams in the morning. Look for symbols, colors, or messages of softness.

Closing Thought

The inner critic may never fully disappear. But it can be unseated from its throne. In grief, our task is not perfection—it is learning to speak to ourselves as a friend would. With kindness. With curiosity. With love.

As Rumi writes:

" Be like a tree and let the dead leaves drop. "

— Rumi

And as Dr. Neff teaches:

Self-compassion is not self-pity. It is *honoring our pain with the dignity it deserves.*

Rumi's wisdom: "The Wound is the Place Where the Light Enters You"

"The wound is the place where the Light enters you."

— Rumi

These eleven words are perhaps the most quoted and most misunderstood in Rumi's vast body of mystical poetry. At first glance, they may seem like a poetic bypass—an encouragement to quickly transform suffering into wisdom. But Rumi's actual meaning, grounded in both his Sufi lineage and deeply embodied experience of loss, is far more profound and layered.

This quote is not about *rushing* to the light. It is about recognizing that **light is found *through* the wound**, not in spite of it.

The Alchemical Wound

In the mystical tradition of Sufism, wounds are not seen as enemies to be hidden, but as openings—cracks through which divine grace enters. The Arabic and Persian roots of many of Rumi's words for "pain" and "wound" (such as *dard* and *zakhm*) share poetic lineage with words for longing, love, and transformation. Pain is not merely a biological response—it is a **portal**.

In modern psychology, we see parallel concepts. Carl Jung[1]'s famous insight, *"There is no coming to consciousness without pain"*, echoes Rumi. In trauma therapy, researchers like Dr. Peter Levine[2] and Dr. Bessel van der Kolk explore how trauma, when met with mindful presence, can be metabolized into **resilience and integration**.

Pain, unresisted and compassionately witnessed, becomes a carrier of meaning.

PSYCHOLOGICAL PARALLEL: Post-Traumatic Growth

The field of **Post-Traumatic Growth (PTG)**, pioneered by psychologists Richard Tedeschi[3] and Lawrence Calhoun[4], offers a science-

---

1. **Carl Gustav Jung** was a Swiss psychiatrist, psychotherapist, and psychologist who founded the school of analytical psychology.

2. **Dr. Peter A. Levine** is a psychophysiologist and the developer of Somatic Experiencing® (SE™), a naturalistic approach to healing trauma by focusing on the body's capacity to process and release trauma.

3. **Richard Tedeschi** is an American psychologist. He is also a professor of psychology and a consultant of the American Psychological Association. Tedeschi is noted for introducing the concept of Post-traumatic Growth.

4. **Lawrence Calhoun** is a licensed psychologist born and raised in Brazil. He is co-author/co-editor of eight books and more than 100 articles published in professional journals. He is a recipient of the Bank of America Award for Teaching Excellence and of the University of North Carolina Board of Governors Award for Excellence in Teaching.

backed view that some individuals emerge from grief with greater strength, purpose, and depth. But crucially, PTG is not about glorifying pain—it's about **what happens when suffering is held with honesty, community, and reflection**.

Key dimensions of PTG include:

- Deeper relationships

- Increased spiritual or existential awareness

- Renewed appreciation for life

- Greater personal strength

- New possibilities for living

These themes resonate throughout Rumi's work. He does not promise a return to what was, but rather, an arrival at something truer, subtler, more awake.

" Sorrow prepares you for joy.

It violently sweeps everything out of your house,

so that new joy can find space to enter. "

— Rumi

SOUL PRACTICE: Light through the Wound Meditation

Length: 10–12 minutes

Objective: To sit with a personal wound and invite light without bypassing pain.

Script Summary:

1. Sit in stillness. Breathe gently.

2. Visualize a wound—emotional or physical—you carry.

3. Place your hand gently over the part of the body where this pain is most felt.

4. Ask gently: *"What has this wound taught me?"*

5. Now imagine a soft golden light surrounding it—not fixing, but *warming* it.

6. Whisper silently: *"Even here, I am loved. Even here, the light can enter."*

Repeat weekly during times of grief flare-ups or transition.

WOUNDED STORIES — Reader Submissions

Nika (48, Georgia):

After losing her daughter to an overdose, Nika returned to a traditional healing ceremony involving rose water and salt—"to cleanse the soul and the eyes." She writes:

> *"The wound will never vanish. But it changed how I see. My daughter's memory now holds light. Not pain-free light—but glowing warmth."*

Elias (61, Lebanon)

In Elias's Christian Maronite background, mourning was woven with incense and ancient chants. After his brother died in the Beirut explosion, Elias began singing those chants softly to himself on walks. He writes:

"I thought my heart had shattered. But those songs made me realize: the shattering was an opening."

These are not stories of resolution. They are stories of reverence. The light is not the removal of pain—it is its transformation.

EXPERIENTIAL TOOL: Wound & Light Mandala

Materials: Watercolors, pen, mandala template (provided)

Steps:

1. In the center of your mandala, write a word or phrase representing your wound (e.g., "abandonment," "loss of control," "loneliness").

2. Radiating outward, write:

   o   Emotions that surround it

   o   What this wound has taught you

   o   What wisdom it carries now

3. Use soft gradients of color moving from dark to light to symbolize the alchemy.

Reflection:

- What new patterns or insights emerged as you created this?

- Where the "light" of your grief might be guiding you?

❧ RUMI'S MIRROR Callout Box

"Keep your heart open. Though it makes you vulnerable, it also makes you luminous."

— **Rumi**

Use this affirmation daily:

"My wounds are not my weakness. They are my becoming."

☽ DREAMWORK RITUAL: Ask the Wound for a Message

Before sleep, whisper this invitation:

"Wound, beloved mirror, what do you want me to know?"
"Speak to me in the language of images and symbols."

Upon waking, write down any imagery, colors, or sensations. Look for unexpected symbols of *light, doorway, healing, or voice*. Over time, a new story may emerge.

Closing Reflection

Rumi does not offer saccharine comfort. He offers holy companionship in the dark. His quote is not a command to smile through pain—it's an invitation to discover that pain itself can carry the sacred.

As one Sufi master wrote:

"The rose's perfume comes from its wounds. Every cut bleeds fragrance."

— Rumi

Grief opens us. And in that opening, the light—however dim at first—begins to seep in.

Meditation, Journaling, and Presence Practices

— We grieve not only with emotion but also with attention

Grief can be chaotic—a flood of emotion, memory, and physiological dysregulation. Often, we are swept away by past regrets or future fears, leaving little room for stillness. In Rumi's world and in contemporary therapeutic practice, there is a shared call: return to the present, where the soul still breathes.

In this section, we explore accessible **meditative, journaling, and mindfulness practices** that create *containers* for the vastness of pain. These tools are not about controlling grief—they are about giving it *room to move and speak* without overwhelming the nervous system.

Why Presence Matters in Grief

In modern psychology, particularly in **Mindfulness-Based Cognitive Therapy (MBCT)** and **Somatic Experiencing**, presence is not passive. It is *active witnessing*. When we become attuned to our moment-to-moment experience—sensations, breath, thoughts, and emotions—we reduce reactivity and create space between stimulus and response.

Research shows that even 10 minutes of mindful awareness a day can:

- Reduce rumination and depressive symptoms

- Strengthen emotion regulation circuits in the brain

- Foster increased self-compassion and reduce anxiety (Kuyken et al., 2016)

✦ RUMI ON PRESENCE: "This moment is all there is"

"With life as short as a half-taken breath, don't plant anything but love."

"Be like a tree and let the dead leaves drop."

— Rumi

These lines are not poetic ornament—they are precise invitations into *this breath, this body, this moment.* Rumi constantly redirects our attention away from abstract suffering and toward embodied experience—the heartbeat of divine presence.

Meditation Practices

1. The Wound-Breath Meditation *(10 minutes)*

Sit comfortably, breathe into the place in the body where grief resides (chest, throat, belly). On each inhale, say internally:

"I allow."

On each exhale:

"I release."

After 3 minutes, shift to:

Inhale: *"This pain is part of love."*

Exhale: *"I am not alone."*

Let each breath become a small act of surrender and connection.

2. "Guesthouse" Body Scan Meditation

Inspired by Rumi's famous poem *The Guesthouse*, this meditation invites all emotions as visitors:

"This being human is a guest house.

Every morning a new arrival..."

— Rumi

Scan your body from crown to feet. For each tension or sensation, say:

"Welcome, anger."

"Welcome, sorrow."

"Welcome, numbness."

Do not push away. Only acknowledge. Let each guest have a voice—and then, gently pass.

3. Open Sky Grief Practice *(Outdoor Recommended)*

Lie beneath the open sky. Place both hands on your heart. Imagine your grief rising into the expanse like clouds—shifting, drifting, not stuck.

Silently repeat:

"Grief is weather, not identity."

"I am the sky that holds it."

This expansive practice is rooted in both somatic grounding and contemplative Sufi mysticism, which often evokes sky, sea, and wind as metaphors for soul presence.

Journaling Practices

1. The Compassionate Letter to Self

Write a letter from the voice of your future self—one who has loved through the grief and become wiser through the wound. Let this voice offer kindness, not solution.

Begin with:

"Dear one, I see how deeply you are hurting…"

Close with:

"And still, you remain whole."

This practice draws from Dr. Kristin Neff's compassion journaling model and is supported by the book of narrative therapy and expressive writing (Pennebaker & Smyth, 2016)[1].

2. The Rumi Companion Page

At the top of a blank journal page, write one of the following Rumi quotes:

"Don't turn away. Keep your gaze on the bandaged place."

"The cure for the pain is in the pain."

— Rumi

Write free-flow for 10 minutes. No editing. Let the quote serve as a doorway into what grief is trying to teach you today.

3. The Three Breaths Journal *(Daily Practice)*

Before bed each night, write:

- **Breath 1:** What pain did I carry today?

- **Breath 2:** What beauty did I notice, however small?

- **Breath 3:** What can I offer myself right now—even if just a kind word?

---

1. **Pennebaker, James W.** Opening Up by Writing It Down: How Expressive Writing Improves Health and Eases Emotional Pain. Guilford Publications, 2016.

This journaling ritual gently fosters presence, resilience, and self-compassion.

Presence Practices

🔔 1. Grief Bell Ritual

Choose a small bell or chime. Ring it once when:

- You feel overwhelmed

- A memory stings sharply

- You forget to breathe

Let the sound mark a return to the present. A sacred "reset." In Sufi circles, bells symbolize the awakening of the soul's awareness.

❀ 2. Five Senses Grounding Ritual

In a moment of emotional flooding, pause and observe:

- 5 things you see

- 4 things you hear

- 3 things you can touch

- 2 things you smell

- 1 thing you taste

This evidence-based trauma grounding tool helps anchor the nervous system in the *now*.

☙ 3. Rumi's Presence Walk *(Inspired by Walking Meditation)*

As you walk slowly:

- On **inhale**, say: *"I am here."*

- On **exhale**, say: *"This moment is enough."*

Each step becomes a prayer. Each breath becomes a homecoming.

Reader Reflection: Presence as an Anchor

Mireya (age 52, Mexico):

"When my father died, I couldn't meditate. I hated stillness. But I started just placing my hand on my chest for one minute a day. That became my anchor. Now, five years later, I still do it. It's my way of saying: 'I am with you, Mireya.'"

✦ Integration Reminder

These practices are not *performative rituals*; they are invitations. Tools to help you return to your body, to your breath, to the part of you that is still alive beneath the weight of sorrow.

As Rumi writes:

"Let yourself be silently drawn by the strange pull of what you really love.

It will not lead you astray."

Sometimes, what we really love is simply being held—by breath, by presence, by the quiet space of now.

Chapter 5 Summary: Embracing Pain with Compassion

Compassion is the salve that softens the ache. Here, we explored how grief transforms when met with kindness, rather than judgment. Drawing from Dr. Kristin Neff's model of self-compassion, and Rumi's timeless reminder—*"The wound is the place where the Light enters you"*—we practiced befriending our inner world. We looked closely at the voice of the inner critic, replacing it with a voice rooted in care. Through meditation, journaling, presence practices, and somatic rituals, we cultivated the ground of mercy within. From this soil, healing becomes not just possible—but inevitable.

Chapter 6:
Loneliness, Emptiness, and the Void

"Don't get lost in your pain, know that one day your pain will become your cure."

— **Rumi**

Chapter Opening

Grief often arrives not only with pain, but with a vast *hollowness*—a haunting inner silence that few people prepare us for. Beyond sadness or shock, what remains for many grievers is a **strange emptiness**: days stretched out in aching quiet, nights without warmth or witness, moments when the absence becomes louder than any presence.

In this chapter, we explore that void—**loneliness, spiritual longing, and emotional disconnection**—not as symptoms to be quickly filled or fixed, but as sacred spaces within the grieving psyche. What modern psychology calls **attachment rupture** and **limbic system dysregulation**, Rumi frames as *"the soul's longing to return to its Source."*

We will examine both the **neuroscientific and poetic frameworks** that make sense of this emptiness—not to pathologize it, but to reframe it as a natural terrain of the soul. Whether you feel emotionally isolated, spiritually adrift, or simply *blank inside*, this chapter offers grounded insights and gentle companionship.

The Neuroscience of Attachment and Grief

"When the soul lies down in that grass, the world is too full to talk about."

— **Rumi**

Grief is often framed in emotional or spiritual terms, but it is fundamentally **biological** as well. Beneath the heartbreak, behind the sleepless nights and aching chest, there lies a complex web of **neurochemical and neurostructural responses**. These reactions are not imagined or metaphorical—they are tangible, measurable, and deeply embedded in the human nervous system. Understanding the **neuroscience of attachment and grief** does not reduce loss to cold science; rather, it helps validate the intensity of the grieving experience and offers insight into how to heal.

At its heart, grief is an **attachment rupture**—the tearing of a neurological bond that was wired into us through repetition, trust, presence, and intimacy. In modern psychology, especially through the lens of **attachment theory**, we understand that human beings are born to seek connection not merely for comfort, but for survival. From the earliest days of infancy, our brains organize themselves around the presence of caregivers. These relationships, whether nurturing or neglectful, sculpt the very architecture of the brain, influencing everything from emotion regulation to stress response to identity formation.

When that attachment is lost, the brain does not simply "miss" the person. It enters into a state of **crisis**.

Attachment as a Brain-Based System

John Bowlby, the founder of attachment theory, proposed that humans are biologically primed to seek closeness to others in times of threat or distress. These attachment behaviors are not just psychological reactions —

they are rooted in the **limbic system**, the brain's emotional hub, particularly the **amygdala**, **hippocampus**, and **hypothalamus**.

When someone we are attached to dies or disappears, the brain cannot immediately register this reality as final. The attachment system continues to search for proximity—hoping for a text, listening for footsteps, reaching out in dreams. Mary-Frances O'Connor, a neuroscientist at the University of Arizona, explains that the **neural pathways of attachment do not deactivate simply because someone dies**. The brain has to gradually "update" its internal maps—a process that can take months or even years.

This update process is known in grief psychology as **"relearning the world"** (Attig, 1996). It is not just the loss of the person, but the reorganization of one's internal and external reality around their absence. This is why mundane tasks—sitting at the kitchen table, walking through a shared grocery aisle—can trigger profound emotional distress. The brain is constantly reminded of the mismatch between expectation and reality.

The Stress Response in Grief

From a physiological standpoint, the loss of an attachment figure activates the **stress response system**—particularly the **hypothalamic-pituitary-adrenal (HPA) axis**. This cascade floods the body with cortisol, the primary stress hormone, which can lead to:

- Decreased immune function
- Increased inflammation
- Heightened anxiety and agitation
- Sleep disturbances and exhaustion

- Impaired memory and concentration

Over time, chronic grief can lead to **long-term changes in brain functioning**. Studies using MRI scans (Gündel et al., 2003)[1] show that areas like the **anterior cingulate cortex** and **orbitofrontal cortex**—associated with emotional regulation and decision-making—are significantly affected during intense mourning. This helps explain why grievers often feel disoriented, emotionally overwhelmed, or unable to think clearly.

Yet perhaps the most haunting neurobiological dimension of grief is its ability to simulate **physical pain**. Research by Naomi Eisenberger and others has shown that the same neural circuitry involved in **social pain** (such as rejection or loss) overlaps with regions responsible for **physical pain**—particularly the **dorsal anterior cingulate cortex**. The ache in your chest, the heaviness in your limbs, the burning behind your eyes: these are not metaphors. They are the echo of lost attachment playing through your nervous system.

Rumi's Neuro-Poetic Intuition

Long before MRI machines or neurochemistry, Rumi intuited what science would one day prove: **that separation wounds not just the heart, but the body and soul together.** His metaphors of severed reeds, burning hearts, and wandering souls are not just literary flourishes. They are phenomenological maps of what it feels like when the attachment system collapses.

---

1. **Gündel H, O'Connor MF, Littrell L, Fort C, Lane RD**. Functional neuroanatomy of grief: an FMRI study. Am J Psychiatry. 2003 Nov;160(11):1946-53. doi: 10.1176/appi.ajp.160.11.1946. PMID: 14594740.

"The moment you accept what troubles you've been given, the door will open."

— Rumi

In this verse, Rumi is not minimizing pain—he is pointing toward the **integration of grief** into the nervous system. To "accept what troubles you" is not passivity; it is the conscious regulation of a dysregulated internal world. In modern terms, this is **emotional processing**, a process that allows the prefrontal cortex to eventually reassert leadership over the amygdala, softening the fear, calming the panic, and making space for meaning.

Rumi also writes:

"I died from minerality and became vegetable;

And from vegetable I died and became animal;

I died from animal and became man.

Then why fear disappearance through death?"

— Rumi

Here, he mirrors the **evolutionary trajectory** of consciousness, a movement not just of the soul, but of brain complexity. Grief, he implies, is not regression—it is an initiation into a more expansive identity.

The Neurobiology of Longing

Perhaps one of the most difficult experiences to explain—and yet one of the most universal—is **longing**. Not simply missing someone, but aching for their presence with a kind of desperate sweetness. Neuroscience suggests that longing is a byproduct of **dopaminergic anticipation** without fulfillment. The **mesolimbic dopamine system**, which governs reward and motivation, fires in anticipation of reunion—but when the person is gone, this circuit becomes a feedback loop of yearning.

Rumi doesn't ask us to kill longing. He asks us to **befriend it**. To let longing be a teacher.

"The grief you cry out from

draws you toward union.

Your pure sadness

that wants help

is the secret cup."

— Rumi

To the brain, longing feels like a lack. To the soul, Rumi says, it is **a chalice—the vessel that draws the Beloved closer.**

EXPERIENTIAL SIDEBAR: "Mapping the Brain in Grief"

Create a somatic-emotional map of your grief experience. On a human silhouette or a blank page:

- Shade the areas where you feel emptiness, tension, heat, or numbness.

- Use color, shape, or texture to express emotion: rage might be jagged red lines; despair might be gray smudges.

- In the margins, annotate: What is your body asking for here? What kind of comfort, movement, or stillness does this pain need?

This practice is not a diagnosis—it is a **self-relationship**.

How Grief Affects the Brain and Body

"I want to see you. Know your voice.

Recognize you when you first come 'round the corner.

Sense your scent when I come into a room you've just left.

Know the lift of your heel, the glide of your foot.

Become familiar with the way you purse your lips

then let them part, just the slightest bit, when I lean in to

your space and kiss you.

I want to know the joy of how you whisper 'more.'"

— Rumi

When someone we love dies or is taken from us, the wound is not merely emotional or spiritual—it is physical. Grief is not confined to memory or sentiment; it embeds itself in the *nervous system, muscles, glands, organs,* and *skin.* It becomes a full-body experience that alters everything from hormone regulation to immune functioning, sleep cycles to cardiovascular rhythms. These physiological reactions are not signs of weakness or dramatization—they are the *body's intelligent attempt* to adapt to overwhelming rupture.

Let us examine the profound and often invisible transformation that grief initiates within both the **brain and the body**, as understood by contemporary neuroscience—and illuminated, in its own timeless way, by Rumi.

The Brain in Grief: Disruption, Chaos, and Rewiring

The grieving brain is under siege. Following a significant loss, the brain must *reconcile absence*—but it cannot do so overnight. It has encoded the presence of the beloved into its neural pathways: the way their voice triggers dopamine release, the memory of their scent stored in the hippocampus, the oxytocin that flooded us when they touched our shoulder or laughed in the kitchen. When they vanish, the brain does not understand *why*.

This discrepancy between internal expectation and external reality leads to a state of **cognitive dissonance**, which creates tremendous stress on the **prefrontal cortex** (the brain's center for planning, meaning-making, and regulation). During early grief, **executive functioning** is impaired. Concentration weakens. Decision-making becomes taxing. Time becomes nonlinear. This is not dysfunction—it is *recalibration*.

A study published in *NeuroImage* (Harald Gündel[1] et al., 2003)[2] demonstrated that grief activates the **posterior cingulate cortex, thalamus, and cerebellum**—regions linked with memory retrieval and emotion. The brain keeps "checking" for the presence of the lost one, much like a search engine reloading a missing link. As a result, those grieving often experience:

- Sudden waves of intrusive memories

- Disorientation in familiar spaces

---

1. **Harald Gündel** is a Professor of Psychosomatic Medicine, University Hospital Ulm.
2. **Gündel H, O'Connor MF, Littrell L, Fort C, Lane RD.** Functional neuroanatomy of grief: an FMRI study. Am J Psychiatry. 2003 Nov;160(11):1946-53. doi: 10.1176/appi.ajp.160.11.1946. PMID: 14594740.

- Nightmares and vivid dreams

- Short-term memory lapses

In long-term grief or *complicated bereavement*, these neural circuits can become stuck in feedback loops of yearning, guilt, and imagined scenarios—leading to prolonged anxiety and depression.

Rumi wrote:

"Why do you stay in prison when the door is so wide open?"

— Rumi

He is not shaming the griever here. Rather, he is naming the psychological trap we fall into when the brain keeps cycling through what "should have been" instead of what *is*. Rumi understood that release comes not from forced forgetting, but from deep, compassionate witnessing—of both memory and mortality.

The Body in Grief: Somatic Shock and Cellular Memory

While the brain processes loss in thoughts and emotions, the **body stores it in flesh and fascia**. The somatic impact of grief manifests in varied and often bewildering ways, such as:

- **Chest tightness** (often mistaken for cardiac issues)

- **Gastrointestinal distress** (the "gut-brain" axis is heavily impacted)

- **Appetite loss or binge eating**

- **Weakened immunity**, making the grieving more vulnerable to illness

- Insomnia, chronic fatigue, or hypersomnia

- Tremors, muscle aches, or numbness

In **polyvagal theory**, developed by Dr. Stephen Porges, we learn that grief often triggers the **dorsal vagal state**—a physiological "shutdown" response where the body moves into withdrawal, numbness, and immobilization. This can resemble depression, but is actually a protective state of **energy conservation** during overwhelm. It is the body saying: *pause everything; we cannot survive this all at once.*

Somatic psychotherapists, like Peter Levine (Somatic Experiencing) and Bessel van der Kolk (The Body Keeps the Score), argue that grief must be metabolized *through the body*, not just the mind. Suppressed emotion doesn't disappear—it becomes pain, inflammation, disconnection.

"Don't turn away. Keep your gaze on the bandaged place.
That's where the light enters you."

— Rumi

Rumi urges us to **tend to the physical wound of loss**. Not to bypass it with rationalization or numb it with busyness, but to *sit beside it*, cradle it like a child, and let it speak.

Heartbreak as Literal Cardiac Stress

The phrase *"broken heart"* is more than a metaphor. In fact, a medically recognized condition—**Takotsubo cardiomyopathy**, or "broken heart syndrome"—occurs in some individuals following acute emotional trauma. It mimics a heart attack: chest pain, shortness of breath, and even changes on an EKG, but without the usual arterial blockages.

This phenomenon reflects how the **autonomic nervous system**, particularly the **sympathetic branch**, floods the heart with stress hormones (notably adrenaline and norepinephrine), leading to physical dysfunction. Though typically temporary, it underscores how grief *literally disrupts the rhythm of life*.

Rumi again:

"Listen to the moan of a dog for its master.

That whining is the connection."

— **Rumi**

Grief is not melodrama. It is a physiological expression of the **love that remains**.

Grief and Hormonal Disarray

Grief also leads to imbalances in the **endocrine system**, notably:

- **Elevated cortisol**, which over time leads to fatigue, anxiety, and memory impairment

- **Decreased oxytocin**, the bonding hormone which can cause feelings of emptiness and isolation

- **Fluctuations in serotonin and dopamine**, resulting in low mood, anhedonia (inability to feel pleasure), and motivation loss

These changes are not signs that something is wrong—they are signs that something *important* has happened. The body mourns with us. It signals to the world: *Something has been lost. Pause. Tend. Honor.*

The Energetic Body and Subtle Grief

For those attuned to the **energetic or spiritual dimensions of the body**, grief may also affect the **chakra system**, meridians, or subtle fields. The **heart chakra** (Anahata), associated with love and connection, may feel blocked or empty. The **root chakra** (Muladhara), linked to safety and survival, may become destabilized. Practices like **breathwork**, **yoga nidra**, and **energy medicine** can help restore flow and containment.

Rumi, though writing in the 13th century, understood the multidimensional nature of being:

"There is a candle in your heart, ready to be kindled.

There is a void in your soul, ready to be filled.

You feel it, don't you?"

— Rumi

That **void**, he implies, is not absence—it is a **space of becoming**. In grief, we return not just to sorrow, but to the raw aliveness of our being.

Experiential Sidebar: "Grief Body Inventory"

Take a quiet moment to sit or lie down. Close your eyes, breathe. Then, scan your body from the top of your head to your toes.

Ask yourself:

- Where does my grief live today?

- What textures does it have? (Sharp? Heavy? Hollow?)

- What color would I paint this pain?

- What does this part of me need—silence, touch, movement?

Gently place your hands over the area. Whisper: *"I am listening."*

Spiritual loneliness vs. emotional isolation

"There's a strange frenzy in my head, of birds flying,

each particle circulating on its own.

Is the one I love everywhere?"

— Rumi

Grief does not only sever human bonds—it can unmoor our very sense of self, purpose, and existence. As the heart grapples with absence, the psyche may find itself in a wilderness of questions: *Who am I without this person? What happens after death? Where is the soul of my beloved?* These are not intellectual inquiries. They are **existential cries**. In grief, we do not merely lose the other—we can lose access to meaning itself.

Modern psychology has long recognized the profound difference between **emotional isolation**—the lack of human connection and support—and **spiritual loneliness**, which is the loss of felt connection to the sacred, to wholeness, to the larger web of existence. Understanding this difference is essential to healing, because each dimension requires a different kind of tending.

Emotional Isolation: The Psychology of Disconnection

Emotional isolation arises when a grieving individual feels *cut off* from others—even when they are physically surrounded by people. It stems not from solitude itself, but from **a perceived inability to be understood, seen, or accompanied** in the depths of sorrow. This kind of isolation has been extensively studied in psychology and is a major risk factor for prolonged grief, depression, and even physical illness.

According to the work of psychologist Julianne Holt-Lunstad, loneliness and social isolation are as harmful to health as smoking 15 cigarettes a day. In grief, this isolation can be intensified by **social avoidance**, **emotional withdrawal**, and the fear of burdening others.

Moreover, cultural norms often reinforce this disconnection. In many societies, grief is privatized, hurried, or pathologized. Grievers are often told to "move on" or "stay strong," which only deepens the silence around sorrow. As a result, mourners may feel they must mask their pain, leading to a fractured inner world—*the outward self pretending, the inward self drowning.*

Emotionally isolated grief may manifest as:

- Inability to express pain to others

- Feeling fundamentally misunderstood or unseen

- Suppressing tears or memories in public

- Believing one must carry the pain alone

This is where **relational psychotherapy**, **grief groups**, and **expressive arts therapies** become vital. They offer "**attunement**, **witnessing**, and **mirroring**"[1]—all essential components for emotional reintegration.

---

1. Attunement, witnessing, and mirroring are psychological and interpersonal concepts that work together to build connection and regulate emotions, often used in therapy and relationships. Attunement is the process of being emotionally in sync with another person, while witnessing is the act of paying close attention to and acknowledging another's experience without judgment. Mirroring involves reflecting back the other person's emotions and behaviors, either verbally or non-verbally, to show understanding and build a sense of shared experience.

Rumi knew the ache of emotional isolation. After the death of Shams, his beloved companion and spiritual mirror, he descended into a prolonged period of madness and sorrow. And yet, he emerged not with bitterness, but with **poetry that universalized his pain**. In doing so, he reminds us that shared expression can turn private pain into collective belonging.

"Don't get lost in your pain,

know that one day your pain will become your cure."

— Rumi

Spiritual Loneliness: The Soul's Exile

Distinct from emotional isolation is **spiritual loneliness**—a deeper, often wordless sense of exile from the **divine, cosmos**, or **inner source**. This form of loneliness arises not just from the absence of a person, but from the disintegration of a once-coherent worldview. It may feel like a severing of the soul's tether—not only "They are gone," but "I no longer know what is real."

Theologian Paul Tillich called this the "existential vacuum"—the abyss that opens when one's foundational sense of being is disrupted. Viktor Frankl, the Holocaust survivor and founder of **logotherapy**, wrote that spiritual suffering arises from a loss of meaning, not just emotion. In grief, this may appear as:

- Questioning God, life, or cosmic order

- A deep sense of being adrift or empty

- Feeling disconnected from intuition or purpose

- Experiencing a silent universe—prayer returns no echo

In neuroscience, such experiences are associated with decreased **default mode network (DMN)** activity—the part of the brain involved in self-referential processing and spiritual awe. Trauma and grief can dampen the DMN, leading to feelings of disconnection from one's core self and the transpersonal field.

Here, **transpersonal psychology**—which bridges the spiritual and psychological—becomes a powerful guide. Psychologists like Stanislav Grof and Frances Vaughan emphasized that spiritual crises should not be pathologized, but understood as **rites of passage**. In their view, spiritual loneliness is not a sign of regression, but of transformation—the breaking down of an old ego-identity to make space for a more integrated, soul-centered self.

Rumi, of course, is one of the most enduring guides through this terrain.

"Listen to the reed, how it tells a tale, complaining of separations:
Ever since I was cut from the reed bed, my wail has caused men and women to weep."'

— Rumi

The *reed* is the soul, cut from its divine source. This longing—this spiritual loneliness—is not pathology. It is *remembrance*. Rumi tells us that to feel exiled is also to feel the pull of return. He writes:

"Why do you stay in prison, when the door is so wide open?"

— Rumi

The prison here is not grief itself, but the illusion of disconnection. Through spiritual practice, presence, and inner listening, we begin to sense the nearness of what seemed lost.

Where the Two Meet: The Liminal Threshold

Emotional isolation and spiritual loneliness often occur together, yet they require distinct forms of compassion. The former seeks **human co-regulation**—being held, heard, and seen. The latter seeks **divine or existential reconnection**—remembering the inner light, the sacred thread, the continuity of love beyond form.

And yet, in some moments, the two entwine. When a mourner says, *"No one understands me, and I don't even understand why I'm still here,"* they are naming both types of loneliness. In such moments, the **role of the therapist, friend, or guide is not to fix, but to accompany**—to hold space in the liminal zone between human sorrow and divine mystery. Rumi writes:

"Try to be like the night, and let your pain enter you slowly."

— Rumi

Here he is inviting not dissociation, but **reverent embodiment**—the act of letting sorrow enter, so that something more ancient can arise: a sense of belonging not to this person, or this life, but to **Being itself.**

Soul Practice: "Sitting in Sacred Longing"

Find a quiet, sacred-feeling space. Light a candle, place a meaningful object before you (photo, stone, letter). Sit in silence and breathe deeply into the heart space.

Repeat internally:

"I feel the absence... and I stay."

"I feel the ache... and I breathe."

"I do not run. I do not numb. I remember."

Let tears come if they do. Let numbness come if that is all that arises. This is **spiritual intimacy with your own longing**.

Rumi's Poetry on Separation and Longing

"Don't grieve. Anything you lose comes round in another form."

— **Rumi**

The experience of grief often feels like being flung into a cavern of absence—a space where the other has vanished, and in their place remains only silence, memory, and longing. This is not just emotional sorrow; it is existential disorientation. Modern psychology and Rumi both grasp the depths of this terrain, though each through its own lens: one empirical and clinical, the other spiritual and poetic. And yet, both arrive at a similar truth: **separation is not the end, but the beginning of a deeper intimacy—** with the self, with the soul, and with the eternal mystery of connection.

The Psychology of Longing: Attachment as the Blueprint

Contemporary psychology, particularly attachment theory, explains why separation hurts so profoundly. From infancy, our nervous systems become wired for closeness—first through the mother's gaze, then through relational attunement and physical touch. This is not simply emotional comfort; it is **neurological regulation**. The presence of a loved one soothes the amygdala, reduces cortisol, and activates oxytocin—the "bonding hormone." When that attachment is ruptured, the brain registers loss **as threat**.

Studies in **affective neuroscience** (Coan et al., 2006) show that the brain processes grief similarly to physical pain. But grief also activates the **dopaminergic reward pathways**—especially the nucleus accumbens—suggesting that the yearning for the lost person persists even in their absence. This yearning is what we commonly call *longing*.

Rumi's poetry exquisitely captures this very state—of craving, of thirst, of the painful sweetness of desire that refuses to vanish:

"My soul is from elsewhere, I'm sure of that, and I intend to end up there."

"You left, and I cried tears of blood.

My sorrow grows with each step you take away."

— Rumi

He is not romanticizing despair. Rather, Rumi invites us to see longing itself as **evidence of the soul's gravity**—its pull toward meaning, toward the Beloved, even in the face of death. For Rumi, every instance of separation is a mirror for the greater Sufi longing for union with the Divine. But this metaphor also aligns closely with the **inner object relations** described by psychoanalyst D.W. Winnicott[1]: the notion that a loved one, even when lost, continues to live inside us as a **psychic presence**, shaping our identity and emotional landscape.

Longing as a Portal to the Self

Grief therapists today—especially those influenced by the **continuing bonds model**—recognize that maintaining a relationship with the deceased

---

1. **Donald Woods Winnicott** was an English paediatrician and psychoanalyst who was especially influential in the field of object relations theory and developmental psychology.

can be not only normal but healing. This might take the form of dreams, inner dialogue, rituals, or even art. These echoes of presence are not delusions; they are how the psyche weaves loss into meaning.

Rumi anticipates this therapeutic insight centuries ahead of time:

"The minute I heard my first love story, I started looking for you,

not knowing how blind that was.

Lovers don't finally meet somewhere.

They're in each other all along."

— Rumi

This line reads like a psychological truth as much as a spiritual one: love never departs. It simply changes form. Even in grief, the loved one remains in the architecture of the mind, in the body's muscle memory, and in the soul's yearning. Thus, longing becomes not just a response to separation but a **gateway to transformation**.

Separation and the Transpersonal Dimension

Grief, in Rumi's hands, becomes **a spiritual education**. In the Sufi tradition, separation (*firāq*) is not the opposite of union (*wasl*)—it is the means by which union becomes possible. The agony of absence draws the lover out of ego and into surrender. Similarly, transpersonal psychology (Jung, Wilber, Grof) views grief as a **threshold moment**: one that can dismantle the ego and bring the self into contact with deeper truths beyond personality.

When Rumi writes:

"This longing you express is the return message.

The grief you cry out from draws you toward union."

— Rumi

He is expressing the paradox echoed in many contemporary therapeutic modalities: grief is not something to be "resolved" but **accompanied**, honored, and even deepened until it becomes **transcendent sorrow**—a sorrow that breaks the heart open wide enough for something new to enter.

This idea finds strong support in **meaning reconstruction therapy** (Neimeyer, 2001), which asserts that grief is the process by which we **re-narrate our identity** after loss. Rumi's metaphors—burning, weeping, emptying—are not signs of weakness but evidence of transformation:

"You have to keep breaking your heart until it opens."

This line is a call to **remain within the alchemical fire**, to not turn away from the ache. In that vulnerable opening lies the very material of spiritual growth.

The Void Is Not Empty—It's Sacred

Modern grief often confronts us with a terrifying silence. After the rituals are over, the texts unread, the casseroles cold—**what remains is space**. That space, often mistaken for meaninglessness, is what Rumi might call **the void**. But in mystical poetry, the void is not empty—it is **pregnant with the divine**. Likewise, in existential psychology (Yalom, May, Frankl), this "void" is seen as the **starting point for deeper authenticity**.

"Don't get lost in your pain.

Know that one day your pain will become your cure."

— **Rumi**

Pain, then, is not the enemy. Nor is longing. Nor is the separation itself. All are **necessary ingredients** in the sacred reshaping of the soul. Rumi urges us to meet these inner voids with presence, compassion, and trust in the unseen process.

Modern Integration Practices

Therapeutically, to live Rumi's truth in a clinical or personal context involves:

- **Dialogue with the lost** (e.g., writing unsent letters or keeping a grief journal)

- **Symbolic rituals of connection** (like lighting a candle at specific times, wearing their jewelry, or cooking their favorite dish)

- **Dreamwork** that explores the unconscious presence of the departed

- **Poetic witnessing**, where Rumi's verses are read aloud and reflected upon as grief companions

These practices mirror both **internal family systems therapy** (IFS), which acknowledges multiple internal voices, including those of grief, and **mindfulness-based grief therapy**, which helps us sit with longing without needing to fix it.

✦ Pull Quote Box: *Rumi's Mirror*

"You were born with wings. Why prefer to crawl through life?"

— Rumi

Sometimes, the person we mourn was our mirror—the one who saw our wings even when we could not. Their absence invites us to now become that mirror for ourselves.

Let longing be a signal of the beauty you still carry forward.

Chapter 6 Summary: Loneliness, Emptiness, and the Void

Grief is not merely a wound of the heart; it is a transformation of the entire being. In this chapter, we journeyed into the inner architecture of grief through the lens of neuroscience, spiritual psychology, and the soul-stirring poetry of Rumi.

We began by exploring the **neuroscience of attachment and grief**, discovering how our earliest bonds shape the brain's circuitry for connection, regulation, and safety. When those bonds are ruptured, the nervous system responds as if under threat—activating pain centers, disrupting focus, and flooding the body with the chemistry of despair. Yet we also saw that the brain is capable of renewal. Through compassion, mindfulness, and co-regulation, the brain can rewire itself, forging new pathways toward healing and wholeness.

Next, we looked at **grief's impact on the body and brain**, from cortisol surges and immune suppression to cognitive fog and visceral aches. We learned that grief is not only emotional—it is physiological. And just as it affects the body, so too can the body become a site of restoration through breath, movement, presence, and gentle attention.

We then turned toward the deeper existential terrain of **spiritual loneliness and emotional isolation**. Emotional isolation often results from cultural stigma, relational withdrawal, or unprocessed trauma. But spiritual loneliness—the kind Rumi spoke of—is the soul's longing for reunion with something greater, often intensified by loss. This kind of emptiness, though painful, can also be a sacred invitation: a hollowing that makes space for the divine.

Finally, we entered Rumi's world of **separation and longing**, where absence becomes a doorway to union. Through his verses, we found companionship for our pain, as well as permission to remain in the ache—not as a failure to heal, but as a form of devotion. Longing, in Rumi's hands, is not weakness but sacred fire—a signal of love still burning in the heart. Modern psychology echoes this, showing how grief can transform from suffering into meaning when we allow it to reshape us.

The core insight of this chapter is this: **the void is not dead space—it is sacred space**. The loneliness we feel in grief is not only for the person who is gone, but for the parts of ourselves that were held, seen, and mirrored in their presence. In that absence lies both sorrow and possibility. As Rumi reminds us again and again, the soul's ache is also its compass. If we listen deeply, longing can become our guide home.

"Be like a tree and let the dead leaves drop."

— Rumi

In the next chapter, we will explore how grief is held in the body—not metaphorically, but literally. Muscles, fascia, posture, breath: all carry the imprint of loss. Chapter 7 invites us to turn inward once more, this time into the realm of **somatic intelligence**, and discover how the body itself can become an instrument of healing.

Part III: Finding Meaning in the Pain, Not Just Moving On

Chapter 7:
Reconstructing a Life Without Them

"With life as short as a half-taken breath, don't plant anything but love."

— Rumi

Reconstructing a life without the person we've lost is not a single task to complete, but a continuous unfolding. In the wake of profound grief, survivors often report a paradoxical sense of inertia and chaos: life around them seems to move forward, while they themselves feel suspended in time, uprooted from a once-familiar narrative. This is because, as modern psychology increasingly affirms, **grief is not just about the person who is gone—it is also about the part of ourselves that was intertwined with them.**

The work of rebuilding a life, then, requires more than resilience. It asks for **narrative reintegration**, **emotional recalibration**, and—most challengingly—**a reimagining of self** in a world irrevocably altered.

THE PSYCHOLOGICAL TERRAIN: When a Life Story is Shattered

Dr. Robert Neimeyer's **Meaning Reconstruction Theory** forms a foundational psychological model for understanding what happens after loss. Neimeyer posits that human beings live within frameworks of **assumptive worlds**—mental models of how life works, who we are, and what we can expect from the future (Janoff-Bulman, 1992)[1]. When someone dies—especially someone central to our lives—these assumptions fracture.

---

1. **Janoff-Bulman**, R. (1992). Shattered assumptions: Towards a new psychology of trauma. Free Press.

We may no longer feel safe. We may question the fairness or logic of the universe. Most importantly, we may no longer recognize ourselves.

The process of **meaning reconstruction**, then, involves three primary tasks:

1. **Sense-making** – trying to make cognitive and emotional sense of the loss.

2. **Benefit-finding** – identifying any personal growth or deeper values that have emerged.

3. **Identity revision** – reshaping the self-concept to reflect life after the loss.

Each of these tasks involves grief work that is neither tidy nor linear. Many people experience setbacks, confusion, or even crises of meaning. But within this destabilization is the possibility for renewal—a theme that Rumi returns to again and again.

"Be like a tree and let the dead leaves drop."

— **Rumi**

This is not a call to forget the loved one or suppress emotion. Instead, it's an invitation to shed the expectations and roles that no longer serve the evolving self. In psychological terms, this aligns with **narrative therapy**, which suggests that healing emerges through **re-authoring one's story** in a way that includes the loss rather than trying to erase or bypass it (White & Epston, 1990)[1].

---

1. **White, Michael**, and **David Epston**. Narrative Means to Therapeutic Ends. New York, NY: W.W. Norton, 1990.

The Invisible Work of Identity Reconstruction

When we lose someone close, our **identity is often interwoven with theirs**. A parent who loses a child may feel untethered from the role that once structured daily life. A partner who loses their spouse might feel the sudden collapse of a shared future. A sibling might feel the erosion of a lifelong mirror. In clinical terms, this is referred to as **role loss,** but its psychological impact is far more profound than the phrase suggests.

Grief, then, is not just emotional suffering—it is **ontological disorientation**: Who am I now?

Modern therapeutic models acknowledge this as one of grief's central challenges. The bereaved must **construct a new self-narrative**—one that honors the person lost, preserves the continuity of love, and yet allows room for forward movement. This does not mean the loss is "resolved," but rather that it becomes **integrated into the evolving sense of self**.

Trauma and grief researchers such as Richard Tedeschi and Lawrence Calhoun have documented the phenomenon of **Post-Traumatic Growth**—a process through which survivors of major losses report increased appreciation of life, deeper relationships, a reorientation of priorities, and spiritual or existential awakening. Importantly, this growth does not negate the pain—it coexists with it.

"Grief can be the garden of compassion. If you keep your heart open through everything, your pain can become your greatest ally."

— Rumi

Here, Rumi touches the very essence of post-loss identity work. The grieving person does not need to become "whole" again in the way they once were. Rather, wholeness is rediscovered through **transformation**, not restoration. In trauma-informed therapy, this is called **adaptive integration**—the capacity to hold both loss and life simultaneously, to be changed but not destroyed.

Rumi's Vision of the Self in Transformation

For Rumi, grief was never the end of the story. His poetry is laced with imagery of breaking, burning, separation, and transformation—all of which mirror the stages of psychological grief. But unlike modern clinical texts, Rumi frames these upheavals not as pathology, but as **necessary phases of the soul's awakening**.

One of his most famous parables is the metaphor of **the chickpea in the pot**:

"A chickpea leaps almost over the edge of the pot
Where it's being boiled.
'Why are you doing this to me?'
The cook knocks it down with the ladle.
'Don't you try to jump out.
You think I'm torturing you.
I'm giving you flavor,
So you can mix with spices and rice.
And be the lovely vitality of a human being.'"

— Rumi

This poem captures in mythic language what grief therapists describe in cognitive terms: the idea that **pain can soften and transform**. The boiling is not punishment; it is **alchemical preparation** for a new kind of offering.

In reconstructing life after loss, we might ask: *What in me is being softened? What new vitality is struggling to emerge from this pain?*

This shift—from victimhood to participation—is not easy. It is the work of months or years. But it is precisely this shift that marks the movement from acute grief to a more **generative mourning**, where the mourner begins to build a life that is **different, but not empty**.

The Ongoing Task of Integration

Reconstructing a life without the loved one does not mean leaving them behind. Rather, it means building a life **with them in a new form**—as memory, as influence, as love that still shapes your decisions.

Psychologist **Dennis Klass** refers to this as maintaining a **"continuing bond"**—a concept that directly counters outdated grief models, which emphasized detachment and closure. Instead, Klass and others argue that healthy mourning involves **finding new ways to stay connected** to the deceased while also forging ahead.

This may include:

- Speaking to them in prayer or meditation

- Carrying forward their values

- Creating rituals of remembrance

- Letting their memory guide future choices

In Rumi's cosmology, this continuing bond is not a metaphor—it is **a spiritual truth**:

"Goodbyes are only for those who love with their eyes.
Because for those who love with heart and soul, there is no such thing as separation."

— **Rumi**

To reconstruct a life without them is not to extinguish the love, but to become its steward in a new form. The final stage is not forgetting—it is **transmission**. The life rebuilt after loss becomes a **living legacy** of the one who is gone.

More Thoughts

Rebuilding life after loss is an act of courage and creativity. It requires both psychological tools and soulful insight. Meaning Reconstruction Theory offers the structure; Rumi offers the soul-language.

And somewhere between science and poetry, between despair and dawn, between what was and what now must be, we begin to find the shape of ourselves again.

"Try to learn to let what is simply be.

The grief you cry out from draws you toward union."

— **Rumi**

Meaning Reconstruction Theory (Robert Neimeyer)

"Grief is not about letting go, but about finding a new place for the deceased in our ongoing life."

— **Robert Neimeyer**

"Don't grieve. Anything you lose comes round in another form."

— Rumi

When someone we love dies, the rupture goes far beyond the absence of their body. What dies with them, often unnoticed by the outside world, are **entire chapters of our life story**—shared dreams, relational identities, routines, and futures that can no longer unfold. The resulting pain is not merely emotional. It is **existential**, striking at the very foundation of how we see the world and ourselves in it. It is this deeper disorientation that modern grief psychologist **Robert Neimeyer** attempts to address through his groundbreaking **Meaning Reconstruction Theory**.

Neimeyer's work marked a decisive shift away from older grief models—like Freud's "grief work" hypothesis, which focused on detachment and emotional closure—and toward a more **constructivist, narrative-based understanding of bereavement**. In Neimeyer's view, grief is not simply about processing emotions or completing stages. Rather, it is about **rebuilding meaning** after a life-altering event has **shattered the assumptive world** of the bereaved (Neimeyer, 2001).

The Shattered Story

At the heart of Meaning Reconstruction Theory lies a deceptively simple insight: **we are storytelling beings**. As human beings, we do not just experience events—we organize them into **narratives**. These stories give us identity, coherence, and a sense of continuity. They help us make sense of the past and project ourselves into the future.

When someone central to our life dies, that story collapses. It is no longer possible to maintain the same narrative trajectory. We may no longer be able to say with certainty who we are, what we value, or where our lives are going. This is what trauma theorists call **narrative disruption**—and in grief, it often results in what Neimeyer calls a **"loss of assumptive world."**

"The wound is the place where the light enters you."

— **Rumi**

Rumi, centuries earlier, offered a remarkably similar psychological truth in poetic language. For him, grief is not merely a sadness over something lost—it is the **rending of illusion**, the breaking open of egoic attachments. When a person we love is taken from us, we are forced to confront the impermanence of all things and the **illusion of control**. The "light" that Rumi says enters through the wound is not comfort in the ordinary sense; it is **awakening**, often harsh, to a new order of being.

In Neimeyer's psychological framework, this awakening begins with a period of **meaninglessness**—a time when the world seems to lose its coherence and structure. But if mourners are able to engage with their grief, rather than deny or bypass it, they may begin to slowly reconstruct meaning through three overlapping processes: **sense-making**, **benefit-finding**, and **identity revision**.

1. Sense-Making: Grasping the Unthinkable

The first dimension of meaning reconstruction is **sense-making**. The attempt to understand why the loss happened and what it means. This does not mean finding a rational or theological justification for the death, but rather crafting a narrative that integrates the loss into the broader story of one's life.

In cases of sudden, violent, or senseless death, this task is especially difficult. Yet, research shows that individuals who are able to articulate even a tentative or provisional meaning tend to show better psychological adaptation over time (Currier, Holland, & Neimeyer, 2006)[1]. For example, someone might come to see their loved one's death as a turning point that deepened their empathy, altered their life priorities, or awakened spiritual inquiry.

Rumi approaches sense-making not through reason, but through metaphor. For him, death is not an error in the design of life, but its hidden architecture. It is not the end, but a **threshold**, a **return**:

"Death has nothing to do with going away. The sun sets and the moon sets, but they are not gone."

"Don't run away from grief, o soul. Look for the remedy inside the pain, because the rose came from the thorn and the ruby came from a stone."

— Rumi

Rumi's metaphors do not minimize the agony of loss. Instead, they **transmute it**. They invite us to enter grief as a **sacred furnace**, where the crude ore of suffering may eventually yield something of depth, beauty, or insight.

Psychologically, this corresponds with a movement from **post-traumatic distress** to **post-traumatic growth**—not as a guaranteed

---

1. **Currier JM, Holland JM, Neimeyer RA**. Sense-making, grief, and the experience of violent loss: toward a mediational model. Death Stud. 2006 Jun; 30(5):403-28. doi: 10.1080/07481180600614351. PMID: 16610156.

outcome, but as a **possibility** that becomes available through active engagement with the pain.

2. Benefit-Finding: Emerging from the Ashes

Once a bereaved person begins to make tentative sense of the loss, a second layer of meaning reconstruction may emerge: **benefit-finding**. This involves identifying any positive transformations that arise from the loss— not in the sense of justifying it, but in the sense of allowing **growth to coexist with grief**.

This might manifest as:

- A deeper appreciation of life

- Greater emotional resilience

- A new calling or life mission inspired by the deceased

- Strengthened relationships or a heightened sense of interdependence

Neimeyer emphasizes that benefit-finding is not the same as "silver-lining" or spiritual bypassing. The benefits do not erase the pain. They exist **alongside it**, creating a **dual awareness** that allows the bereaved to say, *"I wish this had never happened—and yet, it has changed me in ways I could not have imagined."*

This resonates powerfully with Rumi's alchemical view of suffering. Pain, for him, is not an aberration to be escaped, but a teacher to be embraced:

"Sorrow prepares you for joy. It violently sweeps everything out of your house, so that new joy can find space to enter."

258

"Don't get lost in your pain. Know that one day your pain will become your cure."

— Rumi

These lines are not just consolations—they are **psychospiritual directives**. They urge the grieving to remain present to their experience, trusting that if they do not close their hearts, something new may be born from the wreckage. This trust—the belief that something of value can emerge from loss—is not naive. It is an essential feature of **psychological resilience**.

3. Identity Revision: The Rebirth of the Self

Perhaps the most profound element of Meaning Reconstruction is the **revision of identity**. After a major loss, the mourner often faces a crisis of self. The question *"Who am I without them?"* is not rhetorical—it is real, destabilizing, and urgent.

Neimeyer's work emphasizes that the mourner must construct a **new narrative identity**—one that acknowledges the permanence of the loss but reclaims agency over the future. This often involves **integrating the deceased into one's ongoing life story** in a new form—through memory, ritual, values, and continued bonds.

This process is also echoed in Rumi's metaphors of death and rebirth. His writings are filled with references to spiritual metamorphosis:

"Why should I be unhappy? Every parcel of my being is in full bloom."

"You were born with wings, why prefer to crawl through life?"

— Rumi

These are not naive affirmations. They arise from his own profound grief—the death of Shams of Tabriz, his beloved companion, tore Rumi open. Yet it was precisely through that loss that Rumi became a poet and mystic of transcendent depth. The identity he bore before Shams died was transformed—not erased, but **reborn through fire**.

In clinical terms, this is the final stage of meaning reconstruction: **narrative re-authoring**. The mourner does not return to who they were. They become someone new—someone marked by grief, but also by wisdom, presence, and a deeper sense of what it means to live.

Integrating Meaning Reconstruction and Rumi: A Sacred Psychology of Grief

Robert Neimeyer's Meaning Reconstruction Theory offers a roadmap for grieving minds. Rumi offers a lantern for grieving souls. When woven together, they illuminate a path through the darkness—not a way out of pain, but a way **into its transformative depths**.

Meaning-making in grief is not about erasing sorrow. It is about **becoming someone who can carry sorrow with dignity, creativity, and love**. It is about making space for both the presence of absence and the possibility of renewal.

"Don't turn away. Keep your gaze on the bandaged place.

That's where the light enters you."

— Rumi

As we move deeper into this chapter and into the broader arc of this book, let us remember: **grief is not an error in the system of life. It is**

part of its sacred design. And meaning, though not given, can be **made—** patiently, painfully, beautifully—by those brave enough to grieve and rebuild.

Identity changes after loss

"Try not to resist the changes that come your way. Instead, let life live through you."

— Rumi

"Bereavement shatters the self. It doesn't just change what we do—it changes who we are."

— Robert Neimeyer

When someone we love dies, something in us dies too—not in a metaphorical or poetic way, but in the deep existential architecture of the self. The loss does not simply remove a relationship; it rewrites the terrain of identity. Whether the loss is of a spouse, a child, a parent, a sibling, or a close friend, the bereaved often find themselves facing an unfamiliar reflection: **"Who am I now, without them?"**

This identity rupture is one of the most overlooked dimensions of grief. Much of the public and clinical discourse focuses on emotional pain— sadness, loneliness, yearning—but beneath those emotions lies a quieter, often more destabilizing experience: **the collapse or erosion of one's narrative self.** This is where **modern psychology** and **Rumi's mystical insight** converge most powerfully.

The Relational Self and the Mirror of the Other

Contemporary psychological theory emphasizes that the self is not a closed, fixed entity, but a **relational construct**—something shaped and reshaped through interpersonal connection. In **attachment theory**, for example, we learn that close relationships serve as emotional anchors and developmental mirrors. The people we love reflect back parts of ourselves. They help us know who we are.

When someone close dies, the mirror is shattered. We not only lose them—we lose **the version of ourselves that existed in relation to them**. A woman who was a wife becomes a widow. A person who was a son becomes an orphan. A parent who loses a child carries the unfathomable label of bereaved father or mother—a name for a wound.

This phenomenon is echoed in the work of identity theorists such as **George Herbert Mead** and **Kenneth Gergen**, who argue that our identities are co-authored by the relationships around us. We are, in essence, **social beings performing and refining ourselves** in the gaze of others. When a key co-author disappears, the narrative stalls. The roles we once played caregiver, companion, protector, confidant—may vanish or feel suddenly hollow.

Neimeyer articulates this rupture through the lens of "narrative disintegration." The death of a loved one, especially when sudden or traumatic, may produce a **crisis of meaning** so profound that it feels like the very **fabric of the self has unraveled**. Identity, no longer grounded in the continuity of shared life, begins to feel fragmented, disoriented, and undefined.

Rumi and the Dissolution of the Ego

Centuries before the development of identity theory or narrative psychology, **Jalal al-Din Rumi** was already writing of this phenomenon—

but in language both mystical and profoundly psychological. For Rumi, grief and loss are not merely emotional experiences; they are spiritual earthquakes that **dismantle the ego**, the false self we build around attachments and control.

"Be like a tree and let the dead leaves drop."

"Don't get lost in your pain, know that one day your pain will become your cure."

— Rumi

In Rumi's worldview, the self we lose through grief may not be our ultimate self at all. It is the conditioned, ego-bound identity—the self built through roles, titles, and attachments. While the loss feels annihilating, it may also serve as a portal. Through grief, Rumi suggests, the soul is returned to its deeper essence—not in the denial of identity, but in its **transformation**.

"Try to learn to let what is simply be. That is the path of the Beloved."

— Rumi

This path is neither linear nor gentle. Like modern psychology, Rumi does not promise a quick restoration. Instead, he invites us into a **lived encounter with impermanence**, where identity is stripped down, then slowly reformed in the fires of sorrow.

Identity Disorientation: The Liminal Space After Loss

Grief creates what anthropologists and psychologists call a **liminal space**—a threshold state where old identities no longer fit, but new ones have not yet formed. This in-between place is often experienced as a kind of existential vertigo. Mourners may say:

- "I don't know who I am anymore."

- "I don't recognize myself without them."

- "I feel like I'm just going through the motions."

This identity disorientation is especially intense when the relationship was central to one's sense of self—as in the loss of a life partner, child, or long-time friend. The mourner is thrust into a **transitional identity**, sometimes with no societal script to guide them.

Modern grief therapy increasingly recognizes this stage not as pathology, but as a **necessary psychic reorganization**. Therapists working within constructivist or existential frameworks help mourners narrate their identity loss and slowly author new self-concepts. These are not "replacements" for the deceased, but **adaptations**—new ways of being that can carry both love and loss forward.

Rumi beautifully describes this phase as a burning:

"Try to be like the nightingale that sings in the fire."

"You were born with wings, why prefer to crawl through life?"

— Rumi

These lines remind us that the burning of identity is not the end. It is a necessary stage in a deeper unfolding. The grief-stricken self is not static—it is **becoming**. In the fire of loss, something hidden may begin to emerge.

RE-MEMBERING THE SELF: Reconstructing Identity Through Continuity

One of the most healing acts in post-loss identity work is **"re-membering"**—a term coined by narrative therapist Michael White[1]. It refers to the process of keeping the deceased psychologically present in ways that **support the construction of a new self**. This may involve integrating the loved one's values, beliefs, or voice into ongoing life.

For instance, a bereaved daughter may continue her father's humanitarian work. A widow may speak to her late husband when making important life decisions. A grieving sibling may remember the laughter and carry it into their parenting. These acts of re-membering are not delusions—they are meaningful rituals of identity restoration.

Neimeyer and others affirm that healthy identity reconstruction does not require forgetting the deceased. On the contrary, the mourner often **becomes someone new because of the bond, not in spite of it**. This approach rejects the outdated notion of "closure" and honors the continuing relationship in a transformed form.

Rumi speaks of this beautifully:

"The moment you accept what troubles you've been given, the door will open."

"The grief you cry out from draws you toward union."

— Rumi

---

1. **Michael White** was an Australian social worker and family therapist. He is known as the founder of narrative therapy, and for his significant contribution to psychotherapy and family therapy, which have been a source of techniques adopted by other approaches.

In both psychology and Rumi's spiritual philosophy, grief becomes a crucible. Identity is not restored as it was. It is **reforged**—sometimes more honest, more humble, more spacious. The mourner may no longer know themselves in the way they once did, but they begin to know themselves in a deeper way.

Embracing Identity Evolution as Sacred Labor

Loss does not only break the heart. It breaks the structure of the self. The journey forward is not about returning to who we were. It is about **growing into someone who can carry love and loss in the same breath**.

Modern psychology gives us tools to understand this process—through narrative work, attachment theory, and identity reconstruction. Rumi gives us the spiritual language to honor it. Together, they offer a sacred map for mourning—a way to **embrace identity change not as an erasure, but as a metamorphosis**.

"With life as short as a half-taken breath, don't plant anything but love."

— **Rumi**

In the next section—*"Who Am I Now?": Crafting a New Story*—we will explore the intimate act of rebuilding life narrative after loss, and how we might answer this deeply human question not with certainty, but with courageous imagination.

"Who am I Now?": Crafting a New Story

"Grief is not only about the pain of losing another, but also about the pain of losing a former version of oneself."

— **Stephen Fleming**

"You were born with potential. You were born with goodness and trust. You were born with ideals and dreams. You were born with greatness. You were born with wings. Why prefer to crawl through life?"

— Rumi

The question **"Who am I now?"** is not a rhetorical cry in the darkness of grief—it is a genuine identity crisis that emerges in the wake of personal loss. After the death of a loved one, the mourner often finds themselves standing on uncertain ground. The person they used to be—a wife, son, best friend, caregiver, protector—may no longer exist in recognizable form. The loss reverberates not only through the external landscape of one's daily life but also through the **internal map of the self**, destabilizing long-held roles, values, and assumptions.

This question does not arise out of philosophical curiosity; it is born of **existential rupture**. It is a cry for coherence, for continuity, and for a thread of selfhood to carry forward into a future that now seems fundamentally altered.

Narrative Identity and the Role of Story in the Self

Modern psychological research has increasingly affirmed that human beings are, at our core, **narrative creatures**. We do not simply live through events—we make meaning of them by **organizing them into stories**. These stories do not just explain the past—they shape the present and influence how we move into the future. This is what narrative psychologist **Dan McAdams** calls the "narrative identity": a life story that gives us a sense of unity, purpose, and agency across time.

When we lose someone significant, that narrative identity is disrupted. The story we were telling about our life—our roles, goals, and shared dreams—may no longer make sense. As **Robert Neimeyer** explains in his theory of **Meaning Reconstruction**, grief is often experienced as a **story-breaking event**, one that demands we author a new narrative that can account for the loss and give shape to who we are becoming in its wake.

This is not a process of denial or revisionist memory. Rather, it is a courageous and often painful act of **truth-telling**—acknowledging that the life once lived is no longer, and daring to imagine a new life that can emerge from the ashes of the old. The mourner is not just recovering from grief— they are actively engaged in **re-storying the self**.

"Be patient where you sit in the dark. The dawn is coming."

— **Rumi**

The Void and the Threshold: From Disintegration to Possibility

In the immediate aftermath of loss, there is often no story—only a **void**. Grief creates what might be called a narrative silence. For a time, the mourner may feel disoriented, fragmented, or even erased. There is often a desperate clinging to the past, because the future is unimaginable without the one who has died. The present may feel like a fog, empty of direction or meaning.

Psychologists such as Camille Wortman[1] and George Bonanno[2] emphasize that this disruption is normal and necessary. The mourner must

---

1. **Camille B. Wortman** is a clinical health psychologist and expert on grief and coping in response to traumatic events and loss. She is an Emeritus Professor of Psychology at Stony Brook University.
2. **George A. Bonanno** is a professor of clinical psychology at Teachers College, Columbia University, U.S. He is responsible for introducing the controversial idea of resilience to the study

spend time in what some theorists call the **liminal space**—a transitional zone between the death of the old identity and the emergence of the new. It is a time of inner chaos and potential. The story of the self is under revision, but the pen has not yet touched the page.

Rumi, in his deeply spiritual understanding of human transformation, speaks often of this place. He describes it not as a mistake or failure, but as the **womb of spiritual rebirth**:

"Try to learn to let what is simply be. That is the path of the Beloved."

"This moment is all there is. Don't let your thoughts of the past steal your now."

— Rumi

This is a radical reorientation. The mourner is invited not to escape the pain, nor to rush prematurely into "healing," but to dwell fully in this threshold space. In doing so, the foundations of a new identity may begin to reveal themselves—not as a return to who they were, but as an unfolding of who they might become.

Crafting the New Story: The Work of Integrative Meaning-Making

As the grief journey progresses, many bereaved individuals begin to engage—consciously or unconsciously—in the work of **integrative meaning-making**. This is the psychological process of weaving the experience of loss into a broader personal narrative that honors the past, acknowledges the present, and allows for future growth.

---

of loss and trauma. He is known as a pioneering researcher in the field of bereavement and trauma.

This work includes several overlapping efforts:

1. **Revisiting core values and life goals**: The mourner may begin to reevaluate what truly matters to them in the aftermath of loss. Sometimes, the death of a loved one brings clarity to previously hidden longings or buried truths.

2. **Reauthoring identity in light of grief**: The mourner learns to carry the lost relationship in a new form—not as a daily presence, but as a spiritual or symbolic companion. They begin to speak of themselves in a new voice: "I am someone who has lost deeply—and who loves still."

3. **Creating continuity between the old self and the new**: Rather than severing ties with the pre-loss identity, the bereaved find ways to integrate the deceased into their ongoing story. This may involve rituals, memory work, legacy projects, or daily affirmations of what the loved one gave to their life.

Neimeyer refers to this process as **identity reformation**, and narrative therapists often facilitate it through journaling, storytelling, and memory integration. It is a creative act as much as it is a healing one.

Rumi frames this creative transformation in metaphors of weaving, burning, and reassembly:

"Don't you know yet? It is your Light that lights the world."

"The wound is the place where the Light enters you."

— Rumi

Grief is not simply the backdrop to the new story—it is the ink. The mourner crafts their new identity from the very materials of sorrow, longing, memory, and love.

Letting the Old Die So the New May Be Born

A central, painful truth undergirds all identity transformation after loss: **some parts of the self must die** for others to emerge. This death is not literal, but symbolic. It may mean releasing an old dream, surrendering a role that no longer exists, or saying goodbye to the person you once were in order to make space for who you are becoming.

This is not betrayal—it is evolution.

Rumi speaks to this paradox again and again:

"Die before you die, so that when death comes, you will not die."

"Why do you stay in prison when the door is so wide open?"

— Rumi

These are not instructions to detach or forget—they are invitations to grow. They affirm that identity is not fixed. The self, like a soul in motion, is always changing, always emerging from the shadows of yesterday toward the light of now.

Living the New Story: Becoming a Self Who Can Carry Both Love and Loss

Ultimately, the work of "crafting a new story" is not about finding the perfect narrative or achieving closure. It is about learning to live authentically in the presence of both **absence and continuity**, to be a self who is shaped—but not shattered—by loss.

Modern grief psychologists increasingly speak of this as the ability to hold "continuing bonds" while also moving forward in life. It is not a return to normal, but a **movement toward a transformed normal**, where grief becomes an integrated part of the self's evolving journey.

Rumi captures this beautifully:

"You were born with wings. Learn to use them and fly."

— Rumi

And the mourner, after months or years of disorientation, may begin to rise again—not in defiance of their sorrow, but **in companionship with it**. Their story now includes the loved one in a different form—woven into purpose, into daily acts of kindness, into the quiet resilience of continuing to live.

Rewriting the Self: A Sacred Act of Becoming

The question "Who am I now?" is not a question we answer once. It is a question we live into, over and over, as we walk through the valley of grief toward the distant horizon of meaning.

Modern psychology offers the tools to reauthor this story—through narrative identity, meaning-making, and therapeutic integration. Rumi offers the courage and spiritual permission to let ourselves be transformed by love, by loss, and by the deep longing that both invokes.

In the final section of this chapter, *Rumi's Metaphor of Death as Transformation*, we will explore how death is not just an end, but a portal through which the soul—and the self—may awaken to deeper life.

Rumi's Metaphor of Death as Transformation

"Don't grieve. Anything you lose comes round in another form."

— Rumi

"It's not the end of the physical body that should worry us. Rather, our concern must be to live while we're alive—releasing our inner selves from the spiritual death that comes with living behind a façade designed to conform to external definitions of who and what we are."

— Elisabeth Kübler-Ross

For most, death is viewed as a finality—the irreversible severing of connection, meaning, and shared time. But for the mystic, and increasingly for contemporary psychology, **death is not an end—it is a transformation**. In both spiritual and psychological traditions, death invites us not only to mourn but to **evolve**, to let the death of the other transform the self.

No thinker embodies this vision more fully than **Jalal al-Din Rumi**, the 13th-century Persian mystic, who spoke of death not with fear or finality but with intimacy, awe, and an abiding sense of **metamorphosis**.

In Rumi's poetic and theological vision, death is a **threshold, not a terminus**—a spiritual migration from form to formlessness, from visible to invisible presence, from temporal life to eternal belonging. And within this metaphor lies an invitation not only for the deceased, but also for the bereaved: to let death be a teacher, a purifier, and a portal toward deeper life.

Psychological Grief as a Form of Ego Death

From the standpoint of modern psychology, the loss of a loved one often initiates what can be called a **psychological death**—not of the body, but of the self as previously constructed. The mourner loses not only the person they loved, but also a sense of identity, security, worldview, and continuity.

Psychologists such as **Robert Neimeyer**, **Ronald K. Barrett**, and **Stephen Fleming** describe bereavement as a **shattering of the assumptive world**—a collapse of the frameworks that once helped a person navigate life. This collapse mimics the death of the ego as described in many spiritual traditions. The mourner, like the mystic, is forced into a process of deconstruction—one that, if met with courage and compassion, can become a seedbed for personal transformation.

Here, Rumi offers not consolation but **transfiguration**:

"When the soul lies down in that grass, the world is too full to talk about. Ideas, language... even the phrase each other doesn't make any sense."

— Rumi

Death, he says, strips us of all illusions—not only of permanence and possession, but also of the false solidity of our identities. And in doing so, it returns us to what he calls the **Essential Self**, the soul that is neither born nor dies but exists in eternal union with the Beloved.

From this vantage point, the grief-stricken mourner stands in sacred terrain: not in the absence of meaning, but on the **edge of revelation**.

The Chickpea and the Boiling Pot: A Symbol of Spiritual Alchemy

One of Rumi's most famous metaphors for transformation—often overlooked in grief literature—is the parable of the **chickpea boiling in the pot**:

"A chickpea leaps almost over the rim of the pot where it's being boiled,

'Why are you doing this to me?'

The cook knocks it down with the ladle.

'Don't you try to jump out. You think I'm torturing you.

I'm giving you flavor, so you can mix with spices and rice

and be the lovely vitality of a human being.'"

This metaphor captures a profound psychological truth: transformation rarely feels gentle. It feels like burning. The mourner, like the chickpea, cries out in the agony of grief, wondering why the world has become so unrecognizable, so cruel. But Rumi—and many grief psychologists—suggest that this heat is not without purpose. It **softens**. It prepares. It makes one more able to mix with the ingredients of life.

This parallels the modern psychological notion of **post-traumatic growth**, a concept developed by Richard Tedeschi and Lawrence Calhoun, which explores how individuals can experience positive psychological changes following deeply traumatic events—including bereavement. Such growth may manifest as increased emotional depth, redefined priorities, spiritual awakening, or a renewed sense of purpose.

Rumi and Tedeschi, speaking from vastly different worlds, align in this: **suffering is transformative when we allow ourselves to be changed by it.**

WEDDING NIGHT: Death as Union, Not Departure

Perhaps the most radical of Rumi's metaphors for death is his reference to it as the **"Wedding Night" (Shab-e Arus)**—the night of union with the Divine. On the night of his own passing, Rumi instructed his followers not to mourn, but to celebrate, calling death a return to the Beloved.

To many Western ears, this can sound like spiritual bypassing—an attempt to avoid the pain of grief with poetic idealism. But Rumi is not denying the reality of loss—he is **elevating its meaning**. For Rumi, what we call death is merely the lifting of a veil, the moment when the soul is reunited with its original source. His lens is not that of negation, but of **completion**.

"Don't think of those who are dead as gone.

They're not dead. They're alive in another way.

Invisible, yes, but present."

— Rumi

This metaphor finds resonance in many bereaved people's experiences of **continuing bonds**—a contemporary psychological concept popularized by **Dennis Klass**, which recognizes that relationships with the deceased often continue in a transformed, internalized form. The mourner may feel the presence of the loved one, speak to them inwardly, or draw strength from their memory.

What Rumi frames as mystical union, modern psychology frames as **attachment beyond death**—not pathological clinging, but a healthy adaptation of love into a new modality.

From Collapse to Emergence: The Phoenix Within

Rumi's poetic universe is populated with symbols of death and rebirth: the Phoenix that rises from the ashes, the seed that dies to become a flower, the night that gives way to dawn. In each of these, the message is consistent: **what dies makes way for what is truer to emerge.**

This is not only spiritual imagery—it is **neurological and psychological reality**. Neuroscience research on grief, particularly through the lens of **complicated grief therapy (CGT)** and **emotion-focused therapy (EFT)**, shows that healing from bereavement often involves developing a new cognitive-emotional map—one that includes the loss but no longer revolves around it.

The mourner must allow the old attachments, routines, and identities to fall away—not to forget the loved one, but to become someone capable of loving again, living again. In this way, the death of the other becomes the **catalyst for the rebirth of the self**.

Rumi's metaphorical language urges this same movement:

"Try not to resist the changes that come your way.

Instead, let life live through you."

— **Rumi**

In essence, **grief is an alchemical fire**. It burns, but it also refines. It reduces the ego to ash, but from that ash something essential—something real—emerges.

The Mourner as Mystic: Grief as Spiritual Initiation

In Rumi's cosmology, those who grieve are not broken—they are **initiated**. The mourner, like the mystic, is undergoing a radical transformation of perception. The world no longer appears as it once did. Love becomes both wound and compass. Time bends. Presence deepens.

This aligns with what psychologists like **Jordan Peterson** have termed **transformative suffering**—the idea that, if met with courage, grief can awaken a person to their most profound spiritual and psychological depths.

Rumi does not deny the pain of death; he asks us to walk through it with eyes open, to let it transfigure us, to become more—not less—human through its passage.

"You were born with wings, why prefer to crawl through life?"

— Rumi

Death as Transformation, Grief as Rebirth

To live without someone we love is to live in a different reality—one we never chose, yet one that calls us to rise. Rumi, alongside the most thoughtful voices in grief psychology, invites us to see death not as an annihilation, but as **a change of state**, a movement from form to essence.

For the mourner, this means acknowledging that the loss of the other is also a **death of the old self**. But just as the caterpillar dies to become a butterfly, so too does grief invite us into a different kind of becoming.

Transformation is not comfort—it is calling. It is not the erasure of sorrow, but its redemption.

And in this light, the mourner may come to see that even amidst the ashes of what was, something sacred stirs.

"With life as short as a half-taken breath,

don't plant anything but love."

— **Rumi**

Chapter 7 Summary: Reconstructing a Life Without Them

In the quiet wreckage left by loss, the mourner is asked not merely to survive, but to **reconstruct meaning**, identity, and selfhood in the absence of what once gave life its center. This chapter explored how grief is not simply an emotional reaction, but a profound existential rupture—one that invites the mourner to engage in deep psychological and spiritual reconstruction. Through the lens of Robert Neimeyer's Meaning Reconstruction Theory, we saw how grief involves rebuilding the very architecture of our worldviews. We confronted the aching question—"Who am I now?"—and acknowledged the need to author a new narrative that includes the loss, yet reaches beyond it. And through Rumi's metaphors of death as transformation, we reframed grief as a sacred threshold: painful, yes, but also purifying and profound. Death, as Rumi reminds us, is not an end, but a return, a shedding of the visible form into invisible essence. The mourner, too, is transformed—emerging not untouched by sorrow, but **tempered and reawakened** by it. The old self has fallen away, but in its place, something more honest, more compassionate, and more eternal begins to rise.

As we turn to the next chapter, we shift from inner reconstruction to outward integration—from surviving the loss to **living forward**. The question becomes: how do we now carry this love, this pain, this changed self, into the life that continues?

Chapter 8:
Love Doesn't Die: Continuing Bonds and Spiritual Connection

"Goodbyes are only for those who love with their eyes. Because for those who love with heart and soul, there is no such thing as separation."

— Rumi

When someone we love dies, we are told to move on, to find closure, to "let them go." These messages—so common in Western grieving culture—imply that the relationship ends at the moment of death. But for those who mourn intimately and profoundly, this is not how love behaves. Love, as it is lived and experienced, is not erased by absence. It is transformed.

In truth, **love doesn't die**. It changes form, moves inward, takes root in memory and spirit, and becomes a continued presence that speaks in dreams, rituals, symbols, and silences. The grieving do not cling to a ghost—they are answering an unbroken call of the heart. And this experience is not a sign of pathological denial, as some early psychological theories once argued, but a testament to the enduring capacity of the human psyche to sustain bonds beyond the grave.

PSYCHOLOGICAL FOUNDATIONS: From Detachment to Enduring Connection

For much of the 20th century, bereavement psychology was dominated by a **detachment model**, largely shaped by Sigmund Freud's early views. In *Mourning and Melancholia* (1917), Freud suggested that the healthy resolution of grief required a withdrawal of emotional investment from the deceased.

Grief was framed as a temporary disturbance, the goal of which was to sever ties and redirect affection toward new relationships. Under this model, sustained emotional connection with the dead was often pathologized—as something unresolved, regressive, or even neurotic.

However, the rise of **attachment theory**, pioneered by John Bowlby, reframed the way grief was understood. Bowlby emphasized that our bonds with loved ones are rooted in deep biological and emotional systems. These bonds do not simply disappear upon death. Instead, they continue to exert influence, and the mourner must find ways to integrate the loss while maintaining a sense of emotional continuity. This shift opened the door to a new paradigm: **continuing bonds**.

The groundbreaking work of Klass, Silverman, and Nickman in *Continuing Bonds: New Understandings of Grief* (1996) radically reshaped the field by showing that maintaining a relationship with the deceased is not only normal but often central to the grieving process. Instead of severing ties, healthy grieving involves **redefining the connection**, internalizing it, and allowing it to grow alongside the mourner's evolving life.

We do not let go—we **carry forward**. We adapt. We integrate. The love persists, even if the physical presence does not.

RUMI: Presence Beyond the Body

Centuries before psychologists arrived at this understanding, **Jalal al-Din Rumi** was writing poetry that captured this very truth with mystical clarity. Rumi, who endured the devastating loss of his beloved spiritual companion Shams of Tabriz, did not seek to erase his grief or pretend that the bond had ended. Instead, he transformed his sorrow into a lifelong conversation with the invisible.

"When the soul lies down in that grass, the world is too full to talk about.

Ideas, language... even the phrase each other—doesn't make any sense."

— Rumi

Rumi's vision was never one of finality. To him, the boundary between life and death was porous, fluid, and ultimately illusory. Death was not an end but a **threshold**—a shift in form, a reconfiguration of presence. The beloved did not vanish; he became dispersed into everything, diffused through memory, spirit, and sensation.

He writes:

"Don't grieve. Anything you lose comes round in another form."

— Rumi

This is the spiritual essence of continuing bonds. What was once embodied is now unbound. What was once specific becomes diffuse. And yet the intimacy deepens. In Rumi's world, to love after death is not to hold onto a shadow—it is to enter into a deeper kind of union, one that transcends separation altogether.

The Griever as Storyteller, Ritual Keeper, and Listener

To maintain a continuing bond with the deceased is not to live in the past—it is to **enter into a new phase of relationship**, one shaped by memory, imagination, symbol, and ritual. The mourner becomes a kind of steward of love—a bearer of legacy, a keeper of the flame. This relationship evolves, not unlike how a living relationship changes across the years.

Modern therapeutic practices now embrace these inner dialogues. In **narrative therapy**, the mourner is invited to revisit and reshape the story of their relationship with the deceased. Rather than ending the story at the funeral, they are encouraged to **continue it**: to ask, "What would they say to me now?" or "How can I live in a way that honors them?"

Similarly, **ritual practices**—whether spiritual or secular—offer containers in which this love can be expressed and renewed. Lighting a candle on the anniversary of their death, keeping a place for them at the table, speaking to them aloud in moments of stress or gratitude—these are not acts of denial. They are expressions of devotion.

And Rumi's mysticism affirms this relational model. He shows us that when the body is gone, the soul becomes **more accessible, not less**. He teaches that the heart must learn new ways of listening:

"The wound is the place where the Light enters you."

— Rumi

In the wound of loss, we become more permeable to presence. We learn to listen with the inner ear. And it is often in the quiet spaces—dreams, long walks, sudden memories—that we feel the deceased speaking back.

Transformation, Not Closure

The language of "closure" so often invoked in discussions of grief can be cruel in its finality. Closure implies that the book is shut, the door is locked, and the relationship is archived. But this is not how the psyche works. And it is certainly not how the soul grieves.

Continuing bonds represent a **living integration** of the loved one into the mourner's ongoing life. It is not about freezing time, but rather **allowing the relationship to evolve** within the context of a changed world. The deceased may no longer take up physical space, but they occupy an inner one—guiding, comforting, sometimes even challenging the mourner as they move forward.

"Try to be like the turtle – at ease in your own shell."

— Rumi

This shell, our new life without them, must be reshaped to include the invisible presence of the one we've lost. We don't erase them. We sculpt a place for them in our being. And we come to find, slowly and gently, that **the relationship was never about bodies to begin with. It was about love**.

And love doesn't die.

Maintaining Connection Through Memory and Ritual

When someone we love dies, their absence can feel like an overwhelming void—an interruption of every pattern that once sustained our daily lives. The rituals we once shared—the morning coffee, the phone calls before bed, the annual trips or the little private jokes—suddenly disappear, and in their place is a silence that many mourners describe as "deafening." In this silence, the heart longs not just for the person, but for the *relation*—for that ongoing connection that once defined and held meaning in our everyday existence.

The work of grief, then, is not only about mourning a person, but about **grappling with the disappearance of a pattern**, and seeking new ways to preserve connection while simultaneously adapting to the absence. This is where **memory and ritual** become central—not only as acts of commemoration, but as tools of psychological healing and spiritual reorientation.

The Role of Memory in Continuing Bonds

From a psychological standpoint, memory is not a static archive but an **active and dynamic process**. According to cognitive psychology, memories are reconstructed every time we recall them, influenced by our present emotional state, evolving identity, and current relational needs. This fluidity of memory is not a flaw but a feature—allowing us to reshape our relationship with the deceased as we change ourselves.

Robert Neimeyer, a central figure in the meaning reconstruction model of grief, has emphasized that grief is fundamentally a process of **narrative transformation**. Memories are the building blocks of this process. When we revisit a memory, we don't merely re-experience the past—we **reinterpret it** in the light of new understandings. We might remember a conversation with our loved one and hear it differently, as if they are speaking anew through the lens of our current experience. This reshaping is a way of continuing the bond in the language of story and meaning.

In this sense, memory is not just passive recollection—it becomes an *active presence*. It is the voice in the back of your mind when making a hard decision: "What would she say about this?" It is the feeling of warmth at a certain song, the smile provoked by a shared phrase, the instinctive turn of the head when something reminds you of them. These moments are not hallucinations or regressive clinging. Rather, they are forms of

psychological attachment that have shifted from external behavior to internal dialogue.

Memory, then, becomes a sacred terrain—a private space where love can still breathe.

Ritual as a Container of Meaning and Connection

While memory allows for a private and internal continuation of the relationship, **ritual serves as its external embodiment**. Rituals are symbolic actions—often repeated—that help us process complex emotional states, especially those for which language is insufficient. Across cultures and spiritual traditions, rituals have been used to mediate our relationship with death: to honor the departed, to comfort the living, and to maintain an enduring thread between the two.

Psychologists and anthropologists alike recognize the vital function of **ritual as a meaning-making device**. In the work of Victor Turner and Mircea Eliade, rituals are often described as "liminal" experiences—thresholds where transformation occurs. In grief, the mourner stands between two worlds: one where the loved one existed physically, and one where they exist only in spirit and memory. Ritual gives structure to this in-between space. It acknowledges loss, but also invites *continuation*.

Modern grief therapy often encourages the creation of **personal rituals** as a way to support mourning. These can be formal—like visiting a grave or holding a memorial on anniversaries—or informal, like lighting a candle at dinner, journaling letters to the deceased, or playing their favorite music on their birthday. These rituals do not exist to keep the mourner in the past, but to allow them to **carry the relationship forward** in a manageable, meaningful way.

In clinical settings, these rituals have been found to lower anxiety, reduce intrusive grief symptoms, and promote what psychologists call "continuing bonds." Far from being morbid, rituals of remembrance help reintegrate the deceased into the ongoing life of the mourner.

Rumi and the Sacredness of Repetition

Rumi's poetry is infused with the energy of ritual. His practice of the **Sema**, or the whirling dance, was not merely symbolic but deeply experiential. In turning again and again, the dervish participates in a spiritual ritual of remembrance—*dhikr*, or "remembrance of God." For Rumi, repetition was not about monotony but about **sacred attention**. Each turn was a return—just as each memory or ritual we perform in grief is a return to love.

"Come, come, whoever you are.

Wanderer, worshiper, lover of leaving—

It doesn't matter.

Ours is not a caravan of despair."

— Rumi

This invitation from Rumi, repeated across centuries, acts as a **ritual in words**—a call to presence, to reconnection, to meaning even in the face of absence. Rumi saw love as a cyclical motion, not a linear one. The beloved may be gone from the eye, but never from the heart. Ritual allows the heart to stay in motion.

Furthermore, Rumi's writings illustrate that the **ritual of remembrance** is itself a form of reunion:

"The moment I heard my first love story

I started looking for you,

Not knowing how blind that was.

Lovers don't finally meet somewhere.

They're in each other all along."

— Rumi

For Rumi, rituals and memories are not echoes—they are doorways. In participating in the act of remembering, we do not move backward. We move *inward*. And there, within the heart, the beloved still dwells.

Personalizing Rituals for Healing

What emerges in both psychological and spiritual literature is the importance of **personalized, meaningful rituals**. There is no "one-size-fits-all" method for maintaining connection. A mother who lost a child may wear a piece of their clothing. A husband might make his wife's favorite recipe every year on their anniversary. A daughter may journal dreams where she sees her father. These are not sentimental gestures. They are spiritual acts of survival and remembrance.

Grief counselors now encourage clients to **co-create rituals** that reflect the nature of their relationship. This co-creation is empowering—it allows the mourner to become an agent of their own healing, rather than a passive subject of pain.

Rituals do not merely soothe—they **anchor**. In the sea of grief, they offer ground. They tell the mourner: *You are still connected. This love still matters.*

Conclusion: The Ritual of Presence

The practice of remembering and ritualizing our relationship with the deceased is not about resisting change. It is about **honoring continuity within change**. As Rumi's vision reminds us, the soul of the beloved has not vanished—it has only changed address. Ritual becomes the way we keep writing to that new place, knowing that the heart can still send and receive letters even across worlds.

> *"Goodbyes are only for those who love with their eyes.*
>
> *Because for those who love with heart and soul,*
>
> *there is no such thing as separation."*

> **— Rumi**

In this space of remembered love and meaningful action, grief is not just sorrow—it is reverence. It is the ongoing ritual of saying: *You are still part of me. I carry you still.*

Dreaming Of the Deceased, Speaking to Them, Writing Letters

After a profound loss, the boundary between presence and absence often blurs. Even when the physical form of a loved one is no longer with us, the bond does not simply vanish. It shifts, often into subtler forms—into memories, inner dialogue, dreamscapes, and symbolic gestures. Many grieving individuals report continued communication with the deceased, whether through dreams, imagined conversations, or the act of writing letters to them. These experiences, far from being pathological, can serve as vital conduits for **healing, connection, and integration** of the loss.

Modern psychological literature, especially in the realm of **grief therapy**, increasingly validates these experiences. Rather than dismissing them as denial or magical thinking, many contemporary psychologists recognize them as components of what is known as **continuing bonds**—a term used to describe the healthy maintenance of an emotional relationship with the deceased even after death.

Psychological Legitimacy of Post-Loss Communication

For much of the 20th century, Western psychological models emphasized **detachment** as a healthy endpoint in grieving. Influential theories, like Freud's *mourning and melancholia*, framed grief as a process through which the bereaved must sever emotional ties in order to reinvest energy elsewhere. However, starting in the 1990s, this perspective began to evolve, with researchers like Klass, Silverman, and Nickman proposing the **continuing bonds model**. They observed that many bereaved individuals maintained enduring connections with their deceased loved ones—not as a sign of unresolved grief, but as a **normal and adaptive** aspect of their emotional lives.

This model opened the door for a more nuanced understanding of the ways we remain connected. Among the most frequent expressions of continuing bonds are dreams, imagined conversations, and letter writing. Far from being escapist, these acts can help the bereaved reorganize their identity and worldview after loss, provide solace, and even foster post-traumatic growth.

In dreams, for instance, the psyche often processes unresolved emotions or unfinished conversations. Many grieving individuals report **visitation dreams**—vivid, emotionally charged dreams in which the deceased appears, sometimes offering comfort, guidance, or closure. Research by Deirdre Barrett at Harvard and others shows that such dreams are **ubiquitous and cross-cultural**, occurring regardless of religious background or belief systems. They are not hallucinations or pathological events but rather **psychological phenomena deeply rooted in our emotional and symbolic processing systems**.

Similarly, **inner dialogue** or "speaking to the deceased" is common. This may manifest as talking out loud to a photo, whispering a message at a gravesite, or simply hearing the voice of the departed in one's thoughts. Rather than being delusional, these acts are consistent with what psychologists call **internalized representations**. We carry the emotional and cognitive imprints of those we've loved within our mental architecture. Speaking to them is often a form of **internal problem-solving, emotional regulation, and re-attunement to their wisdom**—especially when they served as anchors in our life.

Writing letters to the deceased also serves as a structured form of communication. In **narrative therapy**, clinicians often encourage clients to write letters as a therapeutic exercise. These letters may express love, anger, regret, or gratitude. They can help resolve unfinished business or serve as a container for emotion that has nowhere else to go. The act of writing externalizes the internal world, offering both **emotional release and cognitive clarity**.

Grief experts like Robert Neimeyer and Thomas Attig highlight how such practices can facilitate **meaning reconstruction**, enabling the mourner to integrate the loss into their life story without erasing the emotional bond.

Rumi and the Invisible Conversation

Centuries before modern psychology would validate these practices, **Jalal al-Din Rumi** had already given voice to the inner conversation with the beloved who is "gone." In his mystical worldview, death was never the end of connection. Rather, it was a transition into a subtler form of communion—one not bound by the senses, but illuminated by the heart.

"Why should I fear?

When was I less by dying?"

— Rumi

This question, posed by Rumi, reframes the meaning of death entirely. For Rumi, the beloved is not absent; they have simply become a **formless presence**. Thus, communication with them is not fantasy—it is the deepest act of remembering, of loving beyond the physical veil.

Throughout the *Masnavi* and his ghazals, Rumi frequently speaks to Shams of Tabriz, his lost companion and spiritual mirror. Shams becomes not only a symbol of divine love but also a representation of the **eternal inner dialogue** with someone who transformed one's soul. Rumi's poetry offers constant examples of speaking to Shams—sometimes with longing, sometimes with awe, sometimes with sorrow.

"Don't grieve.

Anything you lose comes round in another form."

— Rumi

Here, Rumi affirms that even though we may no longer hear the voice or feel the touch, something persists—an essence, a frequency of the heart that continues to echo. Speaking to the departed becomes not an act of delusion, but of **devotion**.

In fact, Rumi's own mystical path involved **active engagement with the unseen**. In the Sufi tradition, this is known as *suhbah*—companionship beyond the material. The Sufi seeks connection with the beloved not through the eyes, but through the soul's inner perception. In this way, writing letters or speaking aloud to someone who has died is an act of spiritual faithfulness.

"Try to be a sheet of paper with nothing on it.

Be a spot of ground where nothing is growing,

Where something might be planted,

A seed, possibly, from the Absolute."

— Rumi

This invitation from Rumi speaks to the **state of openness** that allows these post-loss conversations to unfold. In emptiness, there is space for connection. In silence, a whisper can be heard.

Therapeutic Applications and Spiritual Integration

Grief counseling today often draws upon these practices in structured ways. For example:

- Clients may be guided to write **unsent letters** to the deceased to express what was left unspoken.

- Therapists may use **empty chair techniques** from Gestalt therapy, allowing the client to "speak" directly to the loved one.

- In some cases, clients are encouraged to engage in **dream journaling**, reflecting on recurring symbols and messages from the deceased.

These exercises not only offer emotional relief—they can become rituals of **transcendence and transformation**, reweaving the threads of relationship into a new spiritual tapestry.

Moreover, in **cultural psychology**, these practices are recognized as deeply rooted in indigenous, Eastern, and non-Western traditions. Many cultures have long embraced dreams and symbolic communication as legitimate channels of connection. What Western psychology once marginalized is now increasingly acknowledged as **culturally congruent and spiritually meaningful**.

Conclusion: The Conversation That Never Ends

Grief is not about forgetting. It is about **finding new ways to remember**, to speak, to listen, and to love. Dreaming of the deceased, speaking to them in our thoughts or out loud, and writing letters are not signs of pathological attachment—they are expressions of a heart that still knows how to love, even in the dark.

As Rumi reminds us:

"Don't get lost in your pain,

Know that one day your pain will become your cure."

— Rumi

Through these quiet conversations, the mourner does not only find solace. They also find themselves healing—bit by bit, word by word. And perhaps, in that sacred space between silence and speech, they will hear the whispered answer: *I am still with you.*

Psychological Legitimacy of Continuing Bonds

In the aftermath of loss, one of the most enduring questions is whether holding on to a relationship with the deceased—whether through memory, ritual, dialogue, or presence in dreams—is healthy or maladaptive. Historically, much of Western psychology answered this question with skepticism, rooted in the idea that psychological well-being required detachment. But over the past few decades, a significant shift has taken place. The idea of *continuing bonds*—maintaining an enduring, inner relationship with the deceased—has emerged not only as legitimate but as a **profoundly healing and natural part of grief**.

This modern view resonates powerfully with the wisdom of **Jalal al-Din Rumi**, whose mystical worldview anticipated many of these insights by centuries. Rumi's poetry constantly blurs the boundary between life and death, self and other, presence and absence. The beloved may vanish in form, but their essence becomes even more deeply woven into the seeker's soul. The psychological and spiritual threads intertwine: love does not end with death—it transforms.

From Detachment to Connection: A Paradigm Shift in Psychology

For much of the 20th century, prevailing grief models like **Freud's psychoanalytic theory** and **Bowlby's attachment theory** emphasized detachment as the primary goal of grieving. Freud viewed mourning as a process of "withdrawing libidinal energy" from the deceased, eventually freeing the mourner to reinvest in other relationships. Similarly, Bowlby's early formulations focused on how the severance of attachment bonds leads to distress, with resolution being contingent upon relinquishing the old attachment.

However, these models came under increasing criticism for being too narrow, especially in light of findings from cross-cultural and clinical studies. Researchers began to observe that **many bereaved individuals continued to feel connected to their loved ones, often in ways that were emotionally nourishing and adaptive**. These connections didn't signal denial or pathology—instead, they served as sources of resilience, guidance, and identity continuity.

This growing awareness led to the development of the **Continuing Bonds theory**, most notably articulated by Dennis Klass, Phyllis Silverman, and Steven Nickman in their 1996 landmark book *Continuing Bonds: New Understandings of Grief*. They argued that grief is not a process of detaching but of **redefining the relationship** with the deceased. The bond continues, but in transformed ways.

Their research, along with subsequent studies in **constructivist and narrative psychology**, supports the idea that grief is not about forgetting, but about **integrating the loss into one's life story**—often through an ongoing, dynamic relationship with the deceased that persists in memory, dreams, values, and inner dialogue.

The Forms of Continuing Bonds

The psychological literature has identified a wide range of continuing bonds that are developmentally appropriate and emotionally sustaining. These may include:

- **Talking to the deceased** in thoughts or prayer.

- **Dreams** that convey a sense of presence or guidance.

- **Rituals and commemorations**, such as lighting candles or visiting grave sites.

- **Living in accordance with the values or teachings of the deceased**.

- **Sensing the presence** of the deceased in daily life or special moments.

Such experiences help anchor the mourner, especially in situations where the lost relationship was central to one's identity. The key shift is recognizing that **maintaining a relationship is not necessarily about clinging**—it is about **evolving that relationship into a new form**.

Grief experts like **Robert Neimeyer** have incorporated this model into therapeutic practices that emphasize **meaning reconstruction**, where continuing bonds are essential tools in creating a coherent post-loss identity. When these bonds are acknowledged and integrated, mourners are more likely to experience **post-traumatic growth**, spiritual deepening, and even renewed purpose.

Rumi and the Soul's Eternal Dialogue

In Rumi's spiritual philosophy, the idea that love persists after physical separation is not merely poetic—it is metaphysical truth. Death is not the end of relationship; it is the unveiling of a deeper, more intimate form of communion. Rumi does not urge the mourner to forget the beloved but to find them in a new realm of perception.

"The wound is the place where the Light enters you."

— Rumi

Here, the pain of separation becomes an opening—not for closure, but for transformation. Rumi's grief for his lost companion Shams was not resolved through detachment. On the contrary, it was deepened, spiritualized, and eternalized through verse, meditation, and inner presence. Shams became not a memory but a **living archetype**, a guide and flame within.

This mystical stance aligns elegantly with contemporary grief theories that view continuing bonds as a **natural, healing, and necessary process**. Rumi's entire body of work stands as a testament to this truth: love, once ignited, does not end—it *changes form.*

"You left, and I cried tears of blood.

How could I know it was a seed?

Now my chest blooms with roses."

— Rumi

This metaphor beautifully illustrates how psychological suffering can give rise to spiritual blooming, and how the memory of the beloved becomes the soil in which new growth takes place. The mourner, like Rumi, does not shed the past, but **carries it forward**—not as weight, but as light.

Cultural, Clinical, and Ethical Considerations

Across cultures, continuing bonds are not anomalies; they are the norm. In **Japanese traditions**, for instance, the spirits of ancestors are honored in home altars (*butsudan*), and in **Mexican culture**, Día de los Muertos (Day of the Dead) celebrates the return of souls for brief reunions. In **indigenous cultures**, communication with ancestors is an integral part of healing and guidance.

When clinicians embrace continuing bonds, they open space for **culturally sensitive grief work**. Ignoring or pathologizing these experiences risks alienating clients and undermining their natural grieving processes.

Moreover, from an ethical standpoint, validating the mourner's lived experience—especially when it brings comfort and meaning—is essential. The task is not to judge the "reality" of the continued relationship, but to honor its psychological and emotional utility. As **attachment theory** has evolved, researchers like Colin Murray Parkes and John Bowlby's successors have noted that bonds continue throughout life and are **internalized as models that guide future relationships and choices**.

Integration, Not Detachment

The legitimacy of continuing bonds ultimately rests on their role in helping the mourner **integrate loss into a transformed self-concept and worldview**. Whether through dreams, daily dialogue, or moments of spiritual presence, the ongoing relationship can offer:

- **Stability** in identity.

- **Moral guidance** through the internalized voice of the beloved.

- **Emotional regulation** in times of distress.

- **Connection to meaning**, especially when the deceased was a spiritual or moral anchor.

Rather than obstructing healing, these bonds often **facilitate it**, allowing grief to become not a wound to close but a doorway to deeper insight.

As Rumi might suggest, love is not diminished by absence. Instead, it is **refined**, purified, and drawn inward—becoming a source of radiance in the dark night of mourning.

"The moment you accept what troubles you've been given,

the door will open."

— Rumi

In this open door lies the mourner's evolving connection with the beloved—not a ghostly attachment, but a sacred bond reimagined.

Rumi's poetry on reunion, presence beyond form

To speak of grief without speaking of longing is to miss the deepest pulse that runs through both. In the experience of profound loss, what remains after the shock, after the numbness, is a yearning not just for what was, but for **what still is**—in another form. For the mystic Jalāl ad-Dīn Rumi, this yearning was not pathological, nor was it mere sentimentality; it was **the soul's compass pointing to truth**. Rumi's poetry speaks directly to the idea that death is not an end, but a doorway into another form of union, one that transcends the body and sensory world. Through Rumi, we are offered a lens into **the invisible continuation of relationship**, which psychological science is only now beginning to recognize and affirm.

The Mystic's Lens: Form Is Temporary, Presence Is Eternal

In Rumi's universe, form is fleeting. Everything that can be touched, seen, held—these are but garments worn by the deeper truth of being. He writes:

"Don't grieve. Anything you lose comes round in another form."

— **Rumi**, *Masnavi, Book I*

This is not a dismissal of grief but an invitation to re-perceive it. When the form disappears, the essence is revealed. To Rumi, the death of a beloved is not their absence, but their **transfiguration**. The heart still knows them—not through sight, but through **resonance**. Their presence becomes an interior companion, a spiritual imprint that deepens rather than fades.

Modern grief theory, particularly in the domain of **continuing bonds**, increasingly affirms that relationships do not need to end with physical death. Instead, they evolve. People often report sensing the presence of the

302

deceased, experiencing dreams that feel like visitations, or continuing conversations with them in their minds. Far from being unhealthy, these experiences are now understood to be psychologically natural and sometimes essential for **emotional integration and identity continuity**.

Rumi's poetry, rich with metaphors of wind, flame, sea, and sky, gives voice to this form of presence:

"I have died many times, but your breath makes me alive again."

— **Rumi**, *Divan-e Shams-e Tabrizi*

This line does not suggest literal resurrection, but rather **an ongoing, soul-level communion** that infuses the mourner with vitality. The beloved becomes not just a memory but a **source of inner breath**, a spiritual sustenance.

Reunion as a Spiritual Horizon

One of Rumi's most profound and recurring metaphors for death is **reunion**—a homecoming, not a separation. In Sufi cosmology, this worldview is grounded in the idea that the soul originates from the Divine, is briefly housed in a body, and returns after death. The beloved's death, then, is not a vanishing, but a **re-merging** with Source.

"When the soul lies down in that grass,

the world is too full to talk about."

— **Rumi**, *The Great Wagon*

This is the paradox of mystical union: once the individual ego dissolves, there is nothing to grieve, for all is one. For those left behind in the physical world, however, the promise of reunion becomes a powerful **symbol of**

hope and meaning. Contemporary grief theorists such as Robert Neimeyer and Thomas Attig argue that finding meaning in loss—especially spiritual meaning—is one of the key paths to post-loss transformation. Rumi's poetry offers precisely that: a **meaning-rich vision of death** as the rejoining of separated souls.

> *"This moment is all there is.*
>
> *If you miss it, you miss your appointment with life.*
>
> *Don't run after the departed.*
>
> *Look for them in the now."*

— Rumi

The departed are not to be found in some distant realm, but in the **depth of presence**, here and now. This echoes the insights of **mindfulness-based grief therapy**, which encourages the mourner to remain open to the experience of loss without judgment, and to discover the ongoing presence of the beloved in their inner world—not as a ghost of the past but as **a living, inner presence**.

Psychological Parallels: Symbolic Immortality and Internalized Presence

In modern psychological thought, particularly within the existential-humanistic tradition, the idea of *symbolic immortality*—a term coined by Robert Jay Lifton—captures how individuals seek to continue the presence of the deceased through memory, influence, values, and legacy. This aligns with Rumi's spiritual ideal: the beloved lives on in the actions, words, and values we carry forward. When a mourner feels guided by the voice of a deceased parent, partner, or child, it is not fantasy—it is **psychological integration**.

Moreover, **attachment theory**, especially in its contemporary formulations by scholars like George Bonanno and Susan Folkman, suggests that secure attachments do not end with death but become **internalized models of safety and love**. The deceased becomes a secure base not externally but internally—much like Rumi internalized Shams as a voice, a flame, a source of divine insight.

"You were sent for a purpose, and when your work is done,

the candle is snuffed—but the light remains."

— **Rumi**, *Masnavi*

This light is what mourners carry forward: a flame of guidance, an echo of laughter, a standard of courage. Rumi teaches that the form of the beloved may vanish, but **the relationship does not**. It changes, deepens, and becomes less tangible but more enduring.

The Paradox of Absence and Intimacy

One of Rumi's most profound contributions to our understanding of loss is his assertion that **absence intensifies intimacy**. Where modern Western culture often sees grief as a waning connection, Rumi saw it as **a refinement**—a stripping away of illusion, a magnifying of essence.

"The minute I heard my first love story,

I started looking for you, not knowing how blind that was.

Lovers don't finally meet somewhere.

They're in each other all along."

— **Rumi**, *Divan-e Shams-e Tabrizi*

This profound line suggests that the deepest connections transcend space and time. What matters most is not where the beloved is, but **who they have become within you**. Grief becomes not a breaking, but a blending. The veil between worlds, which Rumi refers to often, is not a wall—it is **a mist**, through which the heart can still see, feel, and be guided.

Modern bereavement therapy, particularly in spiritually integrated approaches, encourages clients to develop **an ongoing, living relationship with the deceased**, which includes dialogue, honoring rituals, and internalization of their values. This is not seen as a denial of death, but as a **resilience-building process** that fosters continuity, identity, and meaning. Rumi's mystical worldview anticipated these findings by centuries.

Conclusion: A Poetic-Clinical Synthesis

In Rumi's cosmology, love never ends. The heart's connection to the beloved, once forged, continues through layers of transformation. Modern psychology now affirms what Rumi intuited through ecstasy and longing: the bond with the departed is not a problem to be solved but **a mystery to be lived**.

Rumi gives the mourner not closure, but **continuity**. Not silence, but a new form of conversation. His poems are not just metaphysical musings but blueprints for **psychological healing**—offering a way to move through grief without severing love, and to transform pain into deeper presence.

"Goodbyes are only for those who love with their eyes.

Because for those who love with heart and soul,

there is no such thing as separation."

— Rumi

This teaching, both spiritual and psychological, is at the core of continuing bonds. The body departs. The love remains. And in that love, the beloved is not lost, but **reborn inside the mourner's own becoming**.

Chapter 8 Summary: Love Doesn't Die: Continuing Bonds and Spiritual Connection

In this chapter, we have traversed the delicate terrain where absence meets intimacy, exploring how love endures even after death. Far from being extinguished by loss, the bond with the departed is transformed—continuing in memory, ritual, dream, and the inner dialogue that often deepens over time. Modern psychological thought, increasingly supported by research in attachment theory, grief studies, and narrative psychology, now affirms what Rumi has long whispered to the soul: that death does not end a relationship; it changes its expression. Through meaningful practices—writing letters, recalling memories, invoking rituals, and sensing presence—the mourner carries forward not only the love shared but the essence of the beloved's being. Rumi's poetry offers luminous pathways to understand these bonds not as illusions or denials, but as sacred continuations of intimacy across dimensions. Where traditional grief paradigms once urged detachment and closure, we now embrace connection, fluidity, and the ongoing evolution of love. As Rumi reminds us, "Goodbyes are only for those who love with their eyes." With heart and soul awakened, we learn to see again—not with the eyes, but through the eyes of love, where no separation truly exists.

Chapter 9:
Grief as a Doorway to Spiritual Growth

"Sorrow prepares you for joy. It violently sweeps everything out of your house, so that new joy can find space to enter. It shakes the yellow leaves from the bough of your heart, so that fresh green leaves can grow in their place."

— Rumi

Grief is often regarded as a dark night of the soul—a time of profound sorrow, disruption, and disorientation. In many ways, this framing is accurate. Grief pulls us into the abyss, dismantles the scaffolding of our previous identity, and leaves us standing naked before life's hardest truths. But within the inner chambers of this heartbreak lies a paradox: while grief devastates, it can also awaken. When it is held with reverence, attention, and depth, grief becomes more than an emotional state; it becomes a sacred threshold—one that can lead us into deeper meaning, a renewed sense of self, and spiritual awakening.

This chapter is not about idealizing loss or suggesting that suffering is inherently redemptive. Rather, it acknowledges the raw reality of bereavement and simultaneously explores how, for some, the experience of profound loss becomes a **catalyst for spiritual transformation**. This transformation is not about returning to "normal" or achieving closure. It is about opening the soul to the mystery of life and death and allowing the experience of grief to deepen one's relationship to the sacred.

In contemporary psychology, this process is known as **Post-Traumatic Growth** (PTG)—a concept that will be explored in depth in the next section. But beyond psychological terminology, this chapter also turns to **spiritual**

and poetic insights, particularly those of Jalal al-Din Rumi, to understand how grief can become a gateway rather than a dead end.

Rumi, a 13th-century Persian mystic and poet, is arguably one of the most articulate voices when it comes to the transformational possibilities hidden within sorrow. His entire philosophy is grounded in the belief that **pain is not a punishment but a teacher**, and that the human heart, when broken, becomes more porous to divine love. In a modern secular age where grief is often pathologized or rushed through, Rumi offers a radically different perspective: that grief is not an interruption to life—it is an invitation into its depths.

In therapeutic settings, particularly in existential and humanistic psychology, this dimension of grief is increasingly recognized. Grief therapy no longer exclusively aims at symptom reduction or reintegration into social roles. Instead, contemporary therapists often approach grief as a **meaning-making process**, an existential confrontation, and potentially a **spiritual reorientation**. Scholars such as Robert Neimeyer, Viktor Frankl, Irvin Yalom, and Richard Tedeschi have all contributed to a body of work that understands grief as an experience that shakes the foundations of meaning, identity, and belief—and that can, under certain conditions, give rise to deeper awareness, spiritual insight, and personal transformation.

This approach echoes Rumi's frequent portrayal of grief as both death and birth, as both descent and ascent. In his words:

"With life as short as a half-taken breath, don't plant anything but love."

— **Rumi**

This brief line speaks volumes. In the face of mortality, we are invited to reevaluate everything: our values, our attachments, our understanding of time and presence. Grief, then, becomes a kind of alchemical fire—burning away illusions, superficial concerns, and egoic narratives to reveal what is essential.

The spiritual dimensions of grief are deeply personal and culturally variable, but common themes arise across traditions and psychological research: the confrontation with mortality, the reshaping of identity, the yearning for transcendence, and the possibility of renewed purpose. For some, this path includes returning to or deepening a connection with faith. For others, it may mean stepping into mystery without the framework of religious doctrine—relying instead on intuition, beauty, memory, and presence as their compass.

Importantly, the transformation that grief initiates is rarely linear or clean. It is often cyclical, recursive, and filled with contradictions. One may feel moments of awe and spiritual clarity interspersed with despair and numbness. In fact, the coexistence of pain and growth, sorrow and insight, is not a contradiction but a **hallmark** of spiritual maturity. In modern trauma-informed language, this duality is increasingly recognized: **grief does not need to be "resolved" to be meaningful.** It can remain a living presence in our psyche while simultaneously being a source of spiritual expansion.

Therapist and grief educator Francis Weller refers to grief as "a skill of the soul." He writes that our failure to grieve fully limits our capacity to live fully. This echoes Rumi's spiritual imperative to allow the heart to break open, not to collapse but to expand. In Weller's view, unprocessed grief creates a numbness, while engaged grief deepens intimacy—with ourselves, with others, and with the world.

This is where **Rumi's Sufi mysticism** offers profound guidance. In his cosmology, separation from the Beloved (which can be understood as both God and the soul's essence) is the root of all longing. Grief, then, becomes not a sign of weakness, but of divine yearning. It is not something to be overcome, but something to be embraced as part of the soul's journey home. When Rumi writes, *"Don't grieve. Anything you lose comes round in another form,"* he is not diminishing grief. He is pointing to its evolutionary nature—how loss can transform into new presence, and how love never truly dies.

Grief, in this expanded view, is not an enemy of life; it is an integral part of it. It strips away illusions of permanence and control, and in doing so, invites us to stand in truth. It softens us, humbles us, and opens us to connection, not only with those we've lost, but with life itself. In grief, many discover a profound intimacy with the world—a sensitivity to beauty, impermanence, and the preciousness of the present moment.

In therapeutic practice, when individuals are supported to move through grief consciously—with compassion, spaciousness, and depth— they often report not just healing, but awakening. They speak of a **new inner authority**, a deeper connection to what is sacred, a reorientation toward love, service, and truth. These are not side effects of loss—they are possible fruits of the sacred labor that grief demands.

As we move through this chapter, we will explore in greater depth the psychological concept of Post-Traumatic Growth, the existential questions grief evokes, Rumi's teachings on spiritual liberation, and how cultivating purpose and presence can reweave meaning into a shattered life. Through both science and soul, we will see how grief, while breaking us, may also be building something far greater than we imagined: not the return of the old self, but the birth of a **truer, more spacious self**, capable of holding both sorrow and light.

Let us begin...!

Post-Traumatic Growth (PTG)

In the wake of profound grief or trauma, many people struggle not only with overwhelming sorrow but also with the deeper, unsettling sense that their entire worldview has been dismantled. The assumptions they once held—about the fairness of life, the stability of relationships, the predictability of the future—are called into question. For a time, the inner world resembles a ruin: the landscape of meaning shattered, the structures of belief cracked and swaying.

Yet within this psychic devastation lies a lesser-known possibility: that the very process of breaking down may allow for something new to be built. This possibility is what psychologists Richard Tedeschi and Lawrence Calhoun began to study in the mid-1990s, coining the term **Post-Traumatic Growth (PTG)**. Their research revealed that, contrary to common assumptions, many individuals who endure traumatic loss or life-shattering events do not merely return to baseline functioning—some report profound positive transformations in the aftermath. These transformations are not superficial or wishful thinking. Rather, they often involve five key domains: a greater appreciation of life, more meaningful relationships, increased personal strength, a changed sense of priorities, and deepened spiritual or existential development.

PTG does not mean the trauma or loss itself was good, necessary, or even "worth it." It certainly does not glorify suffering. Rather, it acknowledges a truth seen again and again in human experience: that **while suffering wounds us, it also has the potential to deepen and expand us**—if the conditions for growth are present.

This distinction is important. Growth does not arise automatically from trauma. It is not an inevitable outcome, nor a moral imperative. What determines whether a person experiences PTG depends on a complex interplay of factors: psychological flexibility, emotional processing, social support, and existential engagement. PTG occurs not because of the trauma itself, but because of the inner **struggle to make meaning in its aftermath**.

This is where modern psychology and the mystical wisdom of Rumi converge with remarkable clarity.

Rumi's entire spiritual framework can be seen as a poetic exploration of something akin to PTG. In his verses, pain is not only acknowledged but venerated as a vehicle for transformation. The Sufi path he walked and taught is one of loss—loss of ego, of illusions, of attachments—but it is also a path of expansion. As he writes:

"Don't get lost in your pain. Know that one day your pain will become your cure."

— Rumi

This aphorism captures the essence of PTG. The pain is not denied or rushed through; it is entered fully, consciously, reverently. And in doing so, the soul is not diminished, but opened. This reflects what Tedeschi and Calhoun have emphasized in their clinical work: **PTG is not a replacement for suffering, but a transformation of it.**

Many trauma survivors describe a kind of reordering of their inner world. Priorities shift. Trivial concerns fall away. What once seemed important may no longer matter, while seemingly small things—sunlight on a wall, the sound of a friend's laughter, the memory of a loved one's voice—take on new and sacred significance. These perceptual and existential changes are not uncommon. They signify a realignment of the self, not back to what it was before the trauma, but toward a **new, often more integrated sense of being**.

From a psychological standpoint, PTG involves a **cognitive reconstruction of core beliefs**. Trauma often causes what is known as a "shattering of the assumptive world." As Janoff-Bulman described, this occurs when foundational assumptions—such as the belief in a just world or in one's own invulnerability—are upended. PTG involves reconstructing these beliefs in a way that accommodates both the painful truth of the loss and a more mature, spacious view of life.

This inner reconstruction parallels Rumi's metaphorical architecture. He often speaks of destruction as necessary for true building:

"Be like a tree and let the dead leaves drop."

"Try not to resist the changes that come your way. Instead, let life live through you."

— Rumi

These lines are not about passive resignation, but about an active surrender to the mystery of transformation. Rumi invites us to trust that the shedding of the old self—often through the fire of grief—can lead to a truer and more vibrant self, one that is not built on illusions but on spiritual resilience.

From a clinical perspective, PTG can be supported through therapeutic modalities that facilitate emotional expression, narrative processing, and existential exploration. Meaning-making models of grief therapy, such as Robert Neimeyer's work, align closely with the PTG framework. Therapists guide clients in exploring how their worldview has changed, what values have emerged, and what personal or spiritual truths have come into focus. Importantly, PTG does not require forgetting or minimizing the loss. In fact, it often arises from **an ongoing engagement with the pain**, from holding the grief not as a burden to be cast away but as a companion on the path.

This is precisely Rumi's approach. He encourages a relationship with sorrow—not as an intruder, but as a guide. In one of his most famous lines, he writes:

"This being human is a guest house. Every morning a new arrival... the dark thought, the shame, the malice... meet them at the door laughing and invite them in. They may be clearing you out for some new delight."

— Rumi

PTG is the psychological translation of this guest house metaphor. It is the process by which people learn not only to tolerate pain, but to listen to it. To learn from it. And, eventually, to **let it shape them into someone wiser, deeper, and more attuned to life's fragility and beauty.**

316

Some research even suggests that spiritual growth is among the most significant domains of PTG. In the face of death, many people become more aware of their spirituality, even if they are not religious. They describe a greater sense of connection to others, to nature, to the universe. They become less concerned with dogma and more interested in love, compassion, and presence. This mirrors the path of many Sufi mystics, including Rumi, for whom spirituality is not about belief systems but about **direct, embodied experience of the sacred**—often catalyzed by heartbreak.

Indeed, Rumi's own spiritual journey was ignited by the traumatic loss of his beloved companion Shams of Tabriz. It was in the wreckage of that loss that his greatest poetry emerged. The pain did not disappear—it transfigured. Through grieving Shams, Rumi discovered a love that could not be lost, a divine connection that transcended death. This transformation is the mystical counterpart to PTG.

In both traditions—the psychological and the spiritual—grief becomes the crucible for growth, if we are willing to stay present with it. It is not that the pain becomes "worth it," but that something meaningful can arise from it: a deepening, an awakening, a new sense of purpose. In PTG, this is the new story people begin to tell—not about what happened, but about **who they have become**.

As we continue through this chapter, we will explore how grief engages our most profound existential questions, how Rumi's teachings illuminate the hidden possibilities in sorrow, and how one can cultivate a sense of purpose and spiritual grounding beyond belief systems. PTG, then, is not the end of the grief journey—it is one of its most mysterious and sacred turns.

Grief and Existential Questions

Grief does not only tear through the emotional body; it pierces into the very fabric of one's existential being. In the wake of profound loss—whether through death, separation, or even disillusionment—the mourner is not just faced with absence, but with the overwhelming confrontation of life's most fundamental questions: *What is the meaning of this life? Why do we suffer? Is there anything beyond this world? Who am I, really, when everything I anchored my identity to is now gone?*

These are not questions that lend themselves to quick or tidy answers. In fact, their discomfort often evokes avoidance in modern society. Yet, they are the very questions grief brings to the surface with relentless clarity. And paradoxically, it is in the painful grappling with these questions that many individuals find themselves beginning to awaken—not in spite of grief, but because of it.

In psychological terms, this process of existential reflection following loss is a central theme in **existential psychology**, most notably advanced by figures like **Irvin Yalom, Viktor Frankl**, and **Rollo May**. These thinkers argue that human beings are fundamentally meaning-making creatures, and that suffering—particularly the suffering brought on by loss—forces us to confront the "givens" of existence: death, freedom, isolation, and meaninglessness.

Irvin Yalom, in his existential psychotherapy, identifies death as the "primary source of anxiety" for all humans, even when hidden beneath the surface. The death of a loved one can act as a rupture that tears open this reality. We are faced not just with *their* mortality, but with our own. Suddenly, life feels uncertain, fragile, ephemeral. And this confrontation, while terrifying, can also catalyze a profound transformation.

Similarly, Viktor Frankl, a Holocaust survivor and psychiatrist, observed in his seminal work *Man's Search for Meaning* that suffering—when approached with intentionality and reflection—could lead to the discovery of deeper meaning. For Frankl, meaning was not handed to us; it was something we must *create*, especially in the face of uncontrollable pain. He wrote:

"When we are no longer able to change a situation, we are challenged to change ourselves."

— Viktor Frankl

This is the crux of the existential dimension of grief. We cannot undo the loss, but we can allow ourselves to be reshaped by the questions it opens. And this reshaping often leads people into territories they had not previously explored: spiritual inquiry, philosophical contemplation, or creative expression. The individual begins to wrestle with the mystery of being itself.

It is precisely here where the mystical wisdom of **Rumi** offers a timeless and deeply relevant guide. Rumi's poetry and teachings are filled with existential insight—not in the form of doctrinal conclusions, but as experiential invitations. He does not offer answers so much as doorways: questions that burn, longings that deepen, silences that speak louder than explanations.

One of his most piercing lines asks:

"Why do you stay in prison,

When the door is so wide open?"

— **Rumi**

This line is both literal and metaphoric. The "prison" may be our false sense of control, our attachment to permanence, or our refusal to face the reality of death. The "wide-open door" is the path of surrender, of transformation, of awakening. Rumi's work suggests that existential liberation comes not from avoidance of suffering, but from an intimacy with it—a willingness to let it burn through our illusions.

For Rumi, grief is not the opposite of life—it is part of its hidden architecture. In another verse, he writes:

"Don't run away from grief, o soul.

Look for the remedy inside the pain.

Because the rose came from the thorn

and the ruby came from a stone."

— **Rumi**

This metaphorical framing is remarkably aligned with the psychology of post-traumatic growth and existential inquiry. Grief is not framed as a detour from life, but as a crucible for deeper knowing. It is the classroom where we study impermanence, interconnectedness, and the mystery of being. It invites us to consider not only who or what we have lost, but what remains—what truths have always been there, waiting to be seen once the distractions are stripped away.

Modern existential psychology recognizes that meaning is not static or objective—it is **constructed**. After a loss, the old meaning system often breaks down. The beliefs that once made us feel safe or in control may no longer hold. Some people lose their religious faith; others gain a deeper spirituality. Some become more nihilistic; others become more awakened. What makes the difference often comes down to the willingness to engage these existential questions sincerely and courageously.

It is also important to note that this process does not follow a linear or predictable path. Existential inquiry is often cyclical. Some days are full of clarity and connection; others are consumed by doubt and despair. This is normal. Grief ebbs and flows, and so do the insights it brings. But over time, many people report a quiet emergence of new values, new appreciations, and even a redefined sense of self that is more aligned with their deeper truths.

Rumi's metaphors provide support in this oscillation. He speaks of the soul as a reed flute, hollowed out by longing, made into music only through the carving of emptiness. He does not ask us to bypass the ache, but to listen to it, to *become* it. And in doing so, to discover that the grief we feared was not the end of meaning—but the beginning of a more sacred kind.

In the end, grief becomes a sacred invitation—not to find neat answers, but to **live more fully in the mystery**. This is not just a poetic idea; it is supported by clinical findings. Studies have shown that those who allow themselves to reflect deeply on life's big questions in the wake of loss often experience **greater psychological resilience, improved well-being, and a more profound sense of inner peace**. Existential engagement is not a luxury—it is a necessity for those traversing the terrain of loss.

Thus, the existential questions grief provokes—*Why are we here? What happens after death? Who am I without them?*—are not questions to be feared. They are invitations into the very heart of our humanity. Rumi and modern psychology agree: it is through these questions that we shed our false selves and awaken to something more enduring, more intimate, and more real.

Rumi: "Why Do You Stay in Prison, When the Door Is So Wide Open?"

In the landscape of grief, the feeling of being trapped—emotionally, psychologically, spiritually—is a common and often overwhelming experience. It is not unusual for mourners to describe themselves as "stuck" in sorrow, immobilized by memories, regret, unanswered questions, or a shattered worldview. This metaphor of a prison, of being confined within the limits of one's suffering, captures a psychological truth that many grievers encounter. And yet, Rumi, with his piercing spiritual insight, dares to ask:

"Why do you stay in prison, when the door is so wide open?"

— Rumi

This question is not merely rhetorical. It is a profound invitation to examine the nature of the walls that surround us—walls that may be invisible yet powerfully real—and to awaken to the possibility that liberation, while difficult, is closer than we think. When Rumi speaks of a "prison," he is referring not just to grief itself, but to the **egoic structures**, **attachments**, and **narratives** that we build around our pain. The prison is made of beliefs that say: *I cannot live without them. I am nothing without this relationship. Life no longer has meaning.* These thoughts, left unexamined, can crystallize into a psychological confinement where the mourner becomes defined not by who they are, but by what they have lost.

Modern psychology offers parallel insights into this phenomenon. In particular, **Acceptance and Commitment Therapy (ACT)** and **Cognitive Behavioral Therapy (CBT)** address the cognitive distortions and rigid narratives that can keep individuals trapped in cycles of suffering. ACT, developed by Steven C. Hayes, emphasizes the importance of psychological flexibility: the ability to accept one's thoughts and emotions without becoming entangled in them. In ACT, the "prison" is often our fusion with painful thoughts—taking them as literal truths rather than transient mental events. The "open door" is the possibility of stepping back, observing our inner experience with compassion, and choosing values-based actions even in the presence of pain.

Rumi's wisdom complements this psychological model beautifully. His poetry invites us to see grief not as a terminal state but as a *threshold*. When he asks why we remain imprisoned, he is not diminishing the pain of loss. Rather, he is pointing out that within the sorrow lies a latent potential for **transformation**—if only we dare to step through the door.

From the perspective of **trauma-informed psychotherapy**, this "prison" can also represent unprocessed trauma that gets stuck in the nervous system. According to **Bessel van der Kolk**, author of *The Body Keeps the Score*, trauma survivors—including those grieving the sudden or violent loss of a loved one—may experience a state of physiological freeze, in which the body remains on alert long after the danger has passed. In such cases, the "prison" is somatic as much as psychological. The path out is not only through insight but through embodied healing practices that restore safety and movement to the nervous system.

Rumi, who experienced profound loss in his own life—including the disappearance and presumed death of his spiritual companion Shams of Tabriz—understood this entrapment intimately. Yet, instead of closing off or withdrawing from the world, he turned toward the pain and allowed it to burn through him. He wrote:

"Don't get lost in your pain,

Know that one day your pain will become your cure."

— Rumi

Here, we see Rumi articulating what modern psychologists might call **transformational suffering** or **post-traumatic growth**—the idea that intense emotional upheaval, when processed consciously and compassionately, can lead to a new level of awareness and personal evolution.

But why do so many of us remain in the prison, even when the door is wide open?

There are several reasons. First, because **pain can become familiar**, and familiarity can feel safe, even when it is suffocating. Psychologists call this phenomenon "learned helplessness," first studied by Martin Seligman, in which individuals, after repeated exposure to uncontrollable suffering, begin to believe that change is impossible—even when freedom becomes available. Second, because walking through the open door requires **letting go of identity**—a shedding of the self who was defined by the lost person, the grief, or the past. This letting go, though liberating, can feel like another death.

Rumi recognizes the terror of this process. But he also insists that the soul is **not meant to shrink**. It is meant to expand. He uses metaphors like the chick breaking out of the egg, the moth drawn toward the flame, and the seed cracking open in the dark earth—all to illustrate that **growth often requires a rupture**, and that freedom lies on the other side of surrender.

Psychologist Carl Jung made a similar observation when he wrote:

"There is no coming to consciousness without pain."

— Carl Jung

Both Jung and Rumi are pointing toward an ancient truth: pain can be an initiation. Not a punishment, but an opening. Grief, in this light, becomes a doorway not just to healing but to awakening—awakening to one's deeper self, to the impermanence of all things, and to the spiritual dimensions of reality that transcend the rational mind.

This notion finds support in **transpersonal psychology**, which examines the spiritual aspects of human experience. In this field, grief is not viewed solely as a disorder to be cured but as a **spiritual crisis**—a moment when the soul is forced to question its place in the cosmos. According to scholars like Stanislav Grof, such crises can be disorienting but ultimately lead to greater wholeness if navigated with support and intention.

The key is **conscious choice**. The mourner must choose to approach their grief not merely as a problem to be solved, but as a sacred passage to be walked. The prison door may be wide open, but only the mourner can walk through it. No one else can do it for them.

In this, Rumi offers encouragement laced with love and urgency. He writes:

"Try to be like the sun,

Which opens its door for all

And asks nothing in return."

— Rumi

This, too, is part of the transformation: becoming more compassionate, more open-hearted, not in spite of grief but because of it. Walking through the open door means stepping into a new life, one that honors the past but is not shackled to it. It is a life marked by **presence**, **depth**, and **clarity**— the gifts that grief, paradoxically, can bring.

Ultimately, Rumi's line— *"Why do you stay in prison, when the door is so wide open?"*—is not an accusation. It is an invitation. It is the whisper of the soul calling us toward our own liberation. It is the voice that says: You are not meant to live confined by your suffering. There is more. Step through.

And so the question remains, not just for the mourner, but for all of us: **Will you stay in the prison, or will you walk through the door?**

Cultivating Purpose and Faith Beyond Belief Systems

The death of a loved one can feel like the collapse of an inner world. For many, it is not just the person who is lost, but the very scaffolding of meaning that held life together. Beliefs that once felt secure—about the fairness of the world, the nature of love, the presence of God, or the reliability of the future—can begin to unravel. This unraveling can lead to spiritual crisis, but it can also become a profound opportunity to rebuild one's sense of purpose and faith—not by returning to rigid doctrines or inherited ideologies, but by cultivating something deeper: a living, breathing spirituality that emerges from within and moves beyond belief systems.

This distinction—faith beyond belief—is critical. As modern psychologist James Fowler observed in his seminal work on the Stages of Faith Development, authentic faith does not necessarily depend on religious affiliation or traditional theologies. In fact, many individuals evolve to a stage of faith that is more existential and experiential—a direct, intuitive connection to meaning and transcendence, forged through suffering and inner reflection. Grief often acts as the crucible in which such transformation takes place.

This echoes Rumi's spiritual journey as well. Though deeply rooted in the Islamic mystical tradition of Sufism, Rumi's writings transcend dogma. He does not ask us to adopt a specific belief system. Instead, he invites us to step into the intimate fire of our own longing and to find divinity within the experience itself. In one of his most evocative passages, he writes:

"I searched for God and found only myself.

I searched for myself and found only God."

— Rumi

This profound statement reflects a spirituality that is not about external rules or inherited creeds, but about inner awakening. For Rumi, as for many spiritually awakened individuals across traditions, the goal is not to hold the "right" beliefs but to live in alignment with love, presence, and openness to the mystery.

In contemporary psychology, this shift from belief-based to meaning-based spirituality is supported by growing research in the field of existential and humanistic psychology. Viktor Frankl, the Austrian psychiatrist and Holocaust survivor, argued in Man's Search for Meaning that the primary human drive is not pleasure (as Freud proposed) or power (as Adler proposed), but meaning. According to Frankl, even in the face of devastating loss and suffering, individuals can discover profound purpose by asking themselves not "What can I expect from life?" but "What does life expect from me now?"

Grief, then, becomes a spiritual turning point—a chance to reevaluate what truly matters, to strip away illusions, and to cultivate a form of purpose that is not contingent upon external circumstances. Many who walk through the fire of loss report that their values shift dramatically: from achievement to connection, from security to creativity, from ego to soul. This reorientation often manifests in quiet, courageous acts of service, authenticity, or presence. As psychologist David Kessler notes in his work on finding meaning after loss, the search for purpose is not about replacing the person who has died, but about discovering how we will choose to live in their absence.

Rumi encourages this same movement toward deeper, freer spiritual engagement. He reminds us that the soul's journey is not a straight line and that loss is part of the path:

"Be like a tree and let the dead leaves drop."

— Rumi

What remains when all else is gone? According to both modern psychology and the mystical lens of Rumi, what remains is presence. Not the kind of presence that requires theological certainty, but the kind that arises from direct contact with the rawness of life. Presence that makes room for mystery. Presence that listens, that holds grief without trying to fix it, and that begins to trust the unfolding of the soul's story—even when the future is unclear.

Rumi, again and again, insists that our purpose is not something we must create out of thin air. It is already planted within us, like a seed, waiting for the right conditions—often suffering—to break open and grow. He writes:

"Try not to resist the changes that come your way.

Instead, let life live through you."

— Rumi

From a therapeutic perspective, this insight aligns with Narrative Therapy and Logotherapy, both of which focus on helping clients reconstruct meaning and identity in light of loss. Narrative Therapy, developed by Michael White and David Epston, empowers individuals to separate themselves from problem-saturated stories and to re-author their lives in ways that reflect resilience, agency, and preferred values. Through this lens, faith is not something static—it is a dynamic, unfolding story that the bereaved get to revise with each breath.

In grief counseling, many clients express discomfort with traditional religious platitudes—such as "everything happens for a reason" or "they're in a better place"—and instead crave space for questions, doubts, and authenticity. Therapists trained in spiritually integrated psychotherapy offer that space, encouraging mourners to explore their own lived experiences of meaning, connection, and awe, without the pressure to conform to fixed beliefs. This opens the door for a more inclusive, pluralistic form of faith—one that is not bound by creed but shaped by lived truth.

Rumi himself frequently wrote about God as the Beloved, a presence so vast and intimate that it cannot be captured by words. He did not define God. He danced with God. He wept and laughed with God. He lived his spirituality rather than professing it. In doing so, he modeled what it means to cultivate a faith beyond belief systems: a faith rooted in direct encounter, radical love, and soulful surrender.

This is perhaps the greatest invitation of grief—to let go of inherited answers and to begin listening to the deeper questions that arise from the heart. It is not about rejecting religion, nor about clinging to it out of fear. It is about growing into a spirituality that is both personal and universal, shaped not by certainty but by reverence.

In the end, cultivating purpose and faith beyond belief systems does not mean abandoning tradition. It means moving from secondhand faith to firsthand knowing. From external doctrine to internal flame. From rigidity to openness. From fear to trust.

Rumi says:

"The wound is the place where the Light enters you."

— Rumi

And so grief becomes not only a wound, but also a door. A door into a faith that is wider, wilder, and more awake than anything we may have imagined before.

Chapter 9 Summary: Grief as a Doorway to Spiritual Growth

In this chapter, we have explored grief not merely as an affliction to be endured but as a sacred threshold to deeper spiritual growth. Drawing upon the psychological framework of Post-Traumatic Growth (PTG), we've seen how profound loss can catalyze transformation—inviting us to confront existential questions and to reconstruct lives of greater depth, compassion, and authenticity. Through the lens of Rumi, we are reminded that suffering cracks open the hard shells of ego and illusion, allowing the light of presence and divine love to enter. His timeless invitation—"Why do you stay in prison, when the door is so wide open?"—calls us to walk through the pain not to escape it, but to be remade by it. In doing so, we discover that meaning, purpose, and faith are not found in the rigid certainties of inherited belief systems, but in the intimate, evolving dialogue between our wounded hearts and the sacred mystery of life itself. Grief, when engaged with consciously, becomes a passageway—an alchemical fire in which the soul is both broken and born anew.

Part IV: Returning to Life, Gently

Chapter 10:
Living Again Without Guilt

"Don't grieve. Anything you lose comes round in another form."

— Rumi

There comes a moment in nearly every grieving journey—quiet, conflicted, sometimes unbearably confusing—when one is startled by the feeling of life stirring again. A laugh escapes. A breeze feels good on the skin. Music is no longer unbearable. A desire—perhaps small, perhaps fleeting—emerges to begin again. And with it, too often, comes guilt.

Guilt for surviving. Guilt for smiling. Guilt for moving forward. Guilt for not being crushed every second of the day. Guilt for imagining a future.

In the architecture of grief, guilt can become a hidden load-bearing wall. It may not always scream, but it hums beneath the surface: a belief that to live fully after loss is to commit an emotional betrayal. That joy, pleasure, and healing somehow diminish the memory of the one we lost.

Modern psychology and ancient mysticism agree: this is a false, though deeply human, dilemma. To grieve with integrity and to live with vitality are not opposites. They are two sides of the same devotion—two expressions of the love that binds the soul to life.

Contemporary grief theory, especially as it evolved in the late 20th and early 21st centuries, moved away from rigid stage models (like Kübler-Ross's five stages) and toward more nuanced and compassionate understandings. The dual process model of coping with bereavement (Stroebe & Schut, 1999) proposes that healthy mourning involves oscillating between loss-oriented states (grief, longing, remembering) and restoration-oriented states (engaging with life, adapting, rediscovering). In other words, one does not need to "finish" grieving in order to resume living. The two coexist. Life resumes not as a betrayal of the past but as a way of honoring the endurance of love.

Yet guilt still arises, especially in those who lost someone suddenly, tragically, or during a time of unfinished emotional business. Psychologically, this often reflects what trauma experts call survivor's guilt or moral injury—the painful belief that one's survival is undeserved, or that moving on means leaving the deceased behind. These emotional responses are not irrational, even if they are maladaptive. They are rooted in our deepest social wiring. Human beings are relational creatures; we define ourselves through connection. When a loved one dies, our internal roles, loyalties, and identities are shattered. And sometimes, guilt becomes a misguided attempt to remain loyal to the past.

Rumi, speaking across centuries of mystics and mourners, offers a spiritual invitation to reframe this struggle. In a famous line, he writes:

"Don't grieve. Anything you lose comes round in another form."

— **Rumi**

This is not a denial of pain, nor a demand for premature happiness. It is a reminder that love, once formed, is indestructible—it simply changes form. When we live again after loss, we are not replacing the one who is gone. We are continuing the story they helped shape. The love persists, but like water changing to mist, it moves differently now.

Rumi speaks of the soul as fluid, boundless, and eternal. His metaphors flames, rivers, clouds, wind remind us that life is not static. "Don't get lost in your pain," he writes, "know that one day your pain will become your cure." To live again is not to minimize the pain, but to embody the transformation it brings.

Modern psychology echoes this transformation in the theory of post-traumatic growth (Tedeschi & Calhoun, 2004), which suggests that in the aftermath of profound loss or trauma, people often report increased spiritual awareness, deeper relational empathy, and a stronger sense of life purpose. This growth is not guaranteed. It is not linear. It is not tidy. But it is possible—and often arises only when the mourner dares to step forward, slowly and without certainty, into life again.

Living again, then, becomes a sacred act. Not a selfish one. Not a disloyal one. But a deeply moral one. It is, in a sense, a fulfillment of love—the willingness to keep living the very life that your loved one no longer can. To become a steward of memory and joy. To tend to the garden of this world with hands made tender by grief.

There is no timeline for this return. For some, it begins within months. For others, it takes years. For many, it is not a moment but a process—gradual, uneven, unfolding like a hesitant flower. What matters is not the speed of the blooming, but the permission to bloom at all.

As Rumi says:

"Why do you stay in prison, when the door is so wide open?"

— Rumi

The prison is not the grief. Grief is holy. The prison is guilt. The mistaken belief that love demands perpetual suffering. But love—real love

—wants more for us than misery. It wants expansion. It wants music and dancing. It wants us to wake up again in a world that, though scarred, still pulses with beauty.

This chapter is an invitation to begin. To laugh, without apology. To remember, without being held hostage. To live, not despite what you've lost, but because of what you've loved.

The door is open,

Will you walk through it…?

Joy, Laughter, and New Beginnings as Acts of Healing

"With life as short as a half-taken breath, don't plant anything but love."

— Rumi

There is a sacred rebellion in choosing joy after grief. It defies the heavy narrative that equates sorrow with sincerity and pain with devotion. For many bereaved individuals, the moment they smile without guilt—or laugh without caution—feels both liberating and disloyal. This emotional conflict often creates an internal tug-of-war: how can I be joyful when the person I love is no longer here? But both modern psychological frameworks and Rumi's mystical teachings suggest that joy is not an abandonment of grief—it is a companion to it, a life-affirming act that allows us to metabolize loss into meaning.

Psychologically, joy and laughter serve as vital emotional regulators during times of deep distress. According to Barbara Fredrickson's[1] Broaden-

---

1. **Barbara Lee Fredrickson** is an American professor in the department of psychology at the University of North Carolina at Chapel Hill, where she is the Kenan Distinguished Professor of Psychology.

and-Build Theory of Positive Emotions, positive emotional experiences such as joy, gratitude, interest, and contentment do more than just feel good—they actively broaden our cognitive and behavioral repertoires, and build lasting personal resources such as resilience, social bonds, and psychological flexibility. In the context of grief, this means that moments of joy—no matter how small—can act as crucial psychological "counterweights," helping the individual to step out of the narrow tunnel vision of pain and reengage with the fuller spectrum of life.

Grief, in contrast, tends to narrow our field of attention. It demands silence, depth, introspection. These are necessary stages of integration. But human beings are not designed to live indefinitely in one emotional state. Our nervous systems, shaped by evolution, function best when we are able to oscillate—between sorrow and serenity, remembering and rebuilding. This concept is mirrored in the dual process model of coping with bereavement, which posits that both grieving the loss and re-engaging with life are vital and ongoing processes. One does not cancel the other. Rather, the interplay of the two forms a rhythm that supports healthy adaptation.

Rumi, with his profound attunement to the soul's complexity, speaks to this rhythm with poetic clarity. He writes:

"Sorrow prepares you for joy. It violently sweeps everything out of your house, so that new joy can find space to enter."

— Rumi

This is not a spiritual bypass. It is not about rushing to replace pain with pleasure. Rumi's insight reveals a transformational process—where sorrow itself becomes the womb from which joy is born. It is a joy not rooted in

338

denial, but in depth. One that emerges only after the soil of the heart has been upturned and softened by tears.

In modern grief counseling, clinicians now increasingly normalize the reemergence of positive affect as a sign of healing—not betrayal. In fact, some therapists go as far as to encourage the intentional cultivation of joyful moments as part of therapeutic recovery. Laughter yoga, art therapy, nature immersion, and storytelling are all used in grief interventions to activate the body's parasympathetic nervous system—regulating emotions and reducing chronic stress associated with prolonged mourning.

From a neurological standpoint, joy and laughter stimulate the release of dopamine and oxytocin, neurochemicals linked to pleasure and connection. These natural chemicals serve as gentle correctives to the biochemical imbalances triggered by trauma and prolonged sadness. As such, the reintroduction of joy is not superficial—it's somatic. It's spiritual. It literally changes the internal chemistry of the grieving body.

In the poetic universe of Rumi, joy is not only an acceptable emotion in grief—it is the eventual purpose of grief. In one of his most striking metaphors, he compares the human soul to a reed flute, broken from the reedbed, singing in sorrow. But this lament is not just sadness—it is music. Rumi implies that what we call grief may actually be the soul learning how to sing a new song.

He writes:

"Try to learn to let what is simply be. That's the path to joy."

— Rumi

But this letting-be is not passive. It involves courage. It involves choosing to wake up each day and remain available to beauty, despite the bruises on the heart. It means giving oneself permission to enjoy a meal, to smile at the sun, to dance even if the body still aches. Each of these actions becomes a form of healing—not because they erase grief, but because they help the soul stretch to accommodate both love and loss.

Furthermore, new beginnings, whether they come as new relationships, new passions, or simply new routines, are often infused with both excitement and trepidation. After significant loss, many people describe a strange ambivalence about starting over—as if life is asking them to carry forward a legacy that feels too sacred to touch. Yet, psychological research in narrative therapy shows that creating new stories—with fresh goals, characters, and plots—helps grieving individuals integrate the past into a coherent self-narrative that makes room for a livable future. In other words, joy does not erase the old chapter—it adds a new one.

This, too, is echoed in Rumi's wisdom. He urges us to embrace the ephemeral nature of life, to surrender to the cycles of death and rebirth. In his line:

"Be like a tree and let the dead leaves drop."

— **Rumi**

He is not advocating emotional coldness. On the contrary, he is teaching detachment with reverence. Just as trees must release old foliage to grow new buds, we too must release our grip on perpetual mourning—not to forget, but to renew.

In conclusion, joy, laughter, and new beginnings are not indulgences in the aftermath of loss. They are acts of bravery and reverence. They say: I carry you with me in how I live. They allow the bereaved to become living vessels of the love that was once shared. And in doing so, they transform grief not into forgetfulness, but into a deeper form of presence—one where sorrow and celebration sit at the same table.

Working With Survivor's Guilt

"Don't get lost in your pain, know that one day your pain will become your cure."

— **Rumi**

Survivor's guilt, though most commonly associated with those who have lived through traumatic events such as war or accidents, is a deeply human response often encountered in the grieving process. For many individuals who have lost a loved one, especially to sudden or premature death, the question, "Why them and not me?" becomes a haunting refrain. This emotional phenomenon is not just a psychological byproduct—it is an existential reckoning, a moral anguish born from the unbearable dissonance between life's randomness and the depth of human love.

Modern psychological thought has recognized survivor's guilt as a subset of complicated grief and as a feature of post-traumatic stress. The Diagnostic and Statistical Manual of Mental Disorders (DSM-5) references feelings of self-blame and guilt as common features of bereavement-related depression and trauma responses. In clinical settings, this guilt can manifest as insomnia, chronic self-doubt, emotional numbing, withdrawal from joy or intimacy, and even somatic symptoms. Many survivors unconsciously begin to believe they are undeserving of happiness, as if enjoying life is a betrayal of the deceased.

At its root, survivor's guilt often involves magical thinking—the belief that one could have or should have done something differently to prevent the death. This sense of imagined responsibility, though irrational, is emotionally compelling. It becomes a means of reclaiming control in a situation that felt entirely out of control. In a paradoxical way, guilt offers the bereaved a twisted form of meaning: if I am to blame, then at least there is a reason. Yet such reasoning corrodes the healing process and keeps the survivor locked in a cycle of shame, punishment, and emotional paralysis.

In therapeutic contexts, especially within cognitive-behavioral therapy (CBT) and compassion-focused therapy (CFT), one of the core tasks is to challenge these maladaptive beliefs and gently untangle the knots of guilt and love. Clients are encouraged to question the assumptions beneath their guilt. Did they truly have the power to change the outcome? Would their loved one want them to suffer in this way? What if continuing to live fully is the very honoring of the relationship—not a betrayal of it?

This is where the wisdom of Rumi becomes an invaluable companion. In his mystic vision, love does not end with death, nor does it demand self-denial as proof of devotion. Instead, love is an ever-expanding force that urges us toward wholeness, even when our hearts are broken. Rumi writes:

"You were born with wings, why prefer to crawl through life?"

— **Rumi**

Survivor's guilt makes us crawl—it shrinks us, confines us to emotional imprisonment. Rumi's poetry, however, consistently invites the soul to rise, even in the aftermath of profound loss. He does not negate the pain; he deepens it, reframes it, and ultimately uses it as a vehicle for liberation. He tells us that the grief we carry can become the cure if we are willing to transmute guilt into grace.

From a psychological growth perspective, working with survivor's guilt involves several interrelated tasks:

1. Acknowledging the guilt without self-condemnation: It's essential to give this emotion space, to name it without shame. Grievers must be helped to understand that guilt is not a measure of love; it is often a measure of powerlessness and trauma.

2. Re-authoring the narrative: In narrative therapy, clients learn to see themselves not as villains in the story of their loved one's death, but as complex humans navigating overwhelming circumstances. They are invited to co-author a new narrative that honors both the loss and the life that remains.

3. Connecting guilt to love: Therapists often help grievers see that beneath guilt lies a deep reservoir of love. The very fact that one feels guilty is proof of their empathy and bond. When this love is given new expressions—through service, remembrance, or living well—it begins to transform.

Rumi speaks directly to this transformation in his line:

"Don't grieve. Anything you lose comes round in another form."

— Rumi

This "another form" might be a new purpose, a new relationship, a renewed commitment to living fully. For someone experiencing survivor's guilt, this means redirecting the energy of guilt toward acts of remembrance, generosity, and self-compassion. Rather than being stuck in mourning, the individual learns to move with the grief, to carry the love forward in creative and meaningful ways.

Moreover, many traditions influenced by Rumi's Sufi teachings emphasize that we are not separate from one another, and certainly not from the beloved dead. In this worldview, continuing to live—and to live well— is not just permitted but required. Life becomes a trust, a sacred duty not to be squandered. As he wrote:

"Be like a guard. Be alert, and always be open to the signs of the Beloved."

— **Rumi**

In practical terms, this openness might look like accepting joy without guilt. It might mean allowing oneself to laugh again, to take a new opportunity, to love again. Each of these becomes a quiet act of resistance against the lie that healing is betrayal.

Finally, spiritual traditions and grief therapy alike remind us that guilt must eventually give way to grace. There is no perfect grief, no pure mourning that absolves the pain of separation. But there is a way to walk with that pain—gently, kindly, and with increasing freedom.

Survivor's guilt can be a crucible. If not addressed, it hardens into self-hatred or numbness. But if worked with carefully—with psychological insight and spiritual wisdom—it becomes a passage. A sacred corridor through which the mourner emerges not unscarred, but more human, more awake, and more capable of loving life not in spite of loss, but because of it.

Reclaiming Daily Life and the Present Moment

"Why do you run toward that which you know will hurt you again and again? Why not open to the garden that is always here, now, within?"

— **Rumi**

In the aftermath of profound grief, the present moment can feel like hostile territory. Time itself warps: the past becomes a well of memory and longing, while the future feels uncertain, even uninviting. Many grievers find themselves either trapped in loops of memory or numbed into emotional withdrawal. To reclaim one's daily life, to return fully to the unfolding now, is not a simple task. It is one of the most courageous acts of healing a grieving person can undertake.

From a psychological perspective, grief disturbs our ability to live in the present because the body and mind are in a state of hyperarousal, disorientation, or shutdown. Neurologically, this is tied to the dysregulation of the autonomic nervous system. The brain, particularly the limbic system, keeps triggering reminders of loss. The amygdala perceives threat in normal cues, while the prefrontal cortex struggles to regain cognitive control and regulate attention. This is why something as seemingly simple as making breakfast, answering an email, or taking a walk can feel overwhelming in early grief.

According to mindfulness-based grief therapy, pioneered by psychologists such as Susan Bauer-Wu and Sameet Kumar, the practice of coming back to the present moment is both a remedy and a reawakening.

Mindfulness teaches that we do not have to escape or fix the pain—we simply need to become aware of it, to hold it gently, and to rest in the aliveness of each moment. Grieving minds often ask, "How can I go on living?"—and mindfulness responds, "You are already living, right now. Let's begin here."

This therapeutic approach finds rich echoes in Rumi's work. Again and again, Rumi returns to the theme of presence—of awakening to what is. In his poetic cosmology, the divine lives in the moment, not the memory. He writes:

"This moment is all there is. Open your eyes. Let your heart open like a rose to the sunlight."

— **Rumi**

Reclaiming daily life is not about forgetting or "moving on." It is about reentering life gently, deliberately, with awareness. It means re-inhabiting your body, your breath, your senses. Rumi often uses metaphors of nature—the garden, the sunrise, the flowing river—to signal that presence is not conceptual; it is embodied. Psychological research supports this: trauma and grief are processed not only through talking, but through grounding, movement, and sensory integration.

Reclaiming daily life also involves the rebuilding of routine, which has immense therapeutic value. Rituals and daily habits act as scaffolding that holds a fragmented psyche. Getting out of bed, drinking tea, feeding a pet, folding clothes—these seemingly small acts reconnect a grieving individual with the rhythm of the living world. Over time, routine reestablishes a sense of continuity, a reminder that life—though changed—has not ended.

The existential psychologist Irvin Yalom writes about how the death of a loved one often collapses one's assumptive world. That is, the basic framework of what one expected from life—certainty, safety, meaning—gets shattered. Reclaiming daily life, then, is not merely about doing things again; it is about being in the world differently. It's an invitation to live with deeper awareness, humility, and, eventually, even wonder.

Rumi speaks directly to this transformation when he says:

"Try not to resist the changes that come your way. Instead, let life live through you."

— Rumi

To let life live through us after loss is to allow the morning light to enter again, not as a denial of darkness, but as its complement. The garden grows not because the gardener forgets winter, but because she works with spring.

In therapy, this principle is applied by helping clients reintegrate the self with the world. This might mean returning to social interactions, rediscovering meaningful work, or simply relearning how to be in a quiet room without fear. Acceptance and Commitment Therapy (ACT), for instance, encourages grieving individuals to take small values-based actions even when pain is still present. A grieving parent might cook a loved one's favorite meal, not because they no longer hurt, but because love compels them to engage.

Crucially, reclaiming daily life involves embracing pleasure without guilt. After loss, pleasure can feel like betrayal. A moment of laughter, a joyful experience, or even a peaceful night's sleep can be followed by a wave of shame. Rumi invites us to recognize this as a false imprisonment of the soul. He says:

"Be like a tree and let the dead leaves drop."

— Rumi

The "dead leaves" here are not the memory of the loved one, but the suffering that no longer serves healing. Letting them fall is not abandonment; it is growth. It is nature's way of renewal.

As the daily self reconstitutes, grief softens—not into forgetfulness, but into a sacred intimacy with life itself. The mourner does not return to the life they had before. That life is gone. Instead, they craft a new life, one rooted in what remains: breath, body, time, relationships, meaning. Rumi whispers:

"Try to be like the night that embraces the stars. A darkness that makes light visible."

— Rumi

This is the alchemy of grief—the transformation of the painful present into a meaningful presence. Through patience, ritual, mindfulness, and a slow reengagement with ordinary life, the grieving person learns not just to survive, but to inhabit the world again with grace. The mundane becomes spiritual. The daily becomes sacred. And life, once again, becomes livable—not as it was, but as it is.

Rumi: "Be Like a Tree and Let the Dead Leaves Drop."

At once simple and profound, Rumi's metaphor "Be like a tree and let the dead leaves drop" speaks directly to the soul navigating grief, guilt, and the slow return to life. It suggests a radical act of release, not as forgetfulness or indifference, but as an act of surrender to the natural cycles of transformation. In this line, Rumi invites us to view letting go not as an abandonment of love or memory, but as a sacred yielding to life's rhythm, much like the trees trust autumn.

In modern psychological frameworks, particularly those concerned with grief and trauma, the concept of letting go is often misunderstood. It's not about erasing the past or denying sorrow. Instead, it is about loosening the grip of the emotions or attachments that inhibit growth and restoration. Rumi's metaphor offers a compelling poetic parallel to what psychologists refer to as emotional flexibility—the ability to experience emotions fully without becoming imprisoned by them.

Psychologist George Bonanno, a leading researcher in the field of bereavement, emphasizes the concept of resilience through emotional oscillation. This means that healthy grieving does not demand constant sorrow or full detachment but involves an ongoing movement between holding on and letting go. Just as trees do not forcefully rip their leaves away but allow them to fall when the season turns, so too are we invited to surrender only when the heart is ready—not in haste, but in rhythm with our internal seasons.

Rumi, in his spiritual vision, saw grief as fertile ground for transformation. When he says, "Be like a tree and let the dead leaves drop," he is urging us to trust that whatever has served its time—be it sorrow, self-blame, guilt, or the clinging to what cannot be returned—must eventually be released for something new to grow. Just as trees drop their leaves in order to conserve energy and prepare for renewal, so too must we clear space in our psychic and emotional landscape to allow for regeneration.

From the perspective of existential psychology, letting go is not an abandonment of the deceased or a denial of grief. Rather, it is an acceptance of the impermanence of all things. Viktor Frankl, the Austrian psychiatrist and Holocaust survivor, wrote that suffering ceases to be suffering at the moment it finds meaning. In this way, letting go becomes not a rejection of the loved one, but a deeper honoring of their legacy—a transformation of sorrow into meaning.

In the Acceptance and Commitment Therapy (ACT) model, this process of release is essential. ACT teaches that clinging to certain thoughts—such as "I'll never be okay again," or "I don't deserve happiness now that they're gone"—can lead to psychological inflexibility and prolong suffering. Instead, through mindfulness and values-based action, we can learn to "drop the rope," as ACT therapists put it. Rumi's leaves become the maladaptive narratives, the outdated beliefs, the residual guilt—and the act of letting them drop is not a defeat, but a courageous movement toward healing.

Importantly, Rumi's metaphor retains a tone of gentleness. There is no demand or force. The tree does not tear away its dead leaves—it simply lets them fall. This reflects a compassionate attitude toward one's own process of healing. The grief-stricken heart often tries to hasten recovery or to repress pain. But Rumi's way is one of patience and surrender. His message resonates with contemporary self-compassion practices, such as those developed by Kristin Neff, which encourage the grieving to allow their feelings without judgment, and to extend to themselves the same kindness they would offer to a beloved friend.

In Rumi's poetry, the tree is not alone. It is part of a larger, ever-turning cosmos where loss, decay, and rebirth are all expressions of divine intelligence. Letting the leaves fall is not the end of the story—it is the beginning of renewal. In another of his verses, Rumi writes:

"Don't grieve. Anything you lose comes round in another form."

— Rumi

This is not a minimization of loss, but a mystical reassurance that what was once love does not vanish—it transforms. The dead leaves return to the earth and nourish the roots. Grief, when integrated, nourishes depth, compassion, and a renewed capacity to live.

This vision dovetails with the psychological concept of post-traumatic growth, which we explored in Chapter 9. Through grief, one may experience an increased appreciation of life, deepened relationships, and greater existential clarity. But none of these are possible without the prior act of letting go—of releasing what has completed its course, no matter how beautiful or painful.

There is a quiet courage in this act of release. It is the courage to feel life again, to risk joy again, to trust in the cycles of the heart. Rumi's tree is not barren forever. In time, it will sprout new buds. But that cannot happen if the old leaves remain clinging to dying branches.

This invitation to let the dead leaves drop is ultimately a call to rejoin the living—not by rejecting grief, but by allowing it to take its rightful place in the soil of the soul. The love remains, but the form must change. And in that metamorphosis lies the potential for beauty beyond what we can yet see.

As we approach the closing of this chapter, Rumi leaves us not with a commandment, but with a whisper of grace:

"Try not to resist the changes that come your way. Instead, let life live through you."

— **Rumi**

In letting go, we do not dishonor our loved ones—we become the fertile ground through which their love continues to live.

Chapter 10 Summary: Living Again Without Guilt

In this chapter, we have gently traversed the path from guilt to grace—recognizing that living again after loss is not a betrayal, but a testament to love's enduring presence. Joy, laughter, and the courage to embrace new beginnings are not signs of forgetting but acts of sacred remembering, honoring the fullness of what once was and allowing space for what may yet become. We explored the psychological intricacies of survivor's guilt and the tender art of reclaiming the present moment, drawing from therapeutic frameworks and Rumi's timeless wisdom alike. Rumi's call to "be like a tree and let the dead leaves drop" serves not as an instruction to forget, but as a profound metaphor for transformation—trusting that the shedding of sorrow can prepare the soil of our hearts for new life to bloom. As we prepare to move forward, we do so carrying not just memories, but renewed meaning, and the quiet permission to live again—fully, deeply, and without guilt.

Chapter 11:
Rituals of Remembrance and Release

Grief is not simply an emotion—it is a sacred process. And like any sacred process, it demands structure, space, and rhythm to be fully honored. This is the essence of ritual. Rituals give form to what is formless. They are the vessels through which love, loss, memory, and meaning can be poured, held, and ultimately transformed. In grief, ritual becomes not just a practice, but a language—one that speaks when words fall short and the heart aches to find expression.

In modern psychological thought, rituals are increasingly recognized not as archaic remnants of superstition but as therapeutic interventions grounded in the body and psyche's need for coherence. While grief often feels chaotic, overwhelming, and disordered, rituals bring order—not to control grief, but to hold it safely. They offer a sense of continuity amid rupture, a bridge between the inner world of the mourner and the external world that may have moved on too quickly.

Psychologist Barbara Fiese defines ritual as "a repeated pattern of behavior that is symbolically meaningful," and in this repetition, the mourner finds stability. Whether it's the lighting of a candle each evening, the annual visit to a gravesite, or the simple act of whispering a name before sleep, these rituals create a sacred space in which the mourner may commune with the dead, with memory, and with their evolving self.

Yet these rituals need not be grand or performative. They can be deeply personal, private, and intuitive. What makes them powerful is not the form but the meaning imbued within them. Research from grief scholars such as

Dr. Robert Neimeyer emphasizes that healing in bereavement is intimately linked to the construction of meaning—and ritual is one of the most potent tools for meaning-making. Through ritual, grief becomes more than a response to loss; it becomes a spiritual act of presence, love, and connection.

Rituals also offer a threshold—one that allows for both remembrance and release. In this duality lies their power. They allow the mourner to honor the love that remains without being imprisoned by sorrow. They offer permission to feel, and eventually, to let go—not of the memory or the relationship, but of the pain's grip.

This delicate balance between holding on and letting go was something Rumi understood intimately. After the shattering loss of his beloved friend and spiritual companion Shams of Tabriz, Rumi did not merely mourn—he transformed his grief into a lifelong ritual of poetry, music, and spiritual practice. In this way, his entire body of work can be read as a sustained ritual of remembrance and release. His verses did not deny pain but sanctified it. He gave his sorrow structure, rhythm, and beauty. He danced his grief into whirling prayer.

Rumi's grief was not passive—it was participatory. He allowed sorrow to become a teacher, a fire that refined the soul. He wrote:

"Be like melting snow. Wash yourself of yourself."

— **Rumi**

In this single metaphor, Rumi captures the essence of ritual as release. Just as snow melts into water, so too must grief soften into remembrance. Rituals help facilitate that alchemy. They invite the mourner not just to feel loss, but to move with it—to be reshaped by it rather than destroyed.

355

In therapeutic settings, clinicians often encourage the creation of rituals as part of grief counseling. These may include writing letters to the deceased, setting up memory altars, sharing stories in group sessions, or planting trees in memory of the loved one. These acts are not performative; they are containers for love and longing. They give the mourner a way to continue the bond while slowly finding a new way of living in the world.

Importantly, rituals do not end grief. But they can transform it. They do not erase absence. But they remind us that presence can still be found—not in form, but in meaning. And meaning, as Viktor Frankl taught, is the deepest human need, especially in suffering.

What rituals offer—above all—is a way to stay in relationship with the deceased while also growing in relationship with oneself. They allow grief to become a path of integration rather than fragmentation. A journey of unfolding rather than closure.

Rumi's spiritual path, forged through loss, invites us to view ritual not as mere habit or tradition but as a soul-language, a bridge between the seen and the unseen:

"The wound is the place where the Light enters you."

— Rumi

Rituals, then, become sacred practices through which that light can flow. They allow the wound to breathe, to be witnessed, and eventually to illuminate. Whether in the quiet solitude of lighting a candle, the communal circle of shared prayer, or the private act of writing a name again and again in a journal—these rituals speak to what words cannot say.

In a world that often demands quick closure and stoic endurance, the intentional practice of ritual is a rebellion of the heart. It is a refusal to forget. A refusal to sever. A decision to remember—and to release—on purpose, with presence, with love.

And in the language of Rumi, it is a return to the sacred:

"When the soul lies down in that grass, the world is too full to talk about.

Ideas, language... even the phrase each other—doesn't make any sense."

— Rumi

Grief, through ritual, brings us to that wordless field. A place not beyond pain, but beyond separation. A place where we can remember, weep, smile, release—and begin again.

Creating Personal and Cultural Rituals

Rituals, whether personal or cultural, serve as profound vessels for navigating the uncharted waters of grief. They not only help individuals honor and remember their loved ones but also provide a stabilizing rhythm in the chaos of loss. At their deepest level, rituals are not about formality or performance—they are about meaning. In grief, meaning can be elusive, and ritual becomes the sacred language through which the soul communicates its longing, remembrance, and resilience.

In modern psychological literature, rituals are understood as both *intrapersonal* and *interpersonal* tools. Psychologist and grief scholar Dr. Robert Neimeyer, whose work on meaning reconstruction has informed the modern understanding of bereavement, emphasizes that rituals are key elements in the narrative rebuilding process. When a loved one dies, the mourner's life story is disrupted. Rituals—especially those consciously created or adapted—allow for a reshaping of narrative identity. They bridge the past, present, and future in symbolic acts that help the bereaved locate themselves in a new and evolving life chapter.

Personal rituals, in this context, are deeply individualistic. They are not always visible to others. They may involve lighting a candle at a particular time of day, visiting a meaningful place, cooking a dish the deceased loved, listening to a shared song, or creating a sacred corner at home with photographs and mementos. These acts, however small, carry immense weight. They affirm continuity—the ongoing presence of the departed within the mourner's inner world.

In therapy, clinicians often help grieving individuals design such rituals. These personalized practices allow mourners to express emotions, maintain a connection, and begin to integrate the loss into their daily lives. Importantly, personal rituals respect the uniqueness of each grief journey. There is no one-size-fits-all template for healing. What matters is the intentionality behind the action and the space it creates for presence, memory, and transformation.

Cultural rituals, on the other hand, offer a communal framework for grief. These include funeral rites, mourning periods, memorial services, and religious ceremonies. While they vary across societies and traditions, their purpose is strikingly similar: to honor the dead, comfort the living, and mark the transition from life to death with dignity and sacredness. Cultural rituals provide mourners with collective validation. They affirm that grief is not a solitary burden but a shared human experience.

In many cultures, death is not seen as an end, but as a threshold—a passage into another realm. Cultural rituals, whether Christian funerals, Islamic Janazah (funeral) prayers, Buddhist chanting ceremonies, or Hindu shraddha rites, often carry this metaphysical understanding at their core. They do not merely memorialize the departed; they situate the mourner within a lineage of ancestral memory and spiritual continuity. In doing so, they offer existential comfort—the reassurance that the deceased belongs to a greater mystery, and that the mourner is not alone in their sorrow.

However, in modern Western societies especially those shaped by individualism and secularism—traditional mourning practices have often been minimized or dismissed. The cultural pressure to "move on" quickly or maintain emotional composure has left many bereaved individuals feeling isolated in their grief. This is where the revival or adaptation of ritual becomes a radical and healing act. It allows individuals and communities to reclaim sacred time and sacred space in a world that rushes forward too quickly.

Rumi, who lived within a culture where ritual was woven into the fabric of daily life, understood both the external and internal dimensions of ritual. For him, the whirling dance of the dervish was not mere performance—it was a ritual of remembrance (*dhikr*), a means of transcending the ego and reconnecting with the Divine. After the death of Shams, Rumi transformed his mourning into a poetic and devotional ritual that lasted for decades. His verses became his prayer beads, his way of holding the grief and allowing it to shape his path of love and union.

He wrote:

"There are a thousand ways to kneel and kiss the ground;

There are a thousand ways to go home again."

— Rumi

This line encapsulates the spirit of ritual: there are infinite ways to remember, to return, to honor what is sacred and lost. Ritual does not have to be traditional to be meaningful. It must simply be sincere. It must open the mourner to a deeper conversation—with the departed, with their own soul, with the divine mystery.

Creating new rituals also speaks to the mourner's agency. In grief, where so much feels out of control, the act of consciously designing a ritual—no matter how modest—can be deeply empowering. It says: *I choose to honor this love. I choose to mark this memory. I choose to bring meaning to my sorrow.*

Such rituals can also evolve over time. What begins as a daily journal entry to the deceased may, months later, become an annual letter written on their birthday. A simple act of lighting incense might one day evolve into a community ceremony or a personal day of silence. The mourner grows, and so too does the ritual. It breathes with the healing process.

Modern psychologists such as Dr. Pauline Boss[1], known for her work on ambiguous loss, also highlight how ritual can help navigate the complex, unresolved dimensions of grief—such as when a body is never recovered, or when the relationship with the deceased was strained. In such cases, ritual

---

1. **Pauline Boss**, is a professor emeritus, University of Minnesota; a Fellow in the National Council on Family Relations (NCFR), the American Psychological Association, and the American Association for Marriage and Family Therapy.

allows for symbolic closure. It gives the mourner permission to honor without perfect resolution, to remember even in the face of uncertainty or unfinished business.

Rumi's view of the soul as infinite and love as indestructible aligns beautifully with this psychological understanding. He would remind us that ritual is not about closure in the Western sense—it is about *openness*. An openness to love that continues, to grief that transforms, and to a presence that persists beyond the physical.

"Don't grieve. Anything you lose comes round in another form."

— Rumi

To create personal and cultural rituals, then, is to say yes to the ongoing relationship with the beloved dead. It is to say yes to healing—not by forgetting, but by remembering in a sacred, living way.

As this chapter will continue to explore, the rituals we craft—whether alone or in community—become the soul's architecture. They are not merely about grief. They are about love made visible and love made lasting.

Grieving In Community vs. Alone

Grief is both a deeply personal and inherently social experience. It strikes at the core of one's individuality while simultaneously revealing the threads that connect us to others. Whether one chooses—or is compelled— to grieve in solitude or among others can shape the trajectory of their healing in profound ways. The interplay between private sorrow and collective mourning is a theme richly explored in both modern psychology and mystical literature, especially in the writings of Jalal al-Din Rumi, whose own grief over Shams of Tabriz became both an inward crucible and a communal fire of inspiration.

In contemporary grief psychology, researchers and clinicians recognize that both solitary and communal grieving have their place and value. Neither mode is inherently superior. What matters is the mourner's needs, context, and capacity to process loss in a way that supports emotional integration and meaning-making.

Solitary Grief: The Interior Landscape

Grieving alone offers a certain kind of depth. It allows the mourner to encounter their pain without the pressure of performance or the necessity of language. In solitude, the bereaved can sit with their rawness, listen to the quiet echoes of memory, and explore the private meanings of their relationship with the deceased. Psychologically, this solitude can be fertile ground for introspection, self-reflection, and spiritual encounter. Carl Jung often emphasized the importance of retreat and inner confrontation during periods of psychic crisis. In Jungian terms, grief in solitude can become a confrontation with the shadow and the soul—a descent into the "night sea journey" from which the self may reemerge transformed.

Yet solitary grieving also carries risks. If prolonged or unsupported, it can lead to social withdrawal, emotional stagnation, and a sense of existential isolation. According to the Dual Process Model of Coping with Bereavement (Stroebe & Schut, 1999), healthy grief involves an oscillation between loss-oriented (facing the pain) and restoration-oriented (engaging with life) processes. Without communal touchpoints, the mourner may become stuck in loss-oriented rumination, struggling to reintegrate into a world that continues to move forward.

Rumi, who spent long periods in inner reflection after the loss of Shams, understood both the gifts and limitations of solitude. His verses reveal an intimate dialogue with grief—a private mourning that was also a form of communion with the divine:

"Listen to the silence. It has so much to say."

— Rumi

For Rumi, silence was not emptiness but presence. Solitary grief, when approached with intentionality and spiritual openness, becomes a space where the soul can be shaped by the presence of absence. But he also knew that grief could not remain locked away forever. As his sorrow deepened, he turned his pain outward—into poetry, community, and spiritual teaching. His grief became a bridge rather than a barrier.

Communal Grief: The Power of Shared Mourning

While solitude offers inward depth, communal grieving offers resonance. When mourners come together—whether in funeral rites, support groups, spiritual gatherings, or informal circles of remembrance—they create a container for collective holding. The burden of grief is not erased, but it is shared. And in that sharing, something miraculous happens: suffering becomes solidarity.

Research in bereavement studies consistently supports the healing value of social support. Studies by Margaret Stroebe, Henk Schut, and Camille Wortman have shown that individuals who feel emotionally supported in their grief are less likely to develop complicated grief and depressive symptoms. Community offers validation: the recognition that one's pain is not only real but worthy of being witnessed.

Communal rituals serve this function beautifully. Whether lighting candles during a memorial, chanting sacred songs, or simply sitting in silence together, these acts reaffirm the mourner's place in a web of human connection. In a society that often rushes past grief, community rituals provide a sacred pause—a space where loss is allowed, honored, and sanctified.

Rumi's gatherings—the very origin of the Mevlevi Sufi order, aka, Whirling Dervishes—became such spaces. He did not grieve alone forever. Instead, he created a circle of seekers who danced their sorrow and joy together in the Sema, the whirling ritual of divine remembrance. In the whirling of the dervishes, grief was not repressed—it was elevated, spun into devotion. For Rumi, grief shared was grief sanctified.

"Don't get lost in your pain,

know that one day your pain will become your cure."

— Rumi

This healing often begins when the individual dares to bring their sorrow into the shared light. In modern psychological terms, this aligns with therapeutic group work. Support groups for bereavement, particularly those facilitated by trained professionals, allow mourners to normalize their emotions, draw strength from others, and break the silence that often surrounds death. The simple act of hearing someone else say, "I feel that too," can be profoundly healing.

However, not everyone feels safe grieving in public. Cultural factors, personality traits, and previous relational experiences all shape a mourner's preference. In collectivist cultures, such as those in many parts of Africa, Asia, and the Middle East, communal grieving is the norm and even expected. Mourning periods may last for days or months, and the bereaved are supported by family, neighbors, and spiritual leaders. In contrast, more individualistic cultures often place emphasis on personal responsibility, autonomy, and emotional containment. In such contexts, the mourner may find themselves feeling isolated or even pathologized for displaying overt grief.

Thus, the tension between solitary and communal grieving is also a cultural and historical one. Rumi's world, infused with Sufi mysticism, offered a blend of both. The Sufi path honors the inward journey of the heart, yet it also thrives in communal circles of zikr (remembrance), music, poetry, and shared ecstasy. This integrated model is perhaps the most holistic—honoring the necessity of solitude while also encouraging communal embodiment.

Bridging the Two: Fluid Grieving

The truth is, grief is dynamic. Most mourners will oscillate between private and public modes of grieving. There will be days when silence feels sacred, and others when human presence is the only balm. Psychologists encourage mourners to recognize and honor both impulses. The goal is not to choose one over the other, but to allow oneself to move fluidly between them, based on the rhythms of the heart.

Therapist Francis Weller describes grief as having both a private chamber and a communal threshold. He writes, *"Grief has always been communal. For millennia, we have sat in circles, cried together, and tended to our sorrow in the presence of others."* But he also affirms the need for solitary rituals, time with nature, and silent communion with the soul.

Rumi would have agreed. He would likely counsel the mourner to listen deeply—to the voice of the heart, the ache in the bones, the longing that whispers either for solitude or companionship. And he would remind us that in every form of grief, love remains.

"There is a candle in your heart,

ready to be kindled.

There is a void in your soul,

ready to be filled.

You feel it, don't you?"

— Rumi

To grieve alone is to tend the inner candle. To grieve in community is to bring that flame into the circle, where others light theirs in return. Both are sacred. Both are necessary.

Writing, Art, Music as Healing Tools

Grief resists containment. It spills out of the heart, leaks through language, and seeks expression beyond the bounds of rational thought. When words fail—or when conventional conversations feel insufficient— the arts offer an ancient and instinctive means of navigating sorrow. Whether through writing, painting, or music, the act of creating becomes a lifeline between inner pain and outer world, between the grieving self and the enduring memory of what was lost. For both modern psychology and mystical traditions, such as those expressed by Rumi, creative expression is not merely a coping strategy but a sacred form of transformation.

Writing as a Vessel for Grief

Modern psychological research underscores the therapeutic value of expressive writing, particularly in the context of bereavement. Pioneered by psychologist James Pennebaker, the field of expressive writing therapy demonstrates how structured journaling about emotional experiences can lead to measurable improvements in both psychological and physical health. Pennebaker's studies have shown that individuals who write about traumatic or emotionally significant experiences for even 15–20 minutes a day over a few days often report reduced depressive symptoms, lower anxiety, improved immune functioning, and greater emotional clarity.

In grief work, this form of writing allows the mourner to externalize inner chaos. Writing offers the mourner a private, nonjudgmental space to process conflicting emotions: sorrow, guilt, longing, anger, and even relief. It can serve as a bridge between the living and the deceased—especially when letters are written directly to the loved one who has passed. These letters often provide an outlet for unresolved dialogue, unspoken farewells, or expressions of continuing love and connection. In psychological terms, this practice supports the concept of "continuing bonds," a model of mourning that honors the persistence of attachment beyond death.

Rumi, too, wrote as a means of bearing grief. His poetry was not composed in serenity but born from the tremors of loss. The death (or mysterious disappearance) of Shams of Tabriz shattered Rumi's ordinary world, and it was through the act of writing—poetry composed in a near-ecstatic state—that Rumi metabolized his heartbreak. The *Masnavi* and *Divan-e Shams* are not simply spiritual masterpieces; they are elegies to love lost and rediscovered in divine form.

"Don't grieve. Anything you lose comes round in another form."

— **Rumi**

Rumi's verses are grief transfigured—sorrow shaped into beauty, absence spun into presence. For the mourner, writing can follow this same arc: from pain, through process, to revelation.

Art and the Language of Symbols

Visual art, too, can be a powerful channel for grief. While words often impose linear structure on experience, art allows for the nonlinear, ambiguous, and symbolic dimensions of sorrow to emerge. Art therapy, as developed and formalized by clinicians like Margaret Naumburg and Edith Kramer, recognizes that when trauma overwhelms verbal capacities, drawing, painting, sculpting, and other visual forms become alternative modes of expression. For those grieving, the image becomes a vessel—carrying the unbearable through metaphor and color.

Art allows the mourner to create symbols of memory, to make visible the invisible contours of grief. A drawing of a favorite place once shared with the deceased, an abstract painting representing waves of emotion, or a collage of torn images and textures can articulate what no sentence can convey. The act of making art is not about technical skill but presence. It is a practice of attention, of slowing down, of being with what is.

368

In Sufi tradition, the aesthetic has always been a spiritual path. Calligraphy, architecture, geometric design—each is an act of devotion. Rumi understood that beauty is not a luxury but a necessity, especially in the face of loss. He did not paint in the traditional sense, but his words painted emotion in radiant hues. The metaphors he used—of birds, gardens, wine, the turning wheel—are all symbolic languages through which grief finds elevation.

"Try not to resist the changes that come your way. Instead,

let life live through you."

— Rumi

Art is one of the ways life lives through us, even when we feel hollowed by sorrow.

Music and the Rhythm of Mourning

Music, perhaps more than any other medium, bypasses the intellect and speaks directly to the emotional body. Neuroscientific research confirms what mystics and mourners have always known: that music has a profound impact on brain chemistry and emotional regulation. It can soothe, evoke, release, and even transport. Listening to music associated with a loved one can elicit poignant memories, allowing a person to feel connected across the threshold of death. Creating music—whether singing, playing an instrument, or composing—offers a rhythm to grief, a pulse to follow when the heart falters.

The use of music in grief rituals is as old as human civilization. Laments, elegies, requiems, and dirges serve both personal and communal grieving.

They allow sorrow to be voiced and shared, transforming private pain into collective resonance. In music therapy, individuals grieving a loss may be encouraged to create "musical portraits" of their loved one, write songs of memory, or use improvisation to express emotional states. These techniques can support emotional release, cognitive integration, and spiritual connection.

For Rumi and the Sufis, music (*Sema*) is not an accessory to spiritual life but a core practice. The whirling dervishes do not spin in silence—they turn to music, to the sound of the *ney* (reed flute), the beat of drums, and the chanting of the Divine Names. This musical ritual is not entertainment but embodiment: a way of remembering the Beloved, mourning the distance, and celebrating the return.

In Rumi's view, the reed flute's cry is the voice of separation—the soul's longing to return to union:

"Listen to the reed and the tale it tells,

how it sings of separation."

— **Rumi**

Music becomes the soul's language when the world falls silent. It echoes what the mourner cannot say, carries them when they cannot walk, lifts them toward joy when they fear joy will never return.

The Alchemy of Creation

Across writing, art, and music, one common thread emerges: creation is a form of alchemy. It takes the leaden weight of grief and, through care and attention, transforms it into something with meaning. Psychologically, this process aligns with the principles of post-traumatic growth and narrative identity. Spiritually, it resonates with Rumi's vision of love as a fire that burns away the dross and leaves only the essence.

Creating while grieving does not "fix" the pain. Rather, it dignifies it. It says: this matters. This person mattered. This love mattered. In the end, creation becomes a way not only of surviving grief but of communing with the one who is lost—and, perhaps, with the divine mystery in which they now dwell.

"Don't get lost in your pain. Know that one day your pain

will become your cure."

— Rumi

The arts do not offer closure. They offer continuity, connection, and expression. They give grief a voice, a shape, a sound. And in doing so, they help us heal—not by forgetting, but by remembering creatively.

Annual Remembrance, Birthdays, and Honoring the Legacy

Grief does not end with time; it evolves. And part of this evolution involves weaving the memory of the departed into the ongoing fabric of our lives. Annual remembrances—such as death anniversaries, birthdays, or shared holidays—become sacred markers in this process. They are not simply calendar dates but emotional and spiritual thresholds that invite us to revisit, reimagine, and honor the bond that remains, even after death. Rather than erasing the presence of the deceased from life, these rituals affirm their continuing significance, enabling healing not through detachment but through intentional remembrance.

Psychological Significance of Anniversaries and Birthdays

From a psychological perspective, anniversaries and birthdays of the deceased are often considered "grief spikes" or "anniversary reactions"—predictable emotional intensifications of grief that occur on or near significant dates. These spikes are not pathological; they are deeply human responses to temporal reminders of love and loss. Rather than viewing them as setbacks, contemporary grief research suggests they can be transformed into opportunities for connection, integration, and meaning-making.

The **Dual Process Model of Coping with Bereavement**, developed by Stroebe and Schut, identifies two central processes in grieving: **loss-oriented coping** and **restoration-oriented coping**. Rituals like birthdays and anniversaries often activate the loss-oriented dimension—bringing the mourner back into contact with the absence of the loved one. But these rituals can also serve as restorative acts, especially when they are reframed as occasions to celebrate life, revisit shared memories, or engage in meaningful service in honor of the deceased.

Clinical psychologist Dr. Robert Neimeyer, a leading voice in meaning reconstruction theory, argues that grief work is largely about narrative and identity. Annual commemorations provide a structure for this narrative process. When we light a candle on a birthday, cook a favorite dish, visit a gravesite, or share stories with others, we are not merely remembering—we are **continuing** the story, integrating the past into our current identity.

Honoring the Legacy: A Living Bond

Honoring the legacy of someone who has died involves more than looking backward; it is also about **carrying something forward**. This can take many forms: starting a foundation in the person's name, pursuing a cause they cared about, living by values they modeled, or simply speaking their name regularly in family rituals. What psychology now recognizes as "continuing bonds" is supported by such acts of legacy. These practices not only affirm the value of the deceased's life but also reinforce the mourner's sense of connection, identity, and purpose.

Psychologically, this process supports integration rather than repression. When the dead are honored meaningfully, they remain a part of the living's evolving story—not as frozen memories, but as dynamic presences. This approach directly counters earlier grief models that emphasized detachment and "letting go" as necessary goals for healing. Today's more nuanced understanding acknowledges that mourning can include an **active, evolving relationship** with the deceased—one that supports psychological adaptation and spiritual growth.

Rumi and the Sacred Continuity of Love

For Rumi, remembrance is not about clinging to the past, but about recognizing the **eternal nature of love**. In his vision, death is not a severance but a veil that temporarily obscures the beloved from view. The practice of remembering, for Rumi, is not sorrowful nostalgia but an invitation to touch the timeless. His own rituals of remembrance—poetic recitation, turning in the Sema, or celebrating the "wedding night" (*Shab-e Arus*)—were not elegies to what was lost, but tributes to what still is, now in invisible form.

"The moment I heard my first love story,

I started looking for you, not knowing

how blind that was.

Lovers don't finally meet somewhere.

They're in each other all along."

— **Rumi**

Here, love is not confined by time, space, or even bodily form. Rumi's approach to grief through remembrance reflects a **sacred continuity**—a conviction that the bond between souls is not only unbroken but eternally generative. In this context, a birthday is not just the anniversary of a physical birth—it is a **reminder of soul emergence**, of a spirit that once touched this world and continues to touch it through those who remember.

Rumi himself held annual ceremonies to honor the death of Shams, his beloved friend and spiritual catalyst. Yet these gatherings were not mournful in the modern sense; they were ecstatic events full of music, poetry, and spiritual longing—a celebration of reunion, not just of absence. In Rumi's cosmology, every remembrance is an act of spiritual fidelity, a declaration that love has no expiration.

Modern Applications of Ritualized Remembrance

In therapeutic practice today, clinicians increasingly encourage clients to develop **intentional rituals** around significant dates. These need not be grand or public. A private walk to a shared spot, lighting a candle at sunset, reading an old letter aloud—each can become a form of psychological and spiritual anchor. What matters most is **intention**—the decision to show up for grief, to speak the name of the one who has died, and to allow their memory to be integrated into the mourner's present life.

Digital spaces, too, have become modern altars of remembrance. Social media pages are often preserved and turned into memorials; online remembrance events on death anniversaries are shared across continents. These new forms do not diminish the sanctity of memory—they extend it. As technology evolves, the human longing to remember—and to be remembered—remains constant.

Transforming Grief Through Commemoration

Ultimately, annual remembrance is not about being trapped in the past—it is about honoring a truth that time cannot undo: that love changes form but never ceases. In the same way that a garden grows even after the gardener has left, the impact of a person's life continues to blossom in those they touched. Ritualized remembrance is how we water that legacy.

In Rumi's language, this remembrance is both earthly and divine:

"When you are with everyone but me,

you're with no one.

When you are with no one but me,

you're with everyone.

Instead of being so bound up with everyone,

be everyone. When you become that many,

you're nothing. Empty."

— Rumi

To remember someone deeply is not to isolate in sorrow—it is to expand into the essence they left behind. Their birthday becomes a celebration of love. Their death day becomes a *Shab-e Arus*—a wedding night, a union with the Infinite.

This is the power of ritual remembrance. It lifts grief from the personal to the sacred. It transforms memory into presence. It reminds the living that to love once is to love always, and to remember with depth is to remain in communion with what is truly eternal.

Chapter 11 Summary: Rituals of Remembrance and Release

Rituals are the sacred threads that stitch memory into meaning. Whether shaped by personal need or cultural tradition, these acts of remembrance help transform grief from a silent ache into a living dialogue with love. In this chapter, we have explored how remembrance rituals—be they annual, artistic, communal, or solitary—can serve as vessels for healing, connection, and spiritual continuity. Psychology affirms that grief needs expression, structure, and space to unfold, while Rumi reminds us that the bonds of the heart are never severed by death. When we create rituals of remembrance, we do not merely preserve the past—we sanctify it. We acknowledge that although the physical presence is gone, the essence remains, whispering to us in poems, in songs, in dreams, in laughter. In honoring the legacy of those we have lost, we reclaim love not as something we once had, but as something we still carry. The dead do not disappear; they transform—and so do we, each time we remember them with intention, reverence, and open hearts.

Chapter 12:
The New You: Life After Loss

To arrive at this point in the journey of grief is not to find an end, but a beginning. This chapter does not mark closure in the sense of forgetting or moving on. Instead, it explores what it means to *live forward* after loss, transformed by pain but not defined by it. This is the territory of post-loss integration, where we begin to shape a renewed identity, values, and path through the raw material that grief has handed us.

Loss, by its very nature, fractures identity. When someone we love dies, a part of who we were dies with them. If we were a spouse, a child, a sibling, a best friend—those roles may shift, dissolve, or take on new meaning. What follows is often a period of profound disorientation. But over time, and with conscious engagement, this fragmentation can give rise to something deeper: an emergent self who is more honest, more awake, and more compassionate. The "new you" is not a replacement for who you were. Rather, it is the result of having walked through fire and come out tempered.

Psychological Grounding

Contemporary grief psychology recognizes this shift as part of the **transformational model of bereavement**. In contrast to earlier models that emphasized detachment and emotional closure (such as Freud's "grief work hypothesis"), modern theories understand grief as a **process of integration and growth** rather than the elimination of bonds. Psychologists like George Bonanno (2009) highlight **resilience** as a key human capacity in grieving, and Robert Neimeyer emphasizes **meaning-making** as essential to identity reconstruction.

This rebuilding of the self is rarely linear. Often, it is recursive, involving relapses, setbacks, and periods of stagnation. However, over time, many individuals find themselves developing greater emotional complexity. This includes a more expansive empathy, a deeper appreciation for life, and a clarified sense of purpose. This is not the same as "getting over" a loss—it is more accurate to say that the person learns to carry their grief differently, with grace, tenderness, and resilience.

Rumi's mystical tradition captures this phenomenon with extraordinary clarity. In his poetry, grief is not merely a wound—it is an aperture. Through the rupture of loss, the soul can encounter itself more deeply and align more truthfully with the divine. Rumi writes:

"Don't get lost in your pain,

Know that one day your pain will become your cure."

— Rumi

This is not a romanticization of suffering, but a recognition of its transformative potential. Rumi's spiritual psychology sees the human experience as a field of longing and return. The shattering caused by grief is what breaks the ego's illusion of control, inviting the soul into a deeper alignment with its true nature.

In the Sufi worldview that shapes Rumi's writings, the "self" that grieves and suffers is also the "self" that must die—metaphorically—to reveal the deeper Self, the "*Ruh*" (i.e., the Soul), or divine essence within. In this sense, the "new you" is not just a healed version of the old; it is a more essential version—stripped of pretense, softened by vulnerability, and widened by love. In the language of the mystic, grief is not an interruption to life; it is the curriculum of the soul.

Rewriting the Narrative of the Self

In psychological terms, this evolution often requires what narrative therapists call **"re-authoring" the self-story**. The loss has disrupted the existing narrative of who we are and where we are going. To live again, we must write a new chapter—not in denial of the past, but in communion with it.

This process includes honoring the old self that loved, hoped, and lost, while also being willing to meet the unfamiliar face in the mirror—the one marked by sorrow, but also illuminated by insight. Many individuals report that through grief, they become more compassionate, more attuned to suffering, and more grounded in what really matters.

Rumi speaks directly to this evolution:

"You were born with wings, why prefer to crawl through life?"

The "wings" he refers to are the capacities of the soul—love, courage, imagination, and divine longing. Grief often reveals them precisely because it strips away the noise and distraction of ordinary life. The new you is not simply more functional or stable. The new you is more attuned to the sacred, more aligned with truth, and more willing to embrace both the fragility and the wonder of human existence.

Living with the Paradox

To live again after loss is to live in paradox: to love what is, knowing it is impermanent; to celebrate life, knowing death has left its mark; to move forward without letting go of the one who is no longer physically here. This paradox is not a problem to solve but a reality to embrace.

Modern psychological thought increasingly recognizes the capacity for **dialectical thinking**—holding seemingly opposing truths—as a sign of post-traumatic maturity. The self after grief is one who has learned to live with contradiction, to be both joyful and sorrowful, open and guarded, fragile and strong.

This mirrors Rumi's spiritual vision, where every loss is a veiled gift, every wound a potential portal to divine intimacy. The "new you" in Rumi's cosmology is not separate from the Beloved (God or Spirit), but drawn closer through loss, tenderized by suffering, and awakened by longing.

"Sorrow prepares you for joy.

It violently sweeps everything out of your house,

so that new joy can find space to enter."

— Rumi

In this vision, grief is the sacred gardener, uprooting illusions so that the truth of your being—your soul—can breathe and flourish.

The emergence of a "new you" after loss is one of the most profound outcomes of the grieving process. It is not something you force or fabricate, but something that slowly, organically arises from the depth of your encounter with sorrow. Modern psychology sees it as a transformation through meaning and growth. Rumi sees it as the soul awakening to its own divine origin. Together, they point to the truth that while death ends a life, it does not end relationship, nor does it end the evolution of the one who remains. It only opens the next chapter—one in which love matures, faith deepens, and a new self, softened and strengthened, steps into the light.

Integrating the Experience of Loss

To integrate the experience of loss is not simply to accept that someone is gone. It is to allow the reality of their absence—and the profound meaning of their presence—to become part of the very architecture of who we are. In the psychological sense, integration involves a shift in the self-narrative, wherein the event of loss is no longer a sharp rupture from the storyline of our life, but a woven thread—distinct in color and tone, but fundamentally part of the same tapestry.

In the early stages of grief, integration is not possible. The mind is in a protective fog, the body in shock, the emotions flooded with disbelief, yearning, or numbness. Yet as time unfolds, a space often begins to open for something subtler: the desire not merely to survive, but to understand. This is the foundation of integration—a movement beyond the rawness of mourning into the reflective engagement with what this loss *means* to us, and how it has shaped us.

Psychological Foundations of Integration

Modern grief psychology, particularly in the work of Robert Neimeyer and his model of *meaning reconstruction*, emphasizes that one of the central challenges after loss is to integrate the event into a coherent sense of self and world. Traumatic or unexpected loss, in particular, can shatter core assumptions: that the world is fair, that life is predictable, that we are safe. Neimeyer argues that healing is found not merely in "getting over" a loss, but in finding or constructing meaning *through* it—by updating our assumptions, values, and goals in light of what we've experienced.

In this sense, integration does not erase the wound; rather, it contextualizes it. The death becomes not a hole we endlessly fall into, but a space within us we learn to tend. It may continue to ache, but it becomes familiar, known, and eventually, even sacred.

Other psychological frameworks also support this view. Attachment theory has evolved to recognize that the bonds we form do not necessarily vanish with death. Rather, we internalize them. According to Dennis Klass and colleagues (1996), the *continuing bonds* theory suggests that integrating a loss includes maintaining an inner representation of the deceased—a way of carrying them forward while also continuing to live our own life. Integration, then, is a balance: acknowledging absence while preserving presence in a new form.

Rumi's Perspective: Embracing the Fracture

From the mystical lens of Rumi, integration is not only psychological—it is existential and spiritual. Loss, in Rumi's poetry, is a doorway to divine remembrance, a call to return to the essence beneath form. For Rumi, grief is not an interruption of life, but a deepening into it.

"Don't grieve. Anything you lose comes round in another form."

— Rumi

This aphorism is not a denial of loss—it is a transformation of perspective. Rumi's idea of integration is not about *recovering* what was lost, but about *realizing* the eternal nature of connection. The form is gone, yes—

but the soul, the love, the imprint, the presence—these endure. And more than endure, they become portals to a deeper relationship with the Divine, with others, and with oneself.

In the Sufi cosmology Rumi draws from, the self is not a fixed identity but a flowing stream of experience. Loss, then, is not a tear in the fabric of who we are, but an opening in it. Through that tear, light enters. And what it illuminates is not just the memory of the one who is gone—but the truth of what they revealed in us.

"Try not to resist the changes that come your way.

Instead, let life live through you."

— Rumi

Integration, in this spiritual sense, is surrender—not in the sense of giving up, but in yielding to the deeper currents of being. It is a conscious allowing of loss to shape us—not as victims of fate, but as participants in the mystery of existence.

From Fracture to Wholeness

The psychological process of integration often includes consciously revisiting memories, revising narratives, and reengaging with life in ways that honor both the past and the present. It may involve therapy, journaling, ritual, or storytelling. It often requires support from others who can witness the transformation without rushing it.

In time, people often report a quiet shift: the pain is still there, but it no longer owns them. The memory of the person becomes less of a wound and more of a wellspring. They find themselves doing things the loved one would have appreciated. They embody traits the loved one admired. They make choices informed by the values that death laid bare. The deceased becomes, in many ways, a teacher—not only in life but in death.

Rumi echoes this process of transformation through his metaphor of alchemy. Just as base metal is transmuted into gold through fire, so too is the heart refined through suffering:

"This moment is all there is.

Die to the past every moment.

You will be reborn with a new mind."

— Rumi

Integration is this rebirth—not a forgetting, but a becoming. It is allowing the experience of loss to melt the rigid parts of us, to dissolve illusions, to awaken us to impermanence, and ultimately, to love more freely.

A Gentle Transformation

There is no universal timeline for this process. Some may feel a sense of integration within months; for others, it may take years. And still, the process is never "complete" in the way that tasks are completed. Integration is an ongoing relationship—an evolving conversation between who we were, who we lost, and who we are becoming.

Importantly, integrating loss does not mean we are no longer sad. It means we are no longer afraid of our sadness. We have befriended it. We understand its language. We see that within it lives our love, our longing, and the most tender truths of our souls.

Rumi writes:

"The wound is the place where the Light enters you."

— **Rumi**

In this way, grief is not simply a passage to endure—it is an initiation. Integration is the outcome of that initiation, where the wound becomes wisdom, the silence becomes presence, and the past becomes a foundation rather than a weight.

Growth in Emotional Depth and Empathy

Loss, though devastating in its immediacy, often awakens qualities in the human spirit that might otherwise remain dormant. Among the most profound of these are emotional depth and empathy. These qualities do not simply emerge as byproducts of suffering; rather, they are cultivated through the transformative process of grief, introspection, and spiritual reawakening. They are forged in the crucible of love and longing, pain and reflection.

The psychological journey of mourning gradually shifts from acute pain toward a broader emotional palette—one that includes not only sadness and sorrow, but also awe, tenderness, compassion, and a greater sensitivity to the suffering and beauty of life. As people move through the stages and spirals of grief, their emotional awareness often deepens. They feel more. And crucially, they begin to *feel with* others.

Empathy Through Shared Vulnerability

In modern psychology, empathy is broadly understood as the capacity to understand and share the feelings of another. There are cognitive aspects (understanding another's perspective) and affective aspects (feeling what another feels). The grieving process often enhances both. Studies in trauma and bereavement psychology, including the work of Dr. Brené Brown and Dr. Kristin Neff, suggest that individuals who have undergone significant emotional pain often report greater capacity for empathy. They not only "know" sorrow—they recognize it in the eyes of others. They are more likely to respond with care, rather than judgment.

This shift is not abstract. It changes behavior and relationships. A person who has walked through grief may be more patient with a crying stranger, more present for a friend in crisis, more willing to listen without rushing to fix. The heart, having been broken, becomes less brittle and more supple. In the words of psychologist Carl Rogers, this kind of deep empathy is "a way of being," not merely a skill.

Furthermore, the grief-stricken often describe feeling more emotionally attuned—not only to the suffering of others but also to the quiet moments of joy. Their internal world grows more nuanced. What once seemed trivial may now shimmer with meaning: a child's laughter, the warmth of sun on skin, the chance to say "I love you" one more time. These heightened emotional textures become evidence that one has not only survived loss but has been changed by it.

Rumi and the Heart Broken Open

Rumi's poetry speaks to this awakening of the heart in ways that are both tender and piercing. For Rumi, emotional depth is not merely a reaction to sorrow—it is a sign of spiritual ripening. Grief is not something to escape but something to lean into, for within it lies the potential for transformation.

"The wound is the place where the Light enters you."

— Rumi

This now-iconic line captures a fundamental paradox. The very place that hurts the most, the wound inflicted by loss, becomes the place through which deeper truths are revealed. In Rumi's cosmology, the heart must break open so that divine love can enter. The pain of separation is the beginning of intimacy—not just with the one who was lost, but with the world, the soul, and the divine source.

He writes:

"Keep breaking your heart until it opens."

— Rumi

This is not a call to masochism, but an invitation to trust the process of emotional exposure. The heart that has been cracked by grief is no longer encased in egoic defenses. It becomes more receptive. It listens more closely. It knows what cannot be said in words. This depth is not shallow sentimentality; it is the raw, unfiltered presence that comes when one realizes how fragile—and how sacred—every life truly is.

The Development of Emotional Intelligence

Psychologically, this growth can be understood in the framework of emotional intelligence, a term popularized by Daniel Goleman. Emotional intelligence includes the ability to be aware of, understand, and regulate one's emotions, as well as to manage interpersonal relationships judiciously and empathetically. Research shows that individuals who process grief with support and self-reflection often develop heightened emotional intelligence.

They become more skilled at recognizing emotional states, managing emotional reactivity, and attuning to others.

In this way, grief functions like a mirror. It reflects our own emotional interior and reveals what we had perhaps overlooked: unspoken love, unresolved regrets, or deeper values that had been buried in the rush of daily life. As we integrate the lessons of loss, we become better listeners—not just to others but to ourselves.

Empathy as Sacred Responsibility

For those who have endured great loss, the ability to empathize becomes more than a skill; it becomes a form of service. It is as if the pain has initiated them into a deeper knowing—a spiritual literacy that cannot be taught by books alone. They may feel compelled to reach out to others in mourning, to volunteer, to offer comfort, or simply to be a steady presence in a world that often rushes past grief.

Rumi's work is filled with such sacred responsibility. He understood love not as possession, but as a force that expands us beyond ourselves. In mourning the death of his beloved teacher, Shams of Tabriz, Rumi became not smaller but larger. His grief birthed an ocean of poetry that has consoled millions for centuries. The empathy encoded in his verses was not an abstract virtue—it was born of lived agony, ecstatic love, and surrender to the mystery of existence.

"Your task is not to seek for love, but merely to seek and find all the barriers within yourself that you have built against it."

— **Rumi**

In this light, empathy is not just interpersonal; it is transpersonal. It is a dissolving of the illusion of separation. The one who suffers becomes kin. The boundaries between "my grief" and "your grief" soften, and in their place arises a shared humanity.

A New Emotional Landscape

As the grieving heart opens, the emotional landscape of the mourner begins to change. Anger softens into inquiry. Fear yields to humility. Sadness transforms into reverence. Empathy becomes a language of connection. This evolution may be subtle or seismic, but it is real. And it signifies that the person is no longer merely surviving grief—they are being shaped by it.

The emotional depth that emerges from grief is a form of wisdom. It cannot be rushed. It cannot be faked. But once it is there, it enriches every relationship and every encounter with life. It colors the way we speak, the way we listen, the way we show up in the world.

In the end, the greatest tribute we can offer to those we've lost is not only to remember them, but to allow their absence to deepen our presence. As Rumi might remind us: the heart, once broken, becomes not less whole but more *real*—a place where love and empathy grow in tandem with pain, until the pain, too, becomes a form of love.

"You Were Born with Wings…" – Rediscovering Your Path

"You were born with wings, why prefer to crawl through life?"

— Rumi

In the quiet aftermath of loss, when the world seems unfamiliar and even one's own reflection in the mirror feels like that of a stranger, these words offer not just comfort—but an invitation. They suggest that within the human heart resides a latent capacity to rise, to reimagine, and to return to a path of meaning. But this return is not a going back; it is a movement forward, transformed. This section explores the rediscovery of one's path after grief, how psychological frameworks support that process, and how Rumi's mysticism can guide one through the spiritual terrain of becoming.

The Shattered Compass

After a profound loss, many people describe a sensation akin to wandering without direction. What once brought purpose may feel hollow. Long-term goals may lose relevance. Identity itself may seem fractured. Psychologically, this disruption is referred to by existential theorists such as Viktor Frankl and Irvin Yalom as a form of existential vacuum—an inner void where previous beliefs, values, and meanings no longer provide anchorage.

Frankl, in his seminal work *Man's Search for Meaning*, emphasized that meaning is not given—it must be found. And often, it is through suffering that meaning is most intensely sought. In the face of death or tragic loss, one may confront questions such as: *What now? Why go on? Who am I without them?* These are not signs of despair alone; they are also signals that the psyche is attempting to reorient itself, to find a new center of gravity.

This psychological liminality—being between what was and what will be—is fertile ground for transformation. It is precisely here, in the suspended terrain of grief and identity loss, that Rumi's metaphor of the wings becomes potent. His call is not one of escapism but of remembrance: of soul-potential, of hidden capacities, and of the divine spark within.

Awakening to Inner Resources

"You were born with wings…" is not a poetic exaggeration. In psychological terms, it speaks to the untapped internal resources that trauma and grief can, paradoxically, reveal. Post-Traumatic Growth (PTG) theory, developed by psychologists Richard Tedeschi and Lawrence Calhoun, outlines how individuals who endure psychological struggle following adversity often report positive changes, including a greater appreciation for life, a sense of new possibilities, enhanced personal strength, and spiritual development.

Rediscovering one's path after loss does not mean replacing the old life but forging a deeper one—sometimes simpler, often more authentic. This realignment requires courage and, just as importantly, imagination. Psychologically, it involves reintegration. Grief therapy and meaning-centered approaches such as those pioneered by Robert Neimeyer focus on helping individuals reconstruct their life story with the loss woven into it—not erased, but honored.

It is in the process of this narrative reweaving that individuals begin to sense their "wings." A widow may discover a calling to advocate for hospice care. A bereaved sibling might turn to painting, not to escape their sorrow but to express its depth. A parent who has lost a child might begin working with at-risk youth, channeling their grief into compassion. In each case, a path is not merely found—it is forged through the fire of sorrow.

Rumi's Vision of Becoming

For Rumi, the rediscovery of one's path is inseparable from the journey of the soul back to its origin. He does not view loss as an ending, but as a divine summons. The pain of earthly separation, he argues, is not a punishment but a signal—a reminder of what we are and what we are capable of becoming.

"Don't get lost in your pain, know that one day your pain will become your cure."

— Rumi

This transformation does not deny the wound—it transfigures it. The spiritual path Rumi outlines is one of deep inner alchemy, where sorrow becomes a crucible for the unveiling of the soul. His metaphor of wings implies not only potential but destiny. You were not born to remain ground-bound. You were born to ascend.

This ascent, however, does not mean turning away from the world, or bypassing grief in favor of spiritual platitudes. Quite the opposite: it is through moving honestly through the depths of loss that one earns the right to rise. Rumi's own life was marked by such a transformation. The death of Shams of Tabriz devastated him—and yet, it also birthed the *Masnavi*, a literary ocean of spiritual wisdom and insight. His personal path was discovered not in spite of grief, but because of it.

Embracing the Unknown

Rediscovering one's path also requires embracing uncertainty. The psychological process of reorientation is rarely linear. There are relapses, setbacks, doubts. Old wounds resurface. The future remains unwritten. And yet, something shifts. What was once paralyzing begins to become formative.

Contemporary grief specialists such as David Kessler and Megan Devine emphasize that finding purpose after loss does not mean "moving on" or forgetting. It means carrying the memory forward, with integrity. It means choosing, often daily, to live in alignment with values awakened through suffering—compassion, honesty, presence, gratitude, and the courage to love again, knowing that all things pass.

Rumi's insistence on soul-freedom is a radical counterpoint to our culture's fixation on closure. His poetry says: Let your loss open you. Let it disorient you. Let it awaken what has been asleep. You were not meant to merely survive. You were meant to fly.

"Try not to resist the changes that come your way. Instead, let life live through you."

— **Rumi**

Returning to the World

The return to life after grief often begins in small, trembling steps. Saying yes to a social invitation. Beginning a new project. Visiting a place you once avoided. Laughing. Loving. Trusting. As you rediscover your wings, you may realize that you are not the same person who began this journey. And that is precisely the point.

The "new you" is not a betrayal of the past but a continuation of the soul's unfolding. Rediscovering your path means owning your right to joy, to purpose, to presence—despite, and because of, the depth of your sorrow.

It means living with the knowledge that love never dies, and neither does the call to grow, to serve, and to remember.

Rumi writes:

"Why are you so busy with this or that, or good or bad; pay attention to how things blend."

— Rumi

In the aftermath of grief, everything blends: sorrow and beauty, death and life, memory and becoming. And in that blend, if we are willing to listen, we may hear a new calling. One that says not only *you can go on,* but *you were meant to rise.*

Accepting Life's Impermanence with Open Arms

In the wake of profound loss, one of the hardest truths to confront is impermanence—the transience not only of life, but of every moment, every relationship, and every form we grow attached to. This recognition can be terrifying. It destabilizes the illusion of control and permanence upon which we often build our lives. And yet, paradoxically, embracing this impermanence can also lead to liberation, peace, and a deeper connection to the unfolding of life. This final section explores how accepting life's impermanence becomes a spiritual and psychological act of healing and growth, drawing from both modern psychological frameworks and the timeless wisdom of Rumi.

Grief as a Teacher of Impermanence

Psychologically, grief is not just a response to loss—it is also a teacher that initiates us into the impermanence of all things. The pain of losing someone we love reveals just how fragile life is. Yet, as psychotherapist Francis Weller writes in *The Wild Edge of Sorrow*, grief is not simply about mourning the loss of what was—it is about learning to live in a world that refuses to stop changing. Weller argues that grief teaches us the "grammar of belonging" by forcing us to feel the poignancy of being alive, which includes the reality that nothing, not even love, can prevent eventual endings.

Existential psychology echoes this perspective. The awareness of death and impermanence lies at the heart of existential anxiety, but also at the root of authentic living. Irvin Yalom suggests that coming to terms with mortality allows us to live with greater intentionality and freedom. When we stop trying to resist the fact that life is impermanent, we can start to love more freely, live more fully, and connect more honestly.

Yet this acceptance is not a passive surrender—it is an active and courageous opening to life as it is, not as we wish it to be. It is the difference between clinging to what must fade and embracing the beauty of what is, even as it slips through our fingers.

Rumi and the Spiritual Alchemy of Impermanence

For Rumi, the impermanence of life is not a tragedy but a divine mystery. He invites us to view the passing nature of all things not with resistance, but with wonder. In his poetry, impermanence is a spiritual truth that keeps the heart supple and the soul awake.

"Try to learn to let what is simply be. That is the closest you can get to stillness."

— Rumi

To Rumi, the forms of this world are veils over deeper truths. The beloved may leave the body, but love remains. A rose withers, but its fragrance lingers in memory. The death of a friend does not sever the connection but opens the door to a subtler communion. What dies was never meant to be held; what lives was never confined to form.

In the Masnavi and his ghazals, Rumi often uses metaphors of autumn, fading candlelight, and falling leaves to illustrate the ephemeral nature of life. Yet, always, he speaks of these not with despair, but with reverence. The leaf falls not because it has failed, but because its time has come. The candle flickers not in defeat, but in fulfillment of its offering of light. As he writes:

"Be like a tree and let the dead leaves drop."

— Rumi

This is not nihilism—it is spiritual clarity. It is not indifference—it is intimacy with the real.

Mindfulness and the Present Moment

From a psychological standpoint, the practice of mindfulness offers a parallel path. Rooted in Buddhist psychology and now widely used in clinical settings, mindfulness trains the mind to remain present with the changing flow of experience—without clinging, resisting, or judging.

Jon Kabat-Zinn, founder of Mindfulness-Based Stress Reduction (MBSR), defines mindfulness as "paying attention in a particular way: on purpose, in the present moment, and nonjudgmentally." When applied to grief, mindfulness helps the mourner sit with sorrow without trying to escape it. It allows one to witness the changing waves of emotion—rage, tenderness, longing, emptiness—without becoming overwhelmed by them. And gradually, it teaches a kind of radical acceptance: *This, too, is part of being alive.*

When we practice mindfulness in the context of impermanence, we come to understand that the only place we truly live is here and now. We stop holding life hostage to what was or might be. And in doing so, we rediscover joy—not as a denial of suffering, but as a deeper capacity to be present with whatever arises.

Rumi echoes this psychological truth in mystical form:

"With life as short as a half-taken breath, don't plant anything but love."

— **Rumi**

Each breath is fleeting, and yet, infinitely sacred. When we accept impermanence, we stop wasting time on grievances, on smallness, on what doesn't matter. We begin to invest our presence in what does: connection, beauty, purpose, kindness.

Grief and the Dance of Holding and Letting Go

Accepting impermanence does not mean detachment in the cold or avoidant sense. Rather, it is an invitation to learn the dance between holding and letting go. In grief, we learn how to carry the memory of our loved one without clinging to the pain. We learn to honor the past while stepping into the future.

In *The Paradoxes of Mourning*, psychologist Alan Wolfelt suggests that healthy grieving involves both "doing" and "being." It involves remembering the loved one while also re-engaging with life. This balance—between presence and release, memory and new beginnings—is an expression of mature grief and spiritual resilience.

Rumi encourages the same dual movement. He does not tell us to forget our beloved. Rather, he calls us to let go of the illusion of permanence, to love more purely, without demand. He writes:

"Don't grieve. Anything you lose comes round in another form."

— Rumi

This is not to say that everything lost will be replaced—but that nothing is ever truly lost in the realm of the heart. The forms may change, but the essence, the love, the spirit—these remain, albeit transformed.

A Tender Surrender

Ultimately, to accept impermanence with open arms is to live with a kind of tender surrender. It is to know that we will love and lose, over and over again—and to love anyway. It is to know that we will one day die—and to live with open eyes and a generous heart. It is to realize that we are part of something vast and flowing, and that our task is not to freeze the river, but to dance in its current while we can.

Modern psychological healing and ancient mystical wisdom converge in this simple, difficult truth: When we stop resisting impermanence, we begin to live more deeply. We stop merely surviving and begin to participate in the sacred unfolding of life, just as it is—fragile, luminous, and ever-changing.

Rumi offers us this final reassurance:

"Don't get lost in your pain, know that one day your pain will become your cure."

— Rumi

This is the ultimate turning point in grief. When impermanence is no longer the enemy, but the teacher, we begin to heal not just from loss—but into life itself.

Chapter 12 Summary: The New You: Life After Loss

As we come to the close of this chapter, we recognize that loss is not only an end but also a profound invitation—to evolve, to deepen, and to rediscover ourselves anew. Integrating the experience of grief reshapes the contours of our identity, inviting greater empathy, emotional depth, and spiritual clarity. Rumi's words echo through this transformation: "You were born with wings, why prefer to crawl through life?"—reminding us that we are not meant to remain shackled by sorrow, but to be transfigured by it. Through this metamorphosis, we learn to live not in denial of death, but in celebration of the fleeting miracle of life. Accepting impermanence with open arms is not resignation—it is the doorway to radical presence. It is here, in this acceptance, that we discover a new self not despite our grief, but because of it—a self forged in vulnerability, strengthened by love, and awakened to the sacredness of every moment.

Chapter 13:
Helping Others Grieve

Listening Without Fixing

Grief often arrives as a wordless ache—raw, sacred, and deeply personal. For those standing beside someone in mourning, the impulse to offer solutions, interpretations, or immediate comfort can feel overwhelming. This is particularly true in cultures that emphasize productivity, control, and emotional resolution. Yet, in the landscape of grief, the most healing thing we can do for another is to **listen—not to fix, but to be present**. True listening is an act of **radical humility**, of stepping back from our own discomfort and trusting that bearing witness to pain is often more healing than trying to remove it.

Modern psychology has long emphasized the importance of **active and empathic listening** in therapeutic and interpersonal relationships. Carl Rogers, the pioneering psychologist who developed **person-centered therapy**, posited that the three core conditions for personal growth were *congruence* (authenticity), *unconditional positive regard*, and *empathic understanding*. These principles are especially critical when supporting someone in grief. Rogers taught that simply being deeply heard—without judgment, agenda, or interruption—can facilitate healing in ways that advice or consolation never could.

When someone is grieving, their world feels disoriented. Language itself may feel inadequate. The mourner often needs a safe and compassionate presence to simply hold their experience without analysis or correction. In this space, **listening becomes a sacred act**. As grief expert **David Kessler** puts it, "Each person's grief is as unique as their fingerprint," and the role of the companion is not to edit that grief into something tidy but to **honor its rawness and complexity**.

This approach aligns beautifully with the contemplative wisdom of Rumi, who understood that the human heart unfolds in its own time, not on the schedule of those watching from the outside. In one of his more understated yet profound teachings, he wrote:

"Try not to resist the changes that come your way.

Instead, let life live through you."

— Rumi

This same ethos applies when we are in the presence of another's grief. We must resist the urge to shape, manage, or redirect their process. Instead, we must allow the sorrow to unfold naturally—through tears, silence, or speech—without attempting to contain or transform it prematurely.

Rumi's emphasis on the inner unfolding mirrors a key principle in modern trauma psychology: **the healing must emerge from within**. In the work of **Dr. Peter Levine**, the founder of Somatic Experiencing, we learn that trauma is stored in the body and released only when the nervous system feels safe enough to let go. This safety often comes from a *felt sense of connection*. Being deeply and compassionately listened to, activates the parasympathetic nervous system, signaling that it is safe to express and process emotion.

Unfortunately, many people try to rush the grieving process by offering clichés or "silver linings"—not out of cruelty, but from a discomfort with pain. Phrases like "At least they're in a better place," or "Everything happens for a reason," may be well-intentioned, but they often function as **emotional bypasses**, signaling that the speaker is unwilling or unable to enter the emotional terrain of grief with the mourner. These statements can feel like subtle rejections: instead of allowing the mourner to sit in their truth, they suggest that they should already be moving toward resolution.

In contrast, the art of listening without fixing invites us to **suspend our need to be helpful in a visible way**. This is difficult, particularly for those who feel helpless in the face of suffering. But as Rumi reminds us:

"When the soul lies down in that grass,

The world is too full to talk about.

Ideas, language… even the phrase each other—

Doesn't make any sense."

— Rumi

In the deepest grief, it is not ideas or language that are needed—it is **presence**. The person in mourning is not looking for intellectual clarity or theological resolution. They are looking to be met. To be accompanied. To not be left alone with a pain that is too vast for words.

From a neurological perspective, this kind of listening can be deeply reparative. **Stephen Porges' Polyvagal Theory** explains how humans detect safety not only through words but through tone of voice, eye contact, facial expressions, and body language. When someone listens with soft eyes, an open posture, and a warm tone, they signal "You are safe. I am with you."

This fosters a state of **neuroceptive safety** that is essential for grief processing.

Thus, to listen without fixing is not passive—it is **profoundly active**, though not in the way our goal-oriented minds might expect. It involves deep attunement, self-regulation, and sometimes, great restraint. We must **quiet the inner voice that wants to narrate, offer wisdom, or share our own stories**, and instead give our full attention to the one before us.

This is also a practice of **ego dissolution**, which Rumi often speaks of. In his words:

"The wound is the place where the Light enters you."

— Rumi

By not rushing to close the wound with platitudes or advice, we make space for the Light to do its work. We trust the process. We honor the grief.

In summary, listening without fixing is a radical form of love. It requires us to **make peace with the discomfort of witnessing pain we cannot remove**. It calls us to be mirrors instead of guides, companions instead of saviors. Both Rumi and modern psychology agree: true healing begins when we feel seen, heard, and not hurried. And sometimes, all it takes to be that mirror is to sit quietly and listen, not with the ears alone, but with the entire soul.

The Importance of Presence and Silence

In the sacred terrain of grief, few gifts are more powerful than **presence**, and fewer acts more profound than **silence**. In modern psychological practice, as well as in the mystical teachings of Jalāl ad-Dīn

Rumi, we find that *being*—rather than *doing*—is often the truest balm for a grieving soul.

Contemporary psychology, especially the fields of grief therapy and trauma recovery, has shifted from a model of cognitive problem-solving toward one that prioritizes **co-regulation**, **emotional attunement**, and **relational presence**. This change echoes a deep wisdom that Rumi wrote of nearly eight centuries ago: the idea that healing does not occur through words alone, but through the energy, stillness, and love that can be shared between two people—heart to heart.

In modern clinical psychology, especially within **humanistic and existential psychotherapy**, presence is not a passive stance but a deeply active one. Carl Rogers, a central figure in this tradition, emphasized the power of *unconditional positive regard*, *empathic understanding*, and *genuineness*— qualities that must be **embodied** rather than spoken. To truly be present with someone in grief means offering the safety of non-judgmental space, where no effort is made to correct, distract, or diminish their pain. The grief is allowed to be what it is. The mourner is allowed to be as they are.

Psychologically, this is profoundly healing. When a grieving person is met with pure presence—when they are not rushed or redirected—their **nervous system finds regulation,** and their **sense of isolation begins to soften.** In **attachment theory,** pioneered by John Bowlby and Mary Ainsworth, we learn that safe relationships provide the foundation for resilience and recovery in the face of loss. Presence becomes a **secure base** from which the bereaved can explore the depth of their emotions and begin the journey of reintegration.

Silence plays a pivotal role here. Yet silence is often misunderstood in modern culture, especially in societies that prioritize constant stimulation, verbal processing, and intellectual explanation. Silence is frequently interpreted as awkward, empty, or lacking compassion. But in the realm of grief, silence is not absence—it is **reverence**. It is the sacred pause in which pain can be felt fully, unencumbered by commentary or interruption.

From a neurobiological perspective, silence can be profoundly **regulating**. In grief, the brain's default mode network (DMN)—responsible for internal reflection and memory—becomes highly active. Verbal intrusion can disrupt this natural process of meaning-making. Silence, on the other hand, **amplifies internal space**, allowing the bereaved to encounter their emotions more organically and integrate their loss in a nonlinear but necessary way.

Rumi, with his profound understanding of the soul's architecture, also revered silence not as emptiness, but as a **vessel for divine presence and inner truth**. In his mystical worldview, silence is the language of God, and grief is a doorway to spiritual transformation that cannot always be walked with words. He wrote:

"Silence is the language of God,

all else is poor translation."

— Rumi

And in another poem:

"There is a voice that doesn't use words.

Listen."

— **Rumi**

In the quiet, the mourner can begin to hear that deeper voice—the whisper of their own soul, and perhaps, even the presence of the one they lost. Rumi believed that **the heart speaks best in silence**, and that what cannot be uttered can still be felt, known, and shared in the space between two souls.

Presence and silence, when combined, form a kind of **spiritual container**—a holding environment, to borrow from psychoanalyst D.W. Winnicott's term. In this container, the mourner does not have to justify their sorrow or explain their emotional waves. The presence of another— calm, grounded, and quiet—serves as **a mirror**, not of advice or strategy, but of acceptance and compassion. In this way, silence becomes a form of profound **attunement**.

This mirrors a truth that trauma researcher **Bessel van der Kolk** emphasizes in *The Body Keeps the Score*: the presence of a safe other is the single most important factor in processing trauma and grief. A person doesn't need to be fixed—they need to be felt with.

To sit beside someone and say nothing, to offer no prescriptions, but to make eye contact, to breathe with them, to share space without retreating or distracting, is a spiritual act. It requires **emotional maturity, restraint**, and **trust** in the healing power of presence itself.

Rumi's poetry is replete with images of the beloved sitting in stillness, surrendering to the silence of longing and loss. In this, he teaches us that presence is not about eradicating suffering, but about being willing to **walk into the fire with another**, not as savior, but as companion. He reminds us:

"Be with those who help your being."

— **Rumi**

To be that person for someone else is to offer more than comfort—it is to offer **companionship on the soul's journey**.

In helping others grieve, we must learn to sit in the silence, to hold the ache without diminishing it, and to allow presence—not words—to be our offering. Modern psychology confirms this, but Rumi felt it in his bones: that in the quiet communion of two hearts, the brokenness does not disappear—but it does begin to shine.

What not to say

Grief is not a puzzle to be solved or a wound that words can always soothe. Yet so often, in our discomfort with another's pain, we instinctively reach for words that are meant to console but instead inadvertently isolate or wound further. Knowing what *not* to say is just as important—if not more so—than knowing what to say.

Modern psychology helps illuminate why certain phrases, although well-intended, can feel invalidating to those who are grieving. Grief expert **Dr. David Kessler**, a close collaborator of Elisabeth Kübler-Ross, points out that many common expressions—like "everything happens for a reason," or "at least they lived a long life"—stem not from compassion, but from the speaker's own discomfort. These comments attempt to **bypass the rawness**

of emotion and **reassert cognitive control** over something that is inherently uncontrollable: loss.

Neuroscience also sheds light here. The grieving brain, particularly in the early stages of bereavement, is operating in survival mode. The limbic system—home to emotional regulation, memory, and attachment—becomes highly activated. When a well-meaning friend offers a rational or minimizing remark, it bypasses the emotional core entirely and activates **defensiveness or detachment** instead. Rather than meeting the bereaved where they are—inside their pain—the speaker accidentally attempts to move them out of it too soon.

From the perspective of **trauma-informed care**, such verbal bypassing can even re-traumatize. Comments like "You're strong," "They're in a better place," or "You'll feel better soon" subtly imply that the mourner should not dwell in sorrow or that grief has an expiration date. These phrases create **emotional dissonance**, where the mourner's internal world is denied or invalidated by the external one.

Instead, a grief-informed, psychologically attuned response honors **the mourner's emotional reality as it is**, without agenda. This principle finds deep resonance in **Rumi's mystical philosophy**, which constantly emphasizes emotional truth over pretense, the heart over the intellect, and soul-connection over explanation.

Rumi teaches us that the language of the soul is not bound by logic. When one is grieving, they are in conversation with the deepest layers of their being—what he called the **"tavern of ruins"** where divine wine is poured. Trying to clean up or explain the mess too quickly dishonors its sacredness. He wrote:

"Don't grieve. Anything you lose comes round in another form."

— Rumi

Yet he does not rush us. The statement is not a command to stop grieving, but rather a **gentle invitation** to remain open, even in despair. Rumi understood the **sacredness of pain**, the necessity of its full expression. Elsewhere, he writes:

"Try not to resist the changes that come your way. Instead, let life live through you."

— Rumi

When a mourner hears something like "They're in a better place," it might sound spiritually elevated, but it may also feel like a dismissal. Rumi never invalidates grief in such a way. Instead, he lets sorrow live alongside spiritual insight. He invites the griever to **feel fully**, rather than explain away their experience.

Psychologist and grief counselor **Megan Devine**, author of *It's OK That You're Not OK*, argues that we must abandon the cultural script that tries to fix pain or pull people toward a premature silver lining. She notes that such phrases are more about the speaker's need for emotional resolution than the mourner's need for connection. Instead, she suggests we say things like:

"I see your pain. I'm here with you."

"I don't have words, but I won't leave."

These are not grand statements—they are **anchoring presences**. They do not attempt to move someone out of grief but instead **stand beside them in it**. In this way, the act of helping is about *witnessing*, not *explaining*.

Rumi mirrored this approach beautifully. He did not seek to silence sorrow or to redefine it quickly into a lesson. In fact, many of his most beloved verses come directly from a place of brokenness. In *The Masnavi*, he writes:

"This moment is all there is.

If you are waiting for anything else, you are missing life."

— Rumi

Here, he subtly warns against future-oriented platitudes. Grief unfolds in the **now**, not in some conceptual tomorrow. To respond with future-focused comfort ("You'll find someone else," "Time heals all wounds") is to miss the mourner's real experience, which is located in the immediate ache of absence.

Another common misstep in conversations about grief is **comparison**. "I know exactly how you feel" or "When I lost my dog/grandparent/friend…" may seem empathetic, but often they redirect the emotional focus back to the speaker. Even when pain is shared, it is not identical. Each grief is **idiosyncratic**, shaped by the unique bond lost, the mourner's life history, and the narrative they held about love and meaning. As such, humility is vital.

The essence of what *not* to say, then, rests in this: **avoid anything that tries to control, redirect, diminish, or rationalize the mourner's**

experience. Instead, hold space for what is raw, strange, and ineffable. Speak less, feel more.

Rumi's wisdom is profoundly instructive here. His poetry is filled with *paradox*, *mystery*, and *tenderness*—rarely with solutions. He models a kind of spiritual presence that neither interrupts grief nor runs from it. In fact, he invites us to enter it, to **be with the fire**:

> *"This moment, this love, comes to rest in me,*
>
> *many beings in one being.*
>
> *In one wheat grain a thousand sheaf stacks.*
>
> *Inside the needle's eye, a turning night of stars."*
>
> **— Rumi**

Such language does not fix—it expands. It reminds the grieving heart of its vastness without asking it to be any different. When we hold others in grief, our words should do the same.

In the end, helping others grieve is not about saying the perfect thing, but about **embodying the sacred presence of care, humility, and open-hearted witnessing**. As Rumi and modern psychology both affirm, what heals is not explanation but connection—often wordless, always sincere.

Rumi's Compassion: "Be A Lamp, Or A Lifeboat, Or A Ladder"

To support the grieving is not merely to offer comfort but to become part of their transformation. Rumi's exhortation—"Be a lamp, or a lifeboat, or a ladder"—is not just poetic; it is deeply instructional. It offers three metaphors that illuminate the spectrum of compassionate presence:

illumination, rescue, and elevation. Each image corresponds to a psychological function we can embody for someone in mourning, guiding us toward an ethic of **empathic presence, emotional containment, and empowering support**. Together, they offer a roadmap for relational care grounded in both **Rumi's mystical insights** and **modern psychological principles**.

Be a Lamp: The Role of Illumination in Grief Support

To "be a lamp" is to offer light, not in the sense of fixing someone's darkness, but by holding a steady flame of **awareness, empathy, and presence**. In grief, the mourner often stumbles through an internal night. Their former worldview has been shaken; meaning may feel fragmented. This is where a "lamp" does its work—not by leading the way, but by **gently illuminating the mourner's own path** so they may see more clearly what is already before them.

Modern psychology—particularly **Carl Rogers' person-centered therapy**—emphasizes the importance of **unconditional positive regard**, **accurate empathy**, and **congruence**. These are qualities of a "lamp." The therapist—or compassionate companion—does not tell the mourner what to feel or believe. Instead, they provide a space where the bereaved can safely explore their own feelings and questions. The light comes not from answers but from **attuned presence**. Rogers believed that healing occurs not when we are told what to do, but when we are deeply understood.

In grief work, this illumination also corresponds to what **clinical psychologist Robert Neimeyer** describes as "meaning reconstruction." The bereaved person, he argues, must find a way to make sense of the loss—

not necessarily by resolving it, but by integrating it into a new life narrative. A compassionate companion serves as a lamp by **bearing witness to that meaning-making process**, never imposing, always accompanying.

Rumi's lamp is a quiet one. He does not advocate forcing light into someone's soul, but instead letting it be a **gentle flame**. In one of his verses, he writes:

"Don't you know yet? It is your light that lights the worlds."

— Rumi

Even in grief, the potential for inner illumination exists. Sometimes the greatest gift we can give is to **believe in the light within the mourner**, even when they cannot see it themselves.

Be a Lifeboat: Containing Emotional Turbulence

To "be a lifeboat" is to provide **emotional containment** during times of overwhelm. In early grief, many mourners describe feeling as though they are drowning—lost in a sea of sadness, anger, guilt, or numbness. The lifeboat does not deny the storm; it simply **offers a space that floats within it**, giving the mourner enough steadiness to catch their breath.

In psychological terms, this is closely aligned with the concept of **"holding"**, a term introduced by **Donald Winnicott**, a British psychoanalyst who described the function of a good-enough caregiver as one who emotionally holds the distressed person through consistency, attunement, and non-intrusiveness. In the context of grief, this might mean sitting quietly with someone as they cry, allowing them to rage without judgement, or simply remaining present as they fall into silence.

Being a lifeboat also means recognizing **the mourner's autonomy**. We do not drag them out of the water; we invite them into a space of safety. Grief, in this model, is not pathology—it is an adaptive response to loss. **Complicated grief** or **Prolonged Grief Disorder** emerges not from feeling too much, but often from not feeling safely held or allowed to process fully. A lifeboat supports emotional integration without rushing or repressing it.

Rumi's metaphor also speaks to the **fluidity of grief**. The waters are always moving, and we must not be rigid in how we offer help. In one poem, he says:

"Try to be like the turtle—at home in your own shell."

This is what the lifeboat does: it creates a temporary shell when the mourner's inner home has been shattered. It is not forever—but it is enough for now.

Be a Ladder: Supporting Transformation and Rebuilding

To "be a ladder" is to **empower**, to **offer elevation**, not through escape but through growth. A ladder implies that the mourner may eventually wish to rise—not away from their grief, but through it. It is a gesture of trust in their **capacity to rebuild meaning**, to become someone new after devastation.

In **Post-Traumatic Growth Theory**, psychologists Richard Tedeschi and Lawrence Calhoun outline how individuals who experience profound loss or trauma sometimes undergo deep transformation—experiencing increased relational depth, altered life priorities, and a greater sense of spiritual awareness. This growth is not about "getting over it," but about

growing through it. A ladder, in this sense, is any support that affirms the mourner's ability to grow in their own way and time.

Rumi was perhaps the original theorist of post-traumatic growth. His own grief over the disappearance of Shams of Tabriz catalyzed some of the most extraordinary mystical poetry the world has known. His entire corpus emerged as a ladder built from the ashes of longing. In one radiant verse, he proclaims:

"Don't grieve. Anything you lose comes round in another form."

— Rumi

The ladder is not made from what was lost—but from what *remains*. Memory, love, resilience, wisdom—these become the rungs upon which the mourner may slowly ascend.

Yet, the ladder must be **offered, not forced**. To "be a ladder" is not to urge the mourner upward too quickly. It is to be available when they are ready, to hold steady as they place one foot above the other, no matter how long it takes.

The Ethic of Compassionate Support

Taken together, Rumi's metaphor invites us to embody a **flexible, loving responsiveness** to those in grief. At times, we may need to be a **lamp**—quiet and illuminating. At other times, a **lifeboat**—resilient and protective. And eventually, a **ladder**—hopeful and empowering. Each role requires presence, empathy, and deep listening.

Modern grief psychology aligns seamlessly with this vision. It teaches us that effective support is not about removing pain, but **making space for**

it. It is about validating the mourner's unique experience, offering consistent care, and—when the time is right—encouraging them toward growth, not by force, but by faith.

Rumi's spiritual psychology reminds us that to help another in grief is not to stand above them with answers, but to kneel beside them with **light, refuge, and hope**. In doing so, we don't just help others heal—we awaken our own heart's deepest compassion.

Chapter 13 Summary: Helping Others Grieve

In the quiet work of helping others grieve, we come face to face with the essence of our shared humanity. This chapter has explored how compassion, when offered without the need to fix or solve, becomes a sacred bridge between suffering souls. Listening deeply, honoring silence, and avoiding the well-meaning but wounding clichés of comfort are all acts of profound respect for the mourner's journey. Rumi's timeless words—"Be a lamp, or a lifeboat, or a ladder"—call us not to rescue, but to accompany; not to advise, but to illuminate. Modern psychology reinforces this wisdom: healing arises not from answers but from presence, not from avoidance but from brave empathy. In supporting others through grief, we do not diminish our own sorrows—we expand our hearts. We become, in Rumi's terms, not mere observers but companions on the path, offering steadiness amid the storm and believing in the light that grief itself may one day reveal. Helping others grieve is, in the end, a deeply healing act—for both the giver and the receiver—a quiet miracle of human connection.

Conclusion:
The Light Beyond the Veil

As this book draws to a close, we return to the place where all grief begins—not in death itself, but in love. To grieve is to have loved. To mourn is to carry memory in the heart. And to heal is not to forget, but to remember with grace, to feel without being undone, to continue with reverence. In both modern psychology and the poetic mysticism of Rumi, grief is not an aberration to be fixed—it is a sacred passage, an initiation into a deeper intimacy with life, death, and self.

A Sacred Passage, Not a Problem to Solve

Grief, especially in Western society, is often seen as something to "get over"—a problem, a malfunction of emotions, an unwanted detour from the regular flow of life. But as we have explored throughout this work, grief is not an illness. It is not a pathology. It is a natural and necessary part of human experience. In fact, psychologists such as Dr. Katherine Shear and Dr. George Bonanno emphasize that grief is a form of adaptive emotional processing, not dysfunction. It allows us to recalibrate our sense of self and world after a rupture in attachment.

Rumi, writing from the 13th century yet speaking with stunning relevance to the modern soul, urges us not to resist the sorrow that arrives with loss. In one of his most poignant metaphors, he writes:

"The wound is the place where the Light enters you."

— Rumi

Loss is a wound, yes—but it is also an opening. And in that opening, we are invited to meet ourselves anew. Rumi never promises that pain will

420

disappear; instead, he assures us that pain has a purpose. It is a teacher, a purifier, and ultimately, a vehicle for transcendence.

Beyond the Binary: Life and Death as One Continuum

Psychologically, one of the most healing paradigms in grief work is the shift from viewing death as a binary opposite of life to seeing it as a part of life's continuum. The existential psychologist Irvin D. Yalom teaches that confronting death can lead to a deeper and more meaningful engagement with life. Similarly, mindfulness-based grief therapy encourages us to stay with what is—not to mentally escape the reality of loss but to find presence within it.

Rumi's cosmology echoes this understanding. Death is not seen as the extinguishing of the flame, but as the extinguishing of the lamp because the dawn has come. He writes:

"When the soul lies down in that grass, the world is too full to talk about."

— Rumi

His vision of death is not finality—it is union, return, continuation. This mirrors contemporary grief psychology's movement away from "closure" and toward "continuing bonds," as articulated by Klass, Silverman, and Nickman. We no longer heal by letting go in the traditional sense; we heal by *transforming* the relationship into something that can be carried inwardly.

Light Beyond the Veil: Hope After Darkness

Hope does not mean the absence of grief. It means learning to live with grief in a way that makes space for beauty again. In **Post-Traumatic Growth Theory** (Tedeschi & Calhoun), we see evidence that many who suffer significant loss also develop greater emotional resilience, spiritual awareness, and relational depth. Their sense of meaning often becomes richer, even if their hearts remain tender.

Rumi's poetry speaks often of light—light as divine love, light as understanding, light as the soul's true nature. His metaphor of "the veil" is an ancient one: death as a veil that separates not two opposites, but two different states of being. To see beyond the veil is not to reject the material world or deny grief, but to glimpse the eternity that exists *within* this moment, even in sorrow.

In the psychological sense, this "light" is not fantasy—it is the reawakening of life after devastation. It is what trauma researchers call "meaning reconstruction." It is what mourners describe when they say that their grief slowly becomes a source of empathy, connection, even guidance for others. It is the new path, not chosen but revealed, that emerges from the ashes of the old.

The Invitation: A New Relationship with Grief

The purpose of this book was never to offer steps for forgetting, or formulas for fixing, but to open a deeper dialogue—between you and your loss, between your pain and your potential. In Rumi's world, everything that happens is an invitation to return to the heart. Loss is no exception. The entire journey through grief, for Rumi, is not away from something—it is toward something greater, more inclusive, more loving.

"Be patient where you sit in the dark. The dawn is coming."

— **Rumi**

Modern therapeutic practices have begun to mirror this patience. Therapists working in the **Compassion-Focused Therapy** and **Meaning-Centered Grief Therapy** traditions encourage mourners to approach themselves with kindness and curiosity, rather than urgency. The question is not "How quickly can I move on?" but "What is emerging in me now that loss has carved me open?"

This shift in relationship—from resistance to reverence—is what transforms the experience of grief. It turns mourning into meaning, and despair into depth. And in that space, the veil grows thinner—not because grief ends, but because love becomes more enduring than the pain it caused.

Death Is Not the Opposite of Life, But A Part of It

In both psychological inquiry and the spiritual wisdom of Rumi, a fundamental reframing arises when we come to see death not as the antithesis of life, but as an inseparable dimension of it. This perspective is not merely philosophical—it has profound implications for how we mourn, how we heal, and how we live with meaning in the shadow of impermanence.

The Psychological Lens: Embracing Death to Enrich Life

In modern psychology, particularly within existential and humanistic traditions, death is not treated as a subject to be avoided but as an essential aspect of human awareness. Pioneering existential psychologist **Irvin D. Yalom** writes:

"Though the physicality of death destroys us, the idea of death saves us." This saving, paradoxical as it sounds, lies in the way mortality grounds our choices, sharpens our priorities, and wakes us to the finite beauty of life.

— Irvin D. Yalom

Contemporary grief psychology has also moved away from older models that sought "closure" and instead embraces a more fluid relationship with death. **Continuing bonds theory**, proposed by Klass, Silverman, and Nickman, illustrates that we do not need to sever ties with those who have died in order to live fully. Rather, healthy grieving often involves maintaining an internalized, transformed connection with the deceased—a dynamic relationship that honors the dead while affirming the living. Death becomes not an endpoint, but a doorway into a deeper, evolving relationship with memory, self, and existence.

In **Acceptance and Commitment Therapy (ACT)** and **Mindfulness-Based Cognitive Therapy (MBCT)**, death and loss are invited into consciousness not to be "fixed" but acknowledged as part of the whole picture of life. These therapeutic approaches teach that suffering comes not from the reality of death, but from our resistance to its inevitability. In making peace with death, we paradoxically become more alive.

Rumi's Perspective: Death as Return, Not Rupture

Centuries before modern psychology would embrace these ideas, **Jalal al-Din Rumi** had already woven them into his mystical worldview. For Rumi, death was not a catastrophe to be feared but a **return to source**, a homecoming. One of his most famous lines captures this sentiment with disarming clarity:

"Don't grieve. Anything you lose comes round in another form."

— Rumi

To Rumi, death is not annihilation—it is **transformation**. It is the soul shedding its temporary form and merging back with the Divine, like a drop returning to the ocean. He challenges us to look beyond the visible disappearance of the body and perceive the deeper continuity of spirit, love, and meaning. In his funeral elegy to Shams of Tabriz—his beloved friend and spiritual teacher—Rumi does not mourn as one devastated, but as one awakened:

"Why should I be weary when every cell of my body is bursting with life?"

For Rumi, the death of the physical is not the death of the real. In fact, much of his work dances with this radical idea: that we are more than our flesh, and that death is not the end of the story, but the dissolving of the veil that hides a more luminous truth.

This mirrors modern psychological observations that people who integrate death into their worldview often develop a more transcendent orientation to life—what some researchers call **post-traumatic transcendence**. These individuals not only learn to live with death—they learn to live differently because of it.

Death as a Teacher, Not a Tyrant

To see death as part of life is not to glorify suffering or minimize the ache of separation. It is, instead, to move out of a dualistic mindset that traps us in fear. In Western cultures, which often treat aging and death as enemies to be conquered, there is little room for honest dialogue about impermanence. This aversion can make loss feel more isolating and terrifying than it needs to be.

Psychological studies increasingly show that people who are more **death-aware**—those, who reflect consciously on mortality—tend to experience:

- Greater gratitude

- More authentic relationships

- Increased sense of purpose

- Deeper connection to spiritual values

In one study, psychologists Sheldon Solomon, Jeff Greenberg, and Tom Pyszczynski—pioneers of **Terror Management Theory**—found that when people confront their mortality in safe, reflective ways, they are more likely to live in accordance with their deepest values. In other words, death awareness can serve as a catalyst for meaning.

This echoes Rumi's spiritual psychology. He urges us not to run from death, but to befriend it:

"Die before you die, so that you may truly live."

— **Rumi**

This famous line of his is both enigmatic and electrifying. It suggests that to "die" to ego, illusion, and fear—to let go of false attachments—is to awaken to the eternal now. In this way, psychological and spiritual insights align: the more we accept death, the more fully we engage with life.

Implications for the Bereaved: Integrating Death with Life

When someone we love dies, we are catapulted into a world that no longer feels safe, knowable, or continuous. The psychological rupture is profound. Yet, as grief theorists have shown, **meaning-making** is a critical pathway through this pain. Making sense of loss—without rationalizing it away—often involves reframing death as part of the broader story of love and life.

Rumi offers a poetic model of this reframing. He encourages us to look beyond what the eyes can see and listen for what the heart knows:

"Try not to resist the changes that come your way. Instead, let life live through you."

— Rumi

When the bereaved begin to integrate death into life—not as an intrusion but as a mystery to live with—they often discover that love is not destroyed by death. Instead, it becomes more distilled. Many report that the person they lost continues to inspire them, guide them, and shape who they are becoming. In this way, death births a new form of presence.

This is not metaphorical comfort. It is psychologically grounded and experientially true for many. The dead do not leave us; they live within us, in memory, in action, in legacy.

Closing Reflection

To hold death not as the opposite of life, but as part of its holy architecture, is to live in more courageous intimacy with everything. This reframing allows grief to be not a dark detour, but a sacred corridor through which we deepen our humanity.

Psychology invites us to stay awake to death, not to fall into despair, but to rise into authenticity.

Rumi invites us to dance with death, not to deny loss, but to find the eternal rhythm pulsing underneath.

And together, they remind us: the end of a life is not the end of love. Death closes the eyes, but not the heart. It silences a voice, but not the echo. It removes the form, but not the essence. When we understand this—truly understand it—not only does grief soften, but life becomes more radiant.

In this light, we no longer run from death. We bow to it, walk beside it, and let it teach us how to live.

"This Moment Is All There Is" – Choosing to Live Again

In the wake of profound loss, time becomes strange. The past feels like a vanished dream; the future, a foggy and unreliable landscape. Grief can distort one's sense of reality, pulling the mourner backward into memories or freezing them in emotional paralysis. And yet, it is precisely in the present moment—raw, unpredictable, but always accessible—that healing can begin. This section explores how both modern psychology and the spiritual teachings of Rumi guide us toward the life-saving insight that *this moment*— not yesterday, not tomorrow—is all we truly have. And in this, we are given the astonishing choice: to live again.

428

Mindfulness and the Power of the Present

One of the central practices in modern psychological approaches to trauma and grief recovery is *mindfulness*, defined by Jon Kabat-Zinn as "paying attention, on purpose, in the present moment, non-judgmentally." Within therapies like **Mindfulness-Based Stress Reduction (MBSR)**, **Dialectical Behavior Therapy (DBT)**, and **Acceptance and Commitment Therapy (ACT)**, mindfulness offers an antidote to the psychological time travel that often defines mourning.

In grief, it is natural to revisit the past—reliving final conversations, replaying regrets, or longing for the presence of the deceased. Similarly, the future can be a minefield of anxiety: "How will I go on?" "What will life be like without them?" These thoughts are valid and human. But staying trapped in either realm—past or future—can prolong suffering and disconnect us from the one place we can exert agency: *the now.*

Research shows that present-focused awareness increases emotional regulation, reduces symptoms of anxiety and depression, and even fosters post-traumatic growth. When grieving individuals are supported in returning their attention to the present—not to escape their grief but to ground it in lived experience—they begin to regain a sense of agency. They begin, slowly, to choose life again.

Rumi's Call to Presence

Centuries before the rise of mindfulness in clinical psychology, **Rumi's poetry resounded with its core message**: come back to the now. In his ecstatic vision, the present moment is not merely a clock tick—it is a gateway to the Divine, to love, to reality unclouded by fear or fantasy.

One of Rumi's most direct instructions reads:

"Don't grieve. Anything you lose comes round in another form. But don't go looking back at what's lost. Stay here. Stay now."

— Rumi

This is not a denial of grief—it is an invitation to remain present with it, to let it unfold in this very breath, in this moment of your life, where pain and possibility coexist. For Rumi, grief is not a static thing to be endured, but a current in the river of being, always moving. And the place to meet it—the only place—is here.

In another verse, Rumi says:

"Be like a tree and let the dead leaves drop."

— Rumi

This line, profound in its simplicity, is a meditation on presence. Trees do not cling to what must fall away. They stand rooted in the seasons of change. So too, Rumi says, must we. We do not discard our grief, but we release the resistance to what is. In that release, in that moment of deep presence, we find ourselves again.

Choosing to Live Again: A Psychological and Spiritual Turning Point

"Choosing to live again" does not mean forgetting. It does not mean putting on a happy face or suppressing sorrow. It means **making a conscious, courageous decision to participate in life, even while carrying the wound of loss**.

In psychology, this is often framed through the lens of **post-traumatic growth** (PTG), a term coined by Richard Tedeschi and Lawrence Calhoun. PTG describes the positive psychological change experienced as a result of the struggle with highly challenging life circumstances. It doesn't imply that the loss was "worth it" or that grief is somehow desirable. Rather, it acknowledges that some individuals, after grappling with profound loss, find a renewed appreciation for life, deeper relationships, spiritual development, or a clarified sense of purpose.

This growth begins not with denial but with **radical presence**—a return to the now. It's in this very breath that the mourner says, sometimes silently, sometimes in tears: *I choose to keep living.* And then, again, the next moment. And the next.

Rumi encourages this path with tender defiance:

"Try to learn to let what is simply be. Let it be. This moment is all there is."

— Rumi

In this way, choosing to live again is not a one-time decision but a *practice*—a daily return to presence, a daily reaffirmation of life's preciousness in the shadow of its fragility.

Living the Moment as a Tribute to the Dead

Another profound psychological shift happens when individuals realize that living in the present can become **a form of honoring the dead**, not betraying them. So many mourners carry guilt about continuing to live, love, or laugh after loss. But as existential psychotherapist Viktor Frankl once wrote, "What is to give light must endure burning." The pain one carries is, in part, love that has nowhere to go. By choosing to live again, one gives that love a new channel.

Rumi echoes this truth:

"The wound is the place where the Light enters you."

— Rumi

To live again is not to move on from the beloved, but to let their presence be a light that informs how we love others, how we serve, how we cherish the fleeting beauty of this world.

From Grief to Grace, One Moment at a Time

Grief often feels endless because it cannot be solved by thought. But moment by moment, breath by breath, the mourner can learn to *be* with their pain instead of fighting it. In this gentle being-with, something sacred unfolds: a subtle shift, a quiet joy, a sense that life has not abandoned them. The dead are gone in body, but not in spirit. And life, remarkably, is still here, offering itself.

In Rumi's world, this is not an abstract idea—it is a living truth:

"This moment is your life."

— Rumi

This moment may be quiet. It may be painful. But it is yours. And it contains, however hidden, the seed of rebirth.

A Final Message of Hope from Rumi and the Heart of Psychology

As this book draws to a close, we arrive not at an ending, but at a quiet threshold—a place where the pain of loss and the promise of life meet. The journey through grief is neither linear nor finite. It does not offer a clean closure, but it does offer something else, something infinitely more profound: transformation. Both the teachings of modern psychology and the timeless poetry of Rumi converge here to leave us with a final, radiant message of hope—hope not as naive optimism, but as a deep, resilient commitment to life, meaning, and love even in the face of suffering.

Grief as a Portal to Wholeness

From the lens of contemporary psychology, particularly the schools of **existential therapy**, **trauma-informed care**, and **positive psychology**, grief is not a problem to be fixed but a *process to be honored*. It is part of the human condition, a mirror reflecting our deepest values: our attachments, our vulnerability, our love. Psychologists such as Irvin D. Yalom and Carl Rogers emphasized that the path to healing lies not in avoiding suffering, but in *leaning into it with authenticity and support*, and in discovering meaning even in life's darkest chapters.

This echoes **Rumi's mystical approach**. For him, loss is not a detour—it is the way itself. The heart that has been broken is not discarded but expanded. His poetry is filled with an unwavering trust in the transformative power of sorrow. He writes:

"Don't get lost in your pain, know that one day your pain will become your cure."

— **Rumi**

This is not a metaphorical flourish—it is a spiritual law. What we think will destroy us, when met with presence and love, becomes what transforms us. And transformation is the deeper purpose of grief. As the chrysalis becomes the butterfly not by refusing its darkness but by surrendering to it, so too does the human heart discover its wings through its cracks.

You Are Not Alone, and You Are Not Broken

Modern psychological frameworks stress that **connection is essential to healing**. Whether through group therapy, shared rituals, or deep personal relationships, healing is most effective when it happens in relationship. **Attachment theory** reminds us that our bonds define us—and losing a beloved person can feel like a rupture in the self. But relational neuroscience has shown that new bonds, new meanings, and new stories can repair the emotional circuitry left raw by grief.

Rumi was centuries ahead of this. He did not believe in a solitary path to healing. His verses are filled with images of the beloved, the friend, the companion, the guide. He urged us to seek out kindred souls, to weep together, to dance together, to burn in the fire of love together. In one of his most hopeful lines, he says:

"Be with those who help your being."

— Rumi

This is perhaps the simplest and most profound psychological advice there is: find people who make it safe to be yourself in your wholeness—your laughter and your tears. Healing is not about being "fixed"; it is about being held.

The Light Beyond the Veil

The title of this final chapter speaks to something ineffable: the **mystery that lies beyond death**, and the **light that somehow pierces even the darkest grief**. Modern psychology may not speak in metaphysical terms, but it has increasingly come to respect the inner life—the spiritual, the symbolic, the unseen realms that give people strength when logic falls short. Scholars like Viktor Frankl, who survived the Holocaust, reminded us that the soul must have purpose, even when the world is incomprehensible.

Rumi offers the same insight, but with the language of the mystic. He does not explain death—he invites us to meet it with love:

"When the soul lies down in that grass, the world is too full to talk about. Ideas, language... even the phrase each other—doesn't make any sense."

— Rumi

This is not a denial of loss, but a re-framing: what we lose in form, we may recover in essence. What dies in the physical world may still whisper through dreams, memories, signs, and the quiet intuition that love cannot be extinguished by time or death. Rumi's own grief—particularly over the death of his beloved companion Shams—became the source of some of his most luminous poems. In that loss, he found union with something eternal.

Hope as a Way of Life

The final message of this book, grounded in psychology and Rumi's wisdom, is not that grief ends, but that **you can live again—not despite your grief, but because of it**. The pain that once threatened to destroy you can become a sacred teacher, a reminder of how deeply you loved, and how fully you can still live.

Hope is not the absence of sorrow. Hope is *carrying your sorrow gently enough that your hands are still free to touch joy.* Hope is choosing to return to life, again and again, no matter how fragile that choice feels. Hope is listening to grief when it says, "You are not done yet."

As Rumi urges:

"Try not to resist the changes that come your way. Instead, let life live through you."

— Rumi

This is the final truth: you are not alone. You are not broken. You are not finished. Grief has opened you—but not only to pain. It has opened you to the sacredness of every fleeting moment, to the miracle of loving at all, and to the quiet possibility that within your pain lives the seed of your becoming.

Closing Words from the Beloved Poet: Walking Together Beyond the Last Page

If you have read this far, know that your grief has been honored on every page. The soul of this book is not found in answers, but in echoes— in the mirrored recognition that pain, though deeply personal, is also universally human.

The path forward is not to be unbroken, but to be lived with open eyes and a wide heart. You do not walk alone. Countless others have walked before you, and countless more will walk beside you, carrying their own tender losses and hard-won insights.

Let the words of Rumi be your lamp in those moments when memory feels too heavy or hope feels too distant:

"With life as short as a half-taken breath, don't plant anything but love."

— Rumi

And let the insights of psychology offer the scaffolding to support you: healing is possible. Integration is real. You are allowed to laugh again, love again, and live again—not in denial of grief, but in honor of it.

This is the light beyond the veil.

And it has always been yours.

And so, as you close this book, may you plant love in the soil of your grief, water it with your tears, and watch—however slowly—a new life take root. One breath at a time. One moment at a time. With light beyond the veil, and love that never dies.

Appendices

Grief Resources and Support Groups

One of the most vital truths about grief is that it was never meant to be carried alone. Whether our mourning is private or public, spoken or silent, the path through grief is greatly enriched and eased when we walk it alongside others. This section provides a guide to established grief resources and support systems that reflect both contemporary psychological insight and the heart-centered compassion that Rumi invites us to embody.

Modern psychology recognizes the therapeutic power of community, especially in navigating grief and trauma. **Support groups**, whether in-person or online, offer a space where one can witness and be witnessed in vulnerability. As trauma-informed psychologist Dr. Bessel van der Kolk affirms, "Being able to feel safe with other people is probably the single most important aspect of mental health." Grief groups allow participants to externalize their sorrow, normalize their experience, and feel less isolated.

There are many widely recognized organizations that offer structured support:

- **The Dougy Center** provides grief support programs for children, teens, young adults, and their families.

- **GriefShare** is a faith-based program offering support groups worldwide, blending psychological principles with spiritual reflections.

- **The Compassionate Friends** offers comfort to families grieving the death of a child.

- **Modern Loss,** an online community, uses storytelling and digital media to help people process grief in relatable, contemporary terms.

- **WhatsYourGrief.com** and **Refuge in Grief** provide both practical tools and emotional support for grieving individuals.

In the spirit of Rumi, we might view these groups not merely as services, but as "beloved communities"—places where grief is seen as a sacred rite of passage, and the mourner is not a problem to be solved, but a soul to be accompanied. Rumi writes:

"With life as short as a half-taken breath, don't plant anything but love."

— Rumi

Each support group or community is, in essence, a garden where love and sorrow grow side by side.

Rumi Quotes and Translations Used

Throughout this book, the wisdom of Rumi has served as both compass and companion. His poetry reaches across centuries not because it provides answers, but because it offers presence. As Coleman Barks, one of the most well-known Rumi translators, notes, Rumi's words "don't explain the mystery. They draw you into it."

Rumi's verses have been translated into English by a number of poets and scholars, each offering a slightly different shade of his meaning. The following translations have been primarily drawn from:

- **Coleman Barks** (especially from *The Essential Rumi* and *The Soul of Rumi*)

- **Kabir Helminski** (from *The Rumi Collection*)

- **Jawid Mojaddedi** (for more literal and academically faithful renderings)

Here are a few of the frequently cited Rumi verses used in the chapters above, to support readers in locating their origins and reflecting further:

1. *"The wound is the place where the Light enters you."* – A metaphor for psychological integration through pain.

2. *"Try not to resist the changes that come your way. Instead, let life live through you."*

3. *"You were born with wings, why prefer to crawl through life?"*

4. *"Be like a tree and let the dead leaves drop."*

5. *"Don't grieve. Anything you lose comes round in another form."*

6. *"Be a lamp, or a lifeboat, or a ladder."* – An invocation of service as a form of spiritual and emotional healing.

7. *"This moment is all there is."* – A reflection on presence and impermanence.

These verses were chosen not just for their beauty, but for their resonance with psychological truths about grief, growth, and the continuity of love. Readers are encouraged to explore Rumi's works in full, through a variety of translations, to deepen their own connection to his voice.

Simple Healing Practices and Exercises (Breathing, Journaling Prompts, Meditations)

Healing from grief is not a passive process. While time plays a role, intentional practices can support and accelerate the integration of loss.

Modern psychology emphasizes the value of **mind-body awareness**, **emotional regulation**, and **expressive arts** as pathways to resilience and meaning-making. In parallel, Rumi's spiritual path invites us to cultivate presence, silence, and deep feeling as vehicles for union with the divine.

Here are several practices designed to nurture healing. Each is rooted in evidence-based psychology and infused with the contemplative spirit of Rumi:

1. Breathing Practice: The Pause that Heals

When the nervous system is overwhelmed by grief, deep breathing calms the sympathetic response (the fight-flight-freeze system). Try this:

- Inhale slowly for a count of 4

- Hold for a count of 4

- Exhale slowly for a count of 6

- Repeat for 5 minutes, while silently reciting Rumi's line: "Be like a tree, and let the dead leaves drop."

This practice grounds the body in the now and allows emotional space for feeling and release.

2. Journaling Prompts: Writing as Ritual

Expressive writing has been shown in multiple studies (Pennebaker, 1997) to reduce emotional suppression and promote psychological insight. These prompts can be used regularly:

- What has grief taught me about love?

- What part of me feels forever changed?

- What do I need to say to the one I lost?

- Where can I see their legacy in my life today?

- If I were to speak to my grief as a guest, what would I say?

Invite Rumi's voice into your journaling. Imagine he is reading your words and responding not with answers, but with presence.

3. Guided Meditation: Meeting Grief with Compassion

Find a quiet space. Sit comfortably. Close your eyes and say to yourself:

"Grief, I welcome you. You are a visitor, not a mistake. What have you come to show me today?"

Let images, sensations, or words arise. After a few minutes, imagine Rumi whispering:

"The wound is the place where the Light enters you."

This meditation affirms that even pain has purpose, and that by softening toward it, we begin to heal.

Recommended Books, Poems, and Lectures

No journey of grief is complete without companionship from the voices that understand its terrain. The following works—psychological, poetic, spiritual—have helped countless individuals navigate the path of mourning and rediscovery.

Psychological and Therapeutic Works

- ***On Grief and Grieving:*** *Finding the Meaning of Grief Through the Five Stages of Loss,* by Elisabeth Kübler-Ross, David Kessler, and Maria Shriver.

- *The **Wild Edge of Sorrow**: Rituals of Renewal and the Sacred Work of Grief,* by Francis Weller, Thomas Hübl, and Michael Lerner.

- *The **Body Keeps the Score**: Brain, Mind, and Body in the Healing of Trauma,* by Bessel van der Kolk

- *When **Things Fall Apart**: Heart Advice for Difficult Times,* by Pema Chödrön

- *Man's **Search for Meaning** by* Viktor Emil Frankl

Poetry and Mystical Writings

- *The **Essential Rumi** by* Coleman Barks

- *Love **Poems from God**: Inspirations from Twelve Sacred Voices of the East and West,* (featuring Rumi, Hafiz, and others) by Daniel Ladinsky

- *The **Gift**: Poems Inspired by Hafiz, the Great Sufi Master,* by Daniel Ladinsky

Lectures and Talks

- **Tara Brach** (on radical acceptance and grief)

- **Stephen Jenkinson** (on grief literacy and elderhood)

- **Jack Kornfield** (on mindfulness and compassion in loss)

- **Megan Devine** (*It's OK That You're Not OK*)

Each resource, in its own way, echoes Rumi's invitation:

"Don't turn away. Keep your gaze on the bandaged place. That is where the Light enters you."

— Rumi

Together, these tools, words, and communities form an extended hand to all who grieve—a reminder that grief may be a solitary road, but it need not be walked alone. As Rumi teaches, even in sorrow, we are accompanied by the Beloved.

Rumi Quotes from the Journey

This appendix gathers all the Rumi quotes shared throughout this book—from Chapter 1 through the Conclusion. Each of these quotes was selected with great care and love, for the light it brings to the grieving heart, the clarity it offers to the searching soul, and the companionship it lends to those walking through loss.

Although Rumi composed his poetry in Persian, the quotes presented here appear only in English. This decision was made with both humility and respect. First, many of the quotes used in this book—particularly those translated or adapted by beloved interpreters like Coleman Barks—are not literal translations from the original Persian texts such as the *Masnavi*, *Divan-e Shams*, or *Fihi Ma Fih*. Rather, they are poetic interpretations that seek to capture the emotional and spiritual essence of Rumi's voice. Including a Persian version alongside these paraphrased lines could create confusion or suggest a direct textual correspondence that does not exist.

Second, since this book is written in English and intended primarily for an English-speaking audience, including the original Persian verses might hinder, rather than enhance, accessibility for most readers.

Ultimately, Rumi's teachings transcend language. What matters most is the presence, the fire, and the grace that his words awaken in us. May these quotes serve not as scholarly artifacts, but as spiritual companions—

reminders that love endures, grief transforms, and the soul, like Rumi's poetry, longs always to return home.

"The wound is the place where the Light enters you."

"Don't grieve. Anything you lose comes round in another form."

"This moment is all there is. Don't wait for tomorrow. Dive in now."

"You have to keep breaking your heart until it opens."

"Don't get lost in your pain, know that one day your pain will become your cure."

"Try not to resist the changes that come your way. Instead, let life live through you."

"The minute I heard my first love story, I started looking for you,
not knowing how blind that was.
Lovers don't finally meet somewhere.
They're in each other all along."

"When the soul lies down in that grass, the world is too full to talk about.
Ideas, language—even the phrase each other—
doesn't make any sense."

"Why do you stay in prison when the door is so wide open?"

"Try to be like the night: quiet, empty, transparent, and free."

"Be like a tree and let the dead leaves drop."

"Be patient where you sit in the dark. The dawn is coming."

"With life as short as a half-taken breath, don't plant anything but love."

"Be like melting snow—wash yourself of yourself."

"The moment you accept what troubles you've been given, the door will open."

"Sorrow prepares you for joy. It violently sweeps everything out of your house, so that new joy can find space to enter."

"What hurts you, blesses you. Darkness is your candle."

"The Guest House: This being human is a guest house. Every morning a new arrival…"

"Let yourself be silently drawn by the strange pull of what you really love. It will not lead you astray."

"Don't get tired of doing what is right, even when no one sees. Your soul knows."

"Try to learn to let what is not yours go. Let it go like the autumn leaves."

"Die before you die."

"Be patient where you sit in the dark. The dawn is coming."

"There is a candle in your heart, ready to be kindled. There is a void in your soul, ready to be filled."

"Don't grieve. Anything you lose comes round in another form."

"Goodbyes are only for those who love with their eyes. Because for those who love with heart and soul, there is no such thing as separation."

"Don't you know yet? It is your light that lights the world."

"Try to be a rainbow in someone's cloud. Let that someone be your own soul."

"Be like a tree and let the dead leaves drop."

"Don't get lost in your pain, know that one day your pain will become your cure."

"With life as short as a half-taken breath, don't plant anything but love."

"Why should I be unhappy? Every parcel of my being is in full bloom."

"Try not to resist the changes that come your way. Instead, let life live through you."

"You were born with wings, why prefer to crawl through life?"

"I died as mineral and became a plant, I died as plant and rose to animal... I died as man and became an angel. What have I lost by dying?"

"Don't you know yet? It is your Light that lights the world."

447

"With life as short as a half-taken breath, don't plant anything but love."

"Grief can be the garden of compassion. If you keep your heart open through everything, your pain can become your greatest ally in your life's search for love and wisdom."

"This moment is all there is. Don't wait for the next moment to begin living."

Final Reflection:
The End That Opens

There is a silence that comes when the last page of a book is turned. It is not empty. It is sacred. Like the quiet that follows a prayer, or the hush after a final breath. If you have made it here, dear reader, you have walked with me through shadows and light, through the cracked-open heart and the doorway of longing. You have listened not only with your mind, but with your soul.

And for that, I thank you. Truly.

This book began in silence—not the kind we seek for peace, but the kind that fell like a curtain over my world when my parents died. I lost not just them, but the very thread that stitched meaning through my life. And in that silence, I found myself returning, not to answers, but to poetry. Not to theology, but to Rumi.

What began as a private weeping became these pages. What began as wordlessness became a kind of prayer.

I did not write this book because I had wisdom. I wrote it because I had grief. And I could no longer carry it alone.

If anything here has soothed even a corner of your pain, or offered you breath in the heaviness of mourning, then let us honor that not as mine, but as Rumi's. As love's. As life's, I believe that what is most personal is also most universal. In my sorrow, you may have found your own reflection. In your tears, I hope you have also found light.

We are not meant to rush grief. We are not meant to conquer it. We are meant to *tend* it—as one would tend a sacred fire. Gently. Faithfully. With reverence for all it transforms.

Rumi once said:

"You were born with wings, why prefer to crawl through life?"

— Rumi

I wrote these pages not to teach you how to fly, but to remind you that you already can. Even broken wings remember the sky.

In a world that urges us to move on, may we instead choose to move *in*—into the wound, into the ache, into the presence of those we've lost, who are perhaps closer now than they ever were in life because love doesn't end. It just changes form.

And so, here at the end, I do not say goodbye. I simply open the door. I bow to your grief. I bow to your courage. I bow to the invisible thread that connects us in this very moment—reader and writer, mourner and mourner, soul to soul.

May this be your invitation to die before you die—to surrender what no longer serves, and awaken into the life that remains.

With deepest love,

Mostafa Darvishi

July 2025

www.ingramcontent.com/pod-product-compliance
Lightning Source LLC
Chambersburg PA
CBHW050846150626
46549CB00012B/36